ELBRIDGE GERRY'S SALAMANDER

THE ELECTORAL CONSEQUENCES OF THE
REAPPORTIONMENT REVOLUTION

The Supreme Court's reapportionment decisions, beginning with *Baker v. Carr* in 1962, had far more than jurisprudential consequences. They sparked a massive wave of extraordinary redistricting in the mid-1960s. Both state legislative and congressional districts were redrawn more comprehensively – by far – than at any previous time in our nation's history. Moreover, they changed what would happen at law should a state government fail to enact a new districting plan when one was legally required. This book provides the first detailed analysis of how judicial partisanship affected redistricting outcomes in the 1960s, arguing that the reapportionment revolution led indirectly to three fundamental changes in the nature of congressional elections: the abrupt eradication of a 6% pro-Republican bias in the translation of congressional votes into seats outside the South; the abrupt increase in the apparent advantage of incumbents; and the abrupt alteration of the two parties' success in congressional recruitment and elections.

Gary W. Cox is Professor of Political Science at the University of California, San Diego. He was elected to the American Academy of Arts and Sciences in 1996. His many publications include *Making Votes Count*, winner in 1998 of the Woodrow Wilson Foundation Award, the Best Book (Political Economy) Award, and the Gregory M. Luebbert Prize.

Jonathan N. Katz is Associate Professor of Political Science at the California Institute of Technology. His numerous articles have appeared in journals such as the *American Political Science Review*, the *Journal of the American Statistical Association*, and the *American Journal of Political Science*.

POLITICAL ECONOMY OF INSTITUTIONS AND DECISIONS

Series Editors

Randall Calvert, Washington University, St. Louis
Thrainn Eggertsson, University of Iceland

Founding Editors

James E. Alt, Harvard University
Douglass C. North, Washington University, St. Louis

Other Books in the Series

Alberto Alesina and Howard Rosenthal, *Partisan Politics, Divided Government, and the Economy*

Lee J. Alston, Thrainn Eggertsson, and Douglass C. North, eds., *Empirical Studies in Institutional Change*

Lee J. Alston and Joseph P. Ferrie, *Southern Paternalism and the Rise of the American Welfare State: Economics, Politics, and Institutions, 1865–1965*

James E. Alt and Kenneth Shepsle, eds., *Perspectives on Positive Political Economy*

Jeffrey S. Banks and Eric A. Hanushek, eds., *Modern Political Economy: Old Topics, New Directions*

Yoram Barzel, *Economic Analysis of Property Rights*, 2nd edition

Robert Bates, *Beyond the Miracle of the Market: The Political Economy of Agrarian Development in Kenya*

Peter Cowhey and Mathew McCubbins, eds., *Structure and Policy in Japan and the United States*

Gary W. Cox, *The Efficient Secret: The Cabinet and the Development of Political Parties in Victorian England*

Gary W. Cox, *Making Votes Count: Strategic Coordination in the World's Electoral System*

Jean Ensminger, *Making a Market: The Institutional Transformation of an African Society*

David Epstein and Sharyn O'Halloran, *Delegating Powers: A Transaction Cost Politics Approach to Policy Making under Separate Powers*

Kathryn Firmin-Sellers, *The Transformation of Property Rights in the Gold Coast: An Empirical Analysis Applying Rational Choice Theory*

Clark C. Gibson, *Politics and Poachers: The Political Economy of Wildlife Policy in Africa*

Continued on page following the index

'ELBRIDGE GERRY'S SALAMANDER,

The Electoral Consequences of the Reapportionment Revolution

WITHDRAWI'

GARY W. COX

University of California, San Diego

JONATHAN N. KATZ

California Institute of Technology

CAMBRIDGE
UNIVERSITY PRESS

PUBLISHED BY THE PRESS SYNDICATE OF THE UNIVERSITY OF CAMBRIDGE
The Pitt Building, Trumpington Street, Cambridge, United Kingdom

CAMBRIDGE UNIVERSITY PRESS
The Edinburgh Building, Cambridge CB2 2RU, UK
40 West 20th Street, New York, NY 10011-4211, USA
477 Williamstown Road, Port Melbourne, VIC 3207, Australia
Ruiz de Alarcón 13, 28014 Madrid, Spain
Dock House, The Waterfront, Cape Town 8001, South Africa

http://www.cambridge.org

First published 2002

Printed in the United Kingdom at the University Press, Cambridge

Typeface Sabon 10/13 pt.   *System* QuarkXPress [BTS]

A catalog record for this book is available from the British Library.

Library of Congress Cataloging in Publication Data
Cox, Gary W.
    Elbridge Gerry's salamander: the electoral consequences of the reapportionment
revolution / Gary W. Cox, Jonathan N. Katz.
        p.   cm. – (Political economy of institutions and decisions)
    Includes bibliographical references and index.
    ISBN 0-521-80675-5 – ISBN 0-521-00154-4 (pbk.)
        1. Apportionment (Election law) – United States.   2. Election districts – United
States.   3. United States – Politics and government – 1945–1989.   4. United States –
Politics and government – 1989–   I. Katz, Jonathan N. (Jonathan Neil), 1968–
II. Title.   III. Series.
    JK1341 .C875   2002
    328.73'07345–dc21   2001035899

ISBN   0 521 80675 5   hardback
ISBN   0 521 00154 4   paperback

Contents

List of Tables and Figures

Tables

List of Tables and Figures

Figures

Preface

Elbridge Gerry was governor of Massachusetts from 1810 to 1812. During his term, his party produced an artful electoral map intended to maximize the number of seats it could eke out of its expected vote share. Contemporary observers latched onto one district in particular, in the shape of a salamander, and pronounced it a Gerry-mander.

This book is about a unique episode in the long history of American gerrymandering – the Supreme Court's landmark reapportionment decisions in the early 1960s and their electoral consequences. The *dramatis personae* of our story are the state politicians who drew congressional district lines, the judges on the courts supervising their handiwork, and the candidates competing for congressional office. The plot of our story concerns the strategic adaptation of these actors to the new electoral playing field created by the Court's decisions.

In writing our story, we have incurred numerous debts. Here we thank some of those we should, with apologies to those we have inadvertently forgotten. For conversations about and comments on our project, we thank R. Michael Alvarez, Bruce Cain, Andrea Campbell, Chris Den Hartog, Andrew Gelman, Dave Grether, Bernie Grofman, John Mark Hansen, Simon Jackman, Gary Jacobson, Sam Kernell, D. Roderick Kiewiet, Gary King, Morgan Kousser, Mat McCubbins, Mike McDonald, Jonathan Nagler, Steven Smith, Matthew Spitzer, Simon Wilke, and participants in seminars given at Princeton, UC Berkeley, UCLA, UC Riverside, the Hoover Institution, Northwestern University, the University of Minnesota, Yale University, the University of Chicago, the University of Illinois at Urbana-Champaign, Harvard University, and the University of Rochester. For research assistance, we thank Chris Den Hartog, Mike McDonald, Meredith Rolfe, and the Reference Law

Librarians at the University of Chicago. For clerical assistance, we thank Heather Guyett. For data, we thank Gary Jacobson, Gary King, Simon Jackman, Jim Snyder, and the Inter-University Consortium for Political and Social Research. For financial support, we thank the National Science Foundation (Grants SBR-9730547 and SBR-9729899), the John Randolph Haynes and Dora Haynes Foundation, the John M. Olin Foundation, the Committee on Research at UCSD, and the Caltech-USC Center for the Study of Law and Politics.

Finally, on the home front, Gary thanks his son, Dylan, for enthusiasm, love, and endurance in sometimes trying times. Jonathan thanks Natasha Jantje Unger for all of her love, support, and understanding.

PART I

Introduction

I

Introduction

ELBRIDGE GERRY'S SALAMANDER

The word *gerrymander* describes a distinctively (albeit not uniquely) American practice, that of redrawing district lines to achieve partisan (or other) advantage. The word also has a distinctively American etymology, dating back to Elbridge Gerry's term as governor of Massachusetts (1810–1812), when political observers made sport of a district drawn by his party that looked something like a salamander.

At the broadest level, indicated by its title, this book is about gerrymandering. The principles of our analysis could be applied to the original Gerry-mander or to any of its various and long line of descendants (for one such effort, see Engstrom 2001).

At a narrower and more specific level, indicated by its subtitle, this book concerns what was arguably the most important change in the practice of American gerrymandering since its invention.[1] Whereas previously the game of drawing salamanders with district lines was limited to legislators and governors, the courts standing scrupulously aside, after 1964 the rules changed. A new process emerged, with new strategic consequences and nuances. We examine how these procedural changes help explain two of the biggest stories in congressional elections since the 1960s: the seemingly invulnerable Democratic majority in the House of Representatives before 1994 and the seemingly unfair and bloated advantage of incumbents over challengers.

---

[1] The practice of gerrymandering certainly predated the Gerry-mander, but its origin has not been precisely dated, so far as we know.

THE REAPPORTIONMENT REVOLUTION

The Supreme Court's reapportionment decisions, beginning with *Baker v. Carr* in 1962, were soon hailed by legal scholars as revolutionary (see, e.g., Baker 1966, p. 3; Dixon 1968, p. 99).[2] They reversed decades of court decisions that had consistently held that the drawing of legislative district lines, fraught though it was with malapportionment and gerrymandering, was not justiciable. They opened the door to a long chain of subsequent litigation, which continued into the 1990s, with important decisions regarding racial gerrymandering. For these and other reasons, the reapportionment decisions now occupy a standard niche in textbooks on the Court.

The Court's decisions did not simply rewrite case law, however. They also sparked a massive wave of extraordinary redistricting in the mid-1960s.[3] Both state legislative and congressional districts were redrawn more comprehensively – by far – than at any previous time in our nation's history.

In the immediate aftermath of the Court's decisions and the consequent redistricting, scholars looked carefully for political consequences, yet concluded that they were very small. Neither party seemed to benefit nationwide, as their gains in some states were offset by losses elsewhere. Incumbents did not seem to benefit, as their margins of victory increased even where redistricting did not take place. Policy did not seem to shift toward urban interests in the dramatic way widely anticipated.

These conclusions were surprising, not just because of the magnitude of the judicial shift in doctrine or the depth and breadth of 1960s redistricting action, but also because of two statistical regularities later described in the scholarly literature. First, work on how congressional votes translated into congressional seats outside the South found a consistent pro-Republican bias prior to the 1960s. By one estimate (Erikson 1972, p. 1234), the Democrats could expect to win only 44.6% of the nonsouthern seats when the aggregate vote division was a 50–50 partisan split – indicating a 5.4% pro-Republican bias. This bias abruptly disappeared in the mid-1960s. Second, scholars found that the so-called incumbency advantage – a vote premium putatively derived from the

---

[2] (*Re*)*apportionment* refers to the (re)allocation of seats in the U.S. House of Representatives to the states after each decennial census.

[3] *Redistricting* refers to the drawing up of new district boundaries within each state – typically but not always pursuant to reapportionment.

resources of office – jumped up dramatically in 1966, the year of the first election in which a substantial number of districts had been redrawn under court order (Erikson 1972; Gelman and King 1990). The size and abruptness of these two statistical changes, and their coincidence with widespread court-ordered redistricting, seem more than coincidence. Yet the literature has intensely scrutinized these factors and found no causal link between them and redistricting.

REEXAMINING THE CONSEQUENCES OF THE REAPPORTIONMENT REVOLUTION

This book reexamines the electoral consequences of the reapportionment revolution. The bulk of the previous literature has focused on the primary *substantive* consequence of the Court's decisions – the eradication of malapportionment in U.S. legislative districts at both the state and federal levels. Our work focuses on the primary *procedural* consequences of the Court's decisions – the redefinition of the legally mandated default outcome to the redistricting processes in the 50 states, and the increased regularity and frequency with which redistrictings were undertaken. We use these procedural shifts to explain sea changes in two struggles central to congressional elections: that between Democrats and Republicans, on the one hand, and that between incumbents and challengers, on the other.

Democrats and Republicans

As regards the partisan struggle between Democrats and Republicans, our argument starts by noting that the Supreme Court's decisions fundamentally altered the *reversionary* (or default) *outcome* of the redistricting processes in the states. That is, they altered what would happen at law should the state government fail to enact a new congressional districting statute. Once one controls properly for the nature of the legal reversion when analyzing the impact of redistricting, several consequences of the Court's reapportionment decisions come into focus.

First, these decisions made the courts strategic players in all subsequent redistricting actions. The courts were players in those cases where an explicit suit had been brought, because the courts then determined the reversion. But even where no suit had yet been brought, each party might worry that the other would bring a suit, were the redistricting plan not to its liking, at which point each party had to worry about where the suit would be brought and what reversion the relevant court would impose.

Second, the courts' ability to set the reversion, combined with the latitude they had in the early years after *Wesberry v. Sanders* in deciding when a plan was sufficiently well apportioned, gave them substantial influence over the final districting plans adopted. Thus, the partisan complexion of the federal judiciary in the 1960s played a central role in redistricting outcomes, as will be seen.

Third, the Supreme Court's decisions unleashed a wave of redistricting just after Lyndon Baines Johnson's landslide victory over Barry Goldwater in 1964 had substantially weakened Republican control of nonsouthern state governments and during a period when the federal judiciary was heavily Democratic. Thus, redistricting in the 1960s was conducted *by* state governments that were less often under unified Republican control than had historically been the case and *under the supervision of* courts that were largely Democratic. This combination produced a substantial net partisan advantage for the Democrats, evidenced not only in the abrupt disappearance of pro-Republican bias outside the South but also in the detailed patterns of how vote shares changed when district lines were redrawn.

Our explanation of the partisan consequences of the reapportionment revolution is quite different from those offered in the literature, both in the line of argument pursued (no one has stressed reversionary outcomes and the strategic role of the courts in the previous literature) and in the conclusion reached (that there was a substantial net partisan consequence directly attributable to the reapportionment revolution). We detail our argument and findings in Part II of the book.

Incumbents and Challengers

As regards the electoral struggle between incumbents and challengers, we argue that the key to understanding the dramatic growth in the apparent advantage of incumbents is to recognize that they are strategic agents, deciding whether to seek reelection or not based on their forecast vote shares. We show that much of the incumbency advantage, as previously measured, reflects incumbents' prudence – getting out when the getting is good – rather than their superior campaigning ability or resources.

We then explore how redistricting affected incumbents' prudential exits and challengers' strategic entries. One line of argument concerns anticipations of redistricting. After the Supreme Court's reapportionment decisions, politicians soon realized that redistrictings, rare and not always forseeable beforehand, would now be unavoidable and regular. This recognition, in turn, facilitated better coordination between incumbents and strong challengers, inducing a stronger redistricting rhythm to congressional entry and exit. Better coordination meant that incumbents more often got out in the face of a particularly formidable challenge, increasing the statistical association between running an incumbent and the incumbent party's vote share.

Another line of argument begins by noting that the eradication of pro-Republican bias in the translation of congressional votes into seats resulted in an abrupt decline in the Republicans' probability of attaining a majority of seats in the House of Representatives. This intensification of the Republicans' minority status exacerbated a syndrome of recruitment-related woes for the party, resulting in significantly larger estimated incumbency advantages for the Republicans than for the Democrats. This last finding, nonobvious and unnoticed in the previous literature, is much at odds with previous theories of why the incumbency advantage arose but follows naturally from our emphasis on strategic entry and exit (as will be shown).

Normative Concerns

To the extent that our explanation of the reapportionment revolution's electoral consequences is correct, these consequences do not pose the threats to our system that many scholars, journalists, and politicians have associated with them. Those who have seen the increasing resources attached to congressional office as increasing the incumbency advantage, and hence bolstering the Democrats' perennial majority status, have correctly been worried. Whenever the resources of public office are used to insulate individual politicians from electoral risk, their accountability to their constituents is weakened. Whenever government resources are used to entrench a single party in government, its accountability to the public at large is weakened. Thus, insulation from electoral risk of the kind suspected would, at a single stroke, debilitate the two fundamental accountability relationships of a democratic system of government.

However, by our story, the insulation of House incumbents is more apparent than real. It is not just that incumbents always "run scared," per Mann (1977) and others. It is that they retire when scared off, and this propensity inflates standard estimates of the incumbency advantage. Indeed, by our estimates, the incumbency advantage enjoyed by

Democratic incumbents was never – even after 1966 – statistically discernible from zero. Nor, at the aggregate level, has the Democratic party had an unfair advantage in how votes translate into seats.[4] The major premises of the preceding arguments thus largely disappear.

EXCLUDING THE "SOUTH"

In the first part of this book, we focus on redistricting actions in the period before (1946–1962) and immediately after (1964–1970) the Supreme Court's reapportionment decisions. In this part, we exclude southern states from the analysis. There are two main justifications for doing so.

First, the legal default to the redistricting process plays a central role in our theory, yet this default was entirely different in the South from elsewhere. Following enactment of the Voting Rights Act in 1965, the Section 5 preclearance rules imposed on seven southern states made the Justice Department the primary arbiter of redistricting plans rather than the courts. Moreover, these Section 5 states were subject to unique legal restrictions on their redistricting plans, such as prohibitions on vote dilution and retrogression.

Second, our theory of redistricting assumes that there was a significant level of interparty competition and that both parties were unitary actors seeking to maximize their respective expected seat shares.[5] In the South, however, especially before passage of the Voting Rights Act but also in the early years thereafter, the Democratic party utterly dominated the scene and the Republicans were a hopeless minority. We believe that southern redistricting before and even in the 1960s was much more a matter of factional infighting within the dominant party than partisan gerrymandering fought out between the parties.

All told, the politics of redistricting in the South has been theoretically quite distinctive for most of the postwar era on which we focus. Although the basic principles of our approach could be adapted to study southern redistricting, the specific model we employ cannot. Thus, we leave the South for another time.[6]

---

[4] For a contrary view regarding whether partisan bias has been near zero, see Campbell (1996).

[5] More precisely, we assume that parties seek to maximize the utility they derive from their seats. This allows the model to recognize that parties' attitudes toward risk mattered, as explained in Chapter 3.

[6] For a recent examination of the politics of redistricting in the South, see Canon (1999).

To be consistent, of course, we should exclude *all* states that were subject to Section 5 preclearance or were "uncompetitive." The first criterion (Section 5 preclearance) is not an issue because no nonsouthern states were affected until after the period of focus in the first part of the book (1946–1970). To systematize the second criterion, we consulted the well-known Ranney index of party competition for the period that most closely matched our period of primary focus (viz., 1964–1970, the elections immediately after the relevant reapportionment decision).[7] All states that were more competitive than all of the already-excluded southern states were included in our analyses. Two border states, Maryland and Tennessee, were even less competitive than some already-excluded states, however, and were accordingly also excluded. Thus, our definition of what is "southern" is slightly more expansive than the definition often used in the literature.

OUTLINE OF THE BOOK

This book is divided into four parts: an introduction, two main substantive parts, and a conclusion. The next chapter sets the stage by describing the Court's decisions, the condition of congressional districts before and after redistricting, and the reasons offered in the literature as to why redistricting should have been relatively inconsequential. In the same chapter, we also elaborate on the theoretical importance of the reversionary outcome to redistricting, describe how it changed with the Court's decisions, and argue that this provides the key to a long-standing puzzle about congressional elections in the 1960s.

Chapter 3 begins Part II by presenting the first half of a general model of the redistricting process(es) in the American states. Chapter 4 uses this model to estimate bias and responsiveness in postwar congressional elections outside the South. Our results clearly demonstrate the importance of the reversionary outcome even before the Court's reapportionment decisions. Chapters 5 and 6 extend the model to include the courts as strategic actors, as is appropriate for redistricting actions after *Baker v. Carr*. Our empirical results show that the partisanship of the judges supervising redistricting cases in the 1960s was at least as important as which party controlled state government in affecting the character of the plan adopted.

---

[7] The closest match to the 1964–1970 time period is the index for 1962–1973 published in Ranney (1971).

The findings of Chapters 3–6 can be interpreted broadly as follows: outside the South, the nation's congressional districts were mostly products of Republican gerrymanders before *Baker* but increasingly products of bipartisan plans or Democratic gerrymanders afterward. If this general thesis is correct, it implies some very specific district-level consequences of redistricting in the 1960s. Chapter 7 investigates these implications and finds them to hold.

In Chapter 8, we set the stage for the analyses of Part III in two ways. First, we review classic evidence that congressional incumbents abruptly began winning by larger vote margins in the 1960s, review previous attempts to explain this and the related increase in the *incumbency advantage*, and sketch our own explanation. Second, we show that Republican incumbents' margins increased more than did Democratic incumbents' margins, and that the Republican incumbency advantage increased more than did the Democratic incumbency advantage (when measured, as is typical, in vote shares). We thus add to the list of explananda that a complete model of postwar congressional elections must address: although there was no systematic difference between the two parties' incumbency advantages before the reapportionment revolution, afterward Republicans tended to benefit more from incumbency.

In Chapters 9 and 10, we seek to explain the patterns of growth in the incumbency advantage as consequences of the reapportionment revolution's impact on political recruitment and career planning. Chapter 9 explores how incumbents' ability to enter or exit in light of their vote forecasts affects previous estimates of the incumbency advantage. Chapter 10 demonstrates that entry by strong challengers and voluntary exit by incumbents have followed the redistricting cycle more regularly since the mid-1960s, arguing that this partly explains the increasing success of incumbents and strong challengers at avoiding contests against one another. Chapter 11 argues that the considerable differences between the two parties in recruitment and career paths that emerged after the mid-1960s stem in good part from (1) the reapportionment revolution's eradication of pro-Republican bias (shown in Part II), which (2) intensified the Republicans' minority status and hence (3) drove a wedge between how candidates of the two parties valued House seats. Chapter 12 concludes our discussion of the incumbency advantage and compares our thesis to previous explanations.

In Chapter 13 (Part IV), we review the various consequences of the reapportionment revolution. In understanding both the battle between Republicans and Democrats and that between incumbents and challengers, we stress political expectations. Anticipation of what courts would and would not allow had been irrelevant and abruptly became essential; this, along with the wave of redistricting action, put a sudden end to pro-Republican bias. Anticipation of the next redistricting had been relatively infrequent and difficult and abruptly became regular and easy; this suddenly increased the extent to which conventional measures of the incumbency advantage overestimated its size. Finally, anticipations of the Democrats' probability of securing a majority in the House (either at the next election or over a somewhat longer time horizon) changed after the eradication of pro-Republican bias; this increased several differences between the parties in recruitment, career paths, and campaigning.

2

The Reapportionment Revolution

In this chapter, we first describe the basic facts of the reapportionment revolution: the Court's decisions, the malapportionment problem they addressed, and the wave of redistricting action that followed. We then characterize what the literature has said about the last of these three elements – court-ordered redistrictings in the 1960s. Were these redistrictings simply partisan gerrymanders? Were they mostly incumbent-protecting gerrymanders? Were they a bit of both? Were they neither? Finally, we explain why we believe the answers given in the literature need to be reconsidered.

A SKETCH OF THE REAPPORTIONMENT REVOLUTION

The Court's Decisions

On March 26, 1962, the Supreme Court handed down its decision in the case of *Baker v. Carr* (369 U.S. 186), thus initiating what has since been known as the *reapportionment revolution*. The suit was brought by urban plaintiffs in Tennessee, who challenged their state legislature's failure to reapportion despite widespread population shifts that had made urban districts vastly more populous than their rural counterparts. The ramifications of the case were clearly national, because urban and especially suburban Americans were significantly underrepresented in state legislatures throughout the country (Hacker 1964). Thus, although the Court limited itself to declaring that state legislative reapportionment was justiciable, leaving more specific action in the case to the lower courts, its decision was immediately seen as a revolutionary step – one the Court had repeatedly declined to take (most recently in *Colegrove v. Green* 328 U.S. 529).

The immediate consequence of *Baker* was more litigation. Indeed, within a year of the decision, all but 14 states were involved in reapportionment suits, and the Supreme Court used some of these cases to stake out a clearer substantive position. The Court had opined in *Baker* that inequalities in district populations – that is, malapportionment – might constitute a violation of the Fourteenth Amendment's guarantee of equal protection of the laws to all citizens. In *Gray v. Sanders* (372 U.S. 368), handed down in 1963, the Court invalidated Georgia's unit-rule primary elections specifically on the grounds that they did not give all voters an equal voice and thus violated the Fourteenth Amendment. A year later the Court extended its "one person, one vote" principle to cover elections to both houses of all state legislatures (*Reynolds v. Sims*, 377 U.S. 533) and elections to the U.S. House of Representatives (*Wesberry v. Sanders*, 376 U.S. 1).

The initial reactions to *Reynolds* and *Wesberry* by the two parties were favorable, at least at the national level. The chairman of the Democratic National Committee praised the decisions as "something the Democratic party had long advocated and fought for and certainly welcomes," while the chairman of the Republican National Committee viewed the decisions as being "in the national interest and in the Republican party's interest" (*New York Times*, 17 June 1964, p. 29).

The Republican reaction to *Wesberry* was presumably influenced by a memorandum written after the 1962 election that demonstrated that Republicans did best in the more populous – that is, the more underrepresented – congressional districts (Prendergast 1965). The report showed that the Republicans had won 53% of the seats in districts with populations above 500,000, 42% of the districts with populations between 300,000 and 500,000, and only 27% of the districts with populations below 300,000. Even outside the South, the Republicans won 61% of the oversized districts (those 15% or more above average) and only 40% of the undersized districts (those 15% or more below average). In light of these figures, the national leadership might well have looked forward to the removal of congressional malapportionment.

The Nature of Congressional Malapportionment

In the 88th Congress (elected in 1962), 234 congressional districts deviated by at least 10% from the average district population in their respective states, with the maximum deviation being 118%. Looking only at the 324 districts in nonsouthern states with more than one district (thus

Table 2.1. *Relationship Between Urbanness and Underrepresentation in*
11 Large States, 1962

Independent Variables	Coefficient Estimate	Standard Error
Percent Urban	2.59**	0.48
Percent Urban Squared	−0.016**	0.003

Notes: (1) Only states with at least 10 districts were included in the analysis. (2) For each district in each state (except at-large districts), the district's population was expressed as a percentage deviation from the state average: *Popdev* = 100 × (district population − average population in state)/(average population in state). (3) *Popdev* was then regressed on the percentage of the district's population living in urban areas and the square of this percentage. We also included fixed effects for each state, not reported in the table. (4) Double asterisks indicate significance at the .001 level or better.

excluding Alaska, Delaware, Nevada, Vermont, and Wyoming), one finds that 52% deviated by more than 10% from their respective averages, with a maximum deviation of 85%.

Previous analysis has shown that malapportionment prior to the reapportionment revolution hurt suburban areas the most, with inner-city areas being more or less properly apportioned and rural areas being overrepresented (Hacker 1963, p. 92). If one looks at the relationship between a district's urbanness (measured by the percentage of its population living in urban areas) and underrepresentation (measured by its percentage deviation from the average population of congressional districts in its state) in the 11 nonsouthern states with 10 or more districts, one finds results consistent with this summary. As Table 2.1 reveals, more urban districts tended to be *under*represented. Moreover, the best fit between urbanness and underrepresentation is quadratic. Indeed, the 100% urban districts were not as underrepresented as districts with somewhat lower but still high urbanness. Assuming that the high-but-not-100% urban cases were suburban areas, these results gibe with the conventional wisdom articulated earlier, that suburban areas were the most underrepresented.

The next question is: who lost from malapportionment prior to the reapportionment revolution in partisan terms? Consistent with the Republicans' assessment of the matter, the answer seems to be that malapportionment outside the South slightly hurt the Republicans. On average, districts won by Democrats in 1962 were slightly overrepresented (i.e., smaller), while districts won by Republicans were slightly underrepresented (i.e., larger). Moreover, controlling for the number of districts in each state and each district's urbanness, districts won by Democrats were significantly smaller than Republican-won districts – by about 6.7% relative to the state average.[1]

Does this result mean that the Republicans were wise to welcome the Court's decisions? Not necessarily. What such a conclusion fails to recognize is that, although malapportionment may have benefited the Democrats, the distribution of votes in each state – the result of prior partisan gerrymandering – may have hurt them. Since removing malapportionment would necessarily entail a substantial redrawing of district lines, thus providing great opportunities for distributional artistry, the overall partisan effect of redistricting could turn out to be substantially to the Republicans' detriment – as we shall see that it was.[2]

The Redistrictings

Having sketched the nature of the problem to which the courts demanded a solution, we can now turn to the redistricting actions themselves. In Table 2.2, we outline redistricting actions in each nonsouthern state from 1960 to 1970, identifying which party controlled the process.

How large were the changes wrought by all the redistricting outlined in Table 2.2? In order to address this question, we focus on one redistricting per state: the first redistricting occurring under court pressure in the decade. For a few states, this first court-pressured redistricting occurs in 1964. For most, it occurs later in the decade. To gauge how much each new district has been altered, we proceed as follows. First, we find the old district that was the single largest contributor of population to the new district (the "parent" district). Letting c denote the total population that the parent district had in common with the new district,

---

[1] This result is not driven by the states operating under Democratic redistricting plans; they show a pattern statistically indistinguishable from that observed in other states.

[2] To show how the Democrats could gain, even if malapportionment favored them, an anonymous referee proposed the following example. Imagine a state with five districts, two of which had 400,000 inhabitants and were typically won by Republicans winning 60% of the district vote, and three of which had 300,000 inhabitants and were typically won by Democrats winning 60%. Under the new districting scheme, all five districts will have equal population: 340,000. If one of the new districts is packed with Republicans (say 90% of the district's inhabitants and voters are Republican), and the remaining Republicans are spread evenly throughout the other four districts, then the Democrats can expect 61% in these other districts. Thus, the Democrats will improve their expected seat total from three to four, despite having lost the advantage of malapportionment.

Table 2.2. *Partisan Control of Redistricting, 1960–1970*
(Nonsouthern States)

State	1960	1962	1964	1966	1968	1970
AZ		Democrat		Democrat[a]		Republican
CA		Democrat		Bipartisan		
CO			Republican			
CT			Bipartisan			
ID				Republican		
IA		Republican				
IL		Bipartisan		Bipartisan		
IN				Democrat	Bipartisan	
KS		Republican		Republican		
KY		Democrat		Democrat		
MA		Bipartisan			Bipartisan	
MD		Democrat		Democrat[a]		
ME		Republican				
MI		Bipartisan	Bipartisan			
MN		Bipartisan				
MO		Democrat		Democrat	Democrat	Democrat
MT				Bipartisan[a]		
NE		Bipartisan			Republican	
ND		Republican				
NH						Republican
NJ		Bipartisan		Democrat	Republican[b]	
NM	Democrat				Bipartisan	
NY		Republican			Bipartisan	Republican
OH		Bipartisan		Republican	Republican	
OK					Bipartisan	
OR				Bipartisan		
PA		Bipartisan		Bipartisan		
RI[c]						
SD				Republican		
UT				Democrat		
WA	Democrat				Democrat[d]	
WI			Bipartisan			
WV		Democrat			Democrat	

[a] Court-imposed plan.

[b] Democratic governor, but Republican supermajorities in both houses.

[c] Rhode Island had minuscule redistrictings in 1964 and 1966, which are not included here.

[d] Listed as a Democratic plan, despite a Republican governor, because the Democratic legislature forced the plan to a referendum – over the governor's objections – and won.

p denote the total population in the *parent* district, and *n* denote the total population in the *new* district, we compute a similarity index: $s = c/(p + n - c)$. The denominator in this fraction is the union of the parent and new districts (or, more precisely, the number of persons living in that union). Thus, *s* is simply the population living in the intersection of the parent district and new district divided by the population living in the union of these two districts.

If a new district is basically the same as its parent, having lost a few townships here and gained a few there, then *s* will be near unity. In some cases, however, the parent district is only faintly related to its offspring. In Arizona, for example, the 1966 redistricting created a new district 3. The largest single contributor to this district was the old district 1. But that district (Phoenix) had a 1960 population of 663,510. Thus, even though it gave 207,892 persons to the new district 3, more than the old district 3's contribution of 174,952, it also gave 455,618 to the new district 1. Thus, the overall similarity score between the old district 1 and the new district 3 was a bit less than 25%. Other low similarity scores arise when, for example, the parent district is very small and a lot is added to the new district from multiple sources.

The average similarity score in nonsouthern districts from states with at least five districts is 72.6%. That is, the population shared between parent and child districts averaged 72.6% percent of the union population in the larger northern states. Fully a quarter of the districts had similarity scores less than 58%. Clearly, a good proportion of districts underwent substantial alterations.

The size of the alterations, moreover, shows some systematic patterns. Given that the 1960s redistrictings' raison d'être was to remove malapportionment, it is no surprise that the biggest changes (lowest similarity scores) occur in those districts whose parents were farther from the average district population: these were the ones that needed to be added to or subtracted from in order to bring them into line. It also turns out that the average changes were smaller in states with more districts. In the smaller states, bringing a few districts into line typically entailed more or less substantial changes in every district, whereas in the larger states there could be relatively large subsets of districts that underwent relatively small changes. Finally, holding constant the parent district's deviation from the average population and the number of districts in the state, it turns out that *more urban districts were altered more substantially*. The effect here is substantively fairly large: as between two otherwise similar districts, one completely rural, one completely urban, the urban district's similarity score was on average 21.8% lower.[3] The most thoroughgoing reworking of district lines, therefore, tended to occur in the more urban areas of each state.

POLITICAL CONSEQUENCES OF THE REAPPORTIONMENT REVOLUTION

Most analyses of the political consequences of the reapportionment revolution have focused on its policy effects. The expectations were high. Removing malapportionment was supposed to remove the veto power of intransigent rural legislators, opening the way for slum clearance, labor and welfare legislation, civil rights laws, and other items high on the liberal agenda. These expectations notwithstanding, scholars almost universally found few substantial policy changes traceable specifically to the reallocation of power from rural to suburban/urban areas (for a strenuous dissent as regards congressional policy, see McCubbins and Schwartz 1988). Here our focus is on two other literatures, one concerned with how 1960s redistrictings affected the electoral success of the two major parties, the other concerned with how it affected the relative success of incumbents and challengers.

In the United States during the 1960s, the boundaries of state legislative and congressional districts were established by state laws passed in the usual fashion. Thus, if one party controlled both houses of the state legislature and the governor's mansion, it could draw district lines to advantage its own candidates. In popular and academic jargon, redistricting plans that seek to maximize the gain of the redistricting party are known as *partisan gerrymanders*.

If neither party controls the redistricting process, partisan gerrymanders may give way to *incumbent-protecting gerrymanders*, in which a bipartisan alliance redraws district lines so as to preserve or enhance the electoral prospects of current officeholders. Even when one party does control redistricting, its incumbents may oppose a partisan gerrymander, because typically such gerrymanders transfer "excess" votes from districts the party already holds to districts it wishes to capture.

---

[3] The figure given in the text is based on a tobit regression in which the dependent variable is the similarity score described in the text and the independent variables are absolute deviation of the parent's population from the average across the North in the states with five or more districts; number of districts in the state; and percentage of the parent's population that lived in urban places. Only nonsouthern states are included in the analysis.

The hope is that such transfers lessen only slightly the probability that the incumbent in the transferred-from district will win, while increasing more substantially the probability that one of the party's nonincumbents will win a new district. From a partywide perspective, such transfers make good sense but particular incumbents may neither benefit much from having an additional copartisan nor view the damage to their own electoral prospects as minimal.

The Partisan Effects of 1960s Redistrictings

In 1964–1968, the opportunity for partisan gerrymandering appeared in at least 18 state-years: 10 cases in which the Democrats controlled all branches of the state government or were able to override a Republican governor's veto, 8 cases in which Republicans controlled the process. The natural conservatism of incumbents, moreover, may have been overcome by the requirement that malapportionment be wrung out of the system. As Elliott (1970, p. 483) put it, "radical reapportionment overrides a legislature's instinct for leaving the districts alone yet leaves unchecked the normal disposition of legislators to consult their own interests ... there is every reason to believe that the Reapportionment Revolution brought with it something which none of the experts had thought of – a Gerrymandering Revolution."

To support his view of the 1960s as an opportunity for partisan gerrymandering, Elliott (1970, pp. 486–487) examines congressional election results from 1966 and 1968 in 10 large states with few uncontested seats. He focuses on the parties in each state that won a majority of the popular two-party vote, sorting them into those that had controlled the last redistricting and those that had not. He finds that parties that controlled the last redistricting were able to translate their vote majorities into much larger seat majorities; on average, the percentage of the seats that these parties won exceeded their vote percentages by 14.7%. In contrast, parties that did not control the last redistricting saw their vote majorities translate into somewhat smaller seat percentages – 4.1% smaller on average. Overall, then, Elliott's results suggest "that in the large states the districting power conferred on its possessor an advantage of 18.8 per cent extra seats in the 1966 and 1968 elections."

Elliott (1970, p. 489) notes that "the Reapportionment Revolution took place at a particularly bad time for the Republicans; namely, after the elections of 1964, which had cost the Republicans 101 seats in state senates and 426 seats in state houses of representatives," going on to quote Congressional Quarterly's opinion (voiced in 1966) that "the result may be a built-in Democratic advantage . . . for years to come" (Congressional Quarterly 1966, p. 44). But Elliott provides no evidence that the Democrats did better on average, and Congressional Quarterly can also be quoted later in the same document explaining why there was no net partisan effect either way: "Because the major beneficiaries of redistricting have been suburban areas where both the Republican and Democratic parties are strong, neither party appears to have been greatly helped or harmed by the realignment of Congressional districts along population lines" (Congressional Quarterly 1966, p. 59). To round things out, Noragon (1973, pp. 318–320), in a study of 41 districts whose partisan tendencies were substantially affected by redistricting, finds "almost a ratio of 2.5 : 1 favoring the Republicans."

Both Elliott's study and Noragon's have methodological problems that make it difficult to be sure of their conclusions. Elliott's study does not, for example, control for the "swing ratio" in the states he studies (Born 1985, p. 306). In plurality-rule elections, the largest vote-getting party *generally* gets a higher percentage of seats than votes, even when districts are established by bipartisan commissions and partisan gerrymandering is unlikely (Rae 1971). The swing ratio, or responsiveness, in a particular state is a measure of how fast the big-party advantage grows as the largest party's vote percentage increases past 50%.[4] Large swing ratios mean that a few more percentage points past 50% of the statewide vote yield a good deal more than 50% of the seats, while a small swing ratio means that the largest vote-getting party is still being only slightly over-represented in seats. Did the redistricting parties in Elliott's study do so well simply because redistricting increased the swing ratio without really conferring any specifically partisan advantage? We cannot tell from his study.[5]

Noragon's study is less useful than it might be in part because he selects on the dependent variable (King, Keohane, and Verba 1994). The 41 districts that Noragon chose to study were those that underwent significant political alteration, changing from marginal Democratic to safe Republican seats, for example. But we cannot really conclude from the fact that most of these cases benefited the Republicans that the Republicans did well overall. Perhaps the Democrats handed the Republicans

---

[4] We discuss responsiveness in greater detail in Chapter 3.
[5] Technically, Elliott's study computes bias as something like $E(S | V > .5) - V$, whereas the now-standard procedure is to estimate $E(S | V = .5) - .5$.

big gains in a few districts in return for smaller gains in a larger number, to their net advantage. The small gains do not appear in Noragon's study, and so it is not a reliable guide to the overall impact of redistricting on partisan fortunes.

Despite the methodological weaknesses of Elliott's and Noragon's studies, few studies have since looked at the partisan impact of the 1960s redistrictings with better methods. Most of the "methodologically modern" literature on redistricting has focused on the postcensus redistrictings in 1972, 1982, and 1992. The primary exception is Born (1985), who includes 24 redistricting plans from the period 1964–1970 in a larger study of 91 plans from 1952 to 1982. How do his findings gibe with those reviewed previously?

First, Born finds only relatively moderate partisan effects in the 1952–1982 period. This does not directly contradict Elliott's stronger claims, since Born does not single out the 1960s for separate analysis, but it suggests that Elliott may have overstated his case. Second, Born does not argue for any net partisan advantage one way or the other – either in the overall period or in the 1960s. His primary emphasis is instead on the partisan nature of malapportionment in each state: "the partisan advantage bestowed by post-1964 [redistricting] schemes has come to depend more on which party's districts before redistricting were relatively underpopulated and less on the identity of the party drawing the lines" (Born 1985, p. 317).

If one turns from those studies that look specifically at the 1960s to the more recent redistricting literature, one finds reports of mixed or relatively moderate partisan effects state by state, which cumulate into even smaller net national effects (e.g., Bullock 1975; Abramowitz 1983; Cain 1985; Glazer, Grofman, and Robbins 1987; Niemi and Winsky 1987; Campagna and Grofman 1990). The view now prevailing in the literature is that redistricting is unlikely to produce any net partisan gains at the national level because (1) partisan gerrymanders occur only when one party controls both the legislative and executive branches in a state, making them relatively rare given the high incidence of divided government in the states;[6] (2) partisan gerrymanders sometimes fail; and (3)

---

[6] Even when one party controls the policy-making apparatus, partisan gerrymanders are less likely to occur if the in party has no reason to fear the out party and is factionalized (as in one-party areas of the country). In this circumstance, it is plausible that different factions within the majority are more worried about each other than they are about the minority party.

pro-Republican gerrymanders in some states balance pro-Democratic gerrymanders in other states (Butler and Cain 1992, pp. 8–9).

The Effect of 1960s Redistrictings on Incumbents

Tufte (1973, p. 551) suggested that the Court's reapportionment rulings gave "incumbents new opportunities to construct secure districts for themselves," rather than giving parties new opportunities to seek advantage against one another. As evidence that incumbents took advantage of their opportunities, he showed that the percentage of competitive districts declined in the House as a whole and in four large states that redistricted during the 1960s.

Tufte's idea that 1960s redistricting plans were mostly incumbent-protecting gerrymanders has not, however, been supported in the subsequent literature. Bullock (1975) showed that incumbent reelection rates were no higher in redrawn than in untouched districts during the 1960s. Cover (1977) showed that the vote swing to incumbents was no larger in redrawn than in untouched districts, controlling for the national partisan swing. Ferejohn (1977) showed that the percentage of competitive districts declined about equally in both redistricted and unredistricted states. Since the publication of these studies, no one has argued that the 1960s redistricting laws were primarily incumbent protection acts.

In Part III of the book, we shall reconsider how redistricting has affected incumbents. Our focus will not be on the type of redistricting, whether partisan or incumbent-protecting, but rather on how candidates' anticipations of the fact of redistricting affected their entry decisions.

RECONSIDERING THE REAPPORTIONMENT REVOLUTION

In our view, the wave of redistrictings sparked by the Supreme Court's reapportionment decisions was much more consequential than the previous literature would have it. In this section, we lay the groundwork for the argument spelled out in the next part of the book. Our basic point is that, although eradicating malapportionment might have favored the Republicans slightly outside the South, the political circumstances of the new redistrictings decisively favored the Democrats. We note three circumstances in particular.

First, traditional Republican dominance of the North meant that most redistricting actions in the 1960s overturned districting plans that were favorable to Republicans. Table 2.3 classifies the last prerevolutionary

Table 2.3. *Last Prerevolutionary and first Postrevolutionary Plans in 33 Nonsouthern States*

Prerevolutionary Plans	Postrevolutionary Plans				
	Partisan: Republican	Bipartisan: Republican	Bipartisan: Democratic	Partisan: Democratic	No New Plan Until 1972
Partisian: Republican	CO (4) KS (5) NH (2) SD (2)	MT (2) NY (41) OR (4) CT (6)	—	UT (2) IN (11)	IA (7) ME (2) ND (2) RI (2)
Mixed: Republican	OH (24)	MI (19) WI (10)	—	NJ (15)	—
Bipartisan: Republican	—	MA (12) NE (3) IL (24) PA (27)	—	—	MN (8)
Bipartisan: Democratic	—	—	—	—	—
Mixed: Democratic	—	—	—	—	—
Partisan: Democratic	ID (2)	—	AZ (3) CA (38) OK (6) MD (8) NM (2)	WV (3) KY (7) MO (10) WA (7)	—

Note: The number of districts in each state is indicated in parentheses. The terms *partisan*, *mixed*, and *bipartisan* are explained in the text.

and first postrevolutionary districting plans in each of the 33 nonsouthern states that had more than one district and did not use multimember elections exclusively in the prerevolutionary period.[7] Each districting plan falls into one of six categories: partisan Republican (i.e., a plan passed under unified Republican government); partisan Democratic; mixed Republican (i.e., a plan passed under divided government and an automatic conservative reversion favoring the Republicans);[8] mixed

[7] Throughout the book, we exclude the five single-district states – Alaska, Delaware, Nevada, Vermont, and Wyoming – from our analysis. In addition, we exclude Hawaii because of its exclusive use of multimember elections prior to 1970.

[8] When the existing districting plan was also the legal default, we say that the reversion was *conservative*. When the reversion came into force if and only if the state did not enact a new plan, we say that it was *automatic*. See the later text for further discussion.

Democratic; bipartisan Republican (i.e., a plan passed under divided government and an automatic radical reversion favoring the Republicans);[9] and bipartisan Democratic.

As can be seen, 14 of the 33 plans in place when the reapportionment revolution arrived were Republican. Another nine were modifications of older Republican plans. Less than a third of the prerevolutionary plans were Democratic.

Even Table 2.3's accounting – by which over two-thirds of the prerevolutionary plans potentially favored Republicans – understates the degree of Republican dominance. California and Washington operated under Republican plans until 1961 and 1959, respectively, so that 75% of the total number of nonsouthern state elections between 1946 and 1966 were held under plans that potentially favored Republicans. Moreover, the Republicans dominated most of the larger states, so that over 80% of nonsouthern district elections in this period were contested under partisan Republican, mixed Republican, or bipartisan Republican plans.

Second, interacting with traditional Republican dominance in the North was Lyndon Baines Johnson's landslide victory over Barry Goldwater in 1964 – which meant that the Republicans found themselves at a low point in terms of their state legislative power just as the wave of court-mandated congressional redistricting peaked. One consequence of this electoral disaster was that the 1960s saw the replacement of mostly Republican plans with mostly bipartisan plans and partisan Democratic plans.

Third, the 1960s redistrictings were conducted under the threat of court action should the state legislature and governor not agree on a bill. Indeed, perhaps the single most important consequence of the Supreme Court's decision in *Wesberry* was to change the reversionary outcome of the congressional redistricting process (and the conditions under which it came into force).

Let us explain this last assertion. Since 1913, the U.S. House has had a fixed number (435) of seats (with minor variations in two Congresses). Since 1929, these seats have been automatically apportioned among the states according to population after each decennial census. It has then been up to each state to define the boundaries of its allotted number of districts. Typically, district boundaries have been established by the

---

[9] When the legal default was not conservative, and came into force if and only if the state did not enact a new plan, we say that there was an automatic radical reversion. See the later text for further discussion.

passage of a state law, with legislatures and governors bargaining within the confines of the ordinary statutory processes of their respective states. If the governor and state legislature could not agree on a new plan, then the next election was held under what we call the *reversionary plan* – a legally defined default.

Prior to the reapportionment revolution, the reversionary plan was usually the state's current plan. That is, if no new plan could be agreed upon, the current plan continued in force. The only exceptions to this rule arose when a state gained or lost seats pursuant to the decennial federal census. If a state had *gained* seats, the exception was minor: a state could simply elect the new members at large, preserving all the old districts. This was a relatively painless solution that incumbent members of Congress often found preferable to the disruption of their current districts. If a state had *lost* seats in the reapportionment, however, all members had to be elected at large, absent a new districting plan. This was a much less palatable reversionary plan, and its unpleasantness explains why the bulk of prerevolutionary redistricting action occurred in states that had lost representation in Congress.

When the current plan was also the reversionary plan (or was the main basis for that plan, as in cases where the state had gained seats), we say that the reversion was *conservative*. When the reversion was not conservative, we say that it was *radical*. In these terms, prior to the reapportionment revolution all states not losing seats had conservative reversions, while all states losing seats had radical reversions.[10]

Now consider how the entry of the judiciary altered the strategic situation. The role of the courts in the 1960s varied from case to case, but often things played out as follows. First, a federal or state court would declare a state's current districting plan null and void. The court would then give the state a more or less clear and more or less constraining deadline; if the legislature and governor could not agree on a plan by the deadline, the court would impose a plan. Sometimes the plan that the court planned to impose was clear ex ante, sometimes not. But

---

[10] Technically, at-large elections were illegal from 1842 until 1872, allowable under certain conditions from 1872 to 1929, and then again illegal after 1968. See Martis (1982). The legal basis for the reversions noted in the text appears to go back to some court decisions in 1932 (see Apportionment Act. 1982. *U.S. Code.* Vol. 4, sec. 2a, p. 64). For present purposes, it is sufficient to note that the 1941 Apportionment Act repeated the relevant provisions (and that they were not overturned until the 1960s). See Apportionment Act. 1941. *Statutes At Large.* Vol. 55, sec. 1, p. 762.

the court's plan was never the preexisting plan. Thus, *all redistricting action in the 1960s took place under the threat of a radical reversionary outcome of one kind or another.*

Another important point to note is that all reversions before the reapportionment revolution were *automatic*: a prespecified reversion was to be used when a prespecified condition was met. In contrast, reversions after the reapportionment revolution were *discretionary*: the conditions under which a reversion would be used, and the nature of the reversion itself, were at a court's discretion. Even when the state government produced a new districting plan, a court might decide that the plan produced was unconstitutional and impose its own. Moreover, the plan that a court imposed was restricted only by its interpretation of the relevant judicial criteria.

We explore the consequences of judicial discretion in Chapters 5 and 6. In Chapters 3 and 4 we focus on automatic reversions – in particular, the political consequences of conservative as opposed to radical reversions.

Some indication of the importance of automatic reversionary plans can be gained by considering a few examples. First, when the reversionary plan was conservative, the party favored by the current lines could simply refuse to agree to a new plan and preserve those lines. Missouri provides a case in point. As Short (1931, p. 637) reports, "The Democratic party had a majority in both houses of the General Assembly in 1911; but, inasmuch as the number of Missouri's representatives in Congress was not changed by the reapportionment act of that year, and the existing districts were distinctly advantageous to that party, no serious attempt was made to formulate a redistricting measure which would meet with the approval of the Republican chief executive."[11]

Second, when the reversionary plan was radical, the party favored under the reversion could be empowered. In Michigan, for example, the Republicans controlled both houses of the state legislature and the governorship when a three-judge federal court declared, on 27 March 1964, that the state's 1963 redistricting plan was unconstitutional in light of *Wesberry*. The state legislature was preoccupied with its own redistrict-

---

[11] The Democrats were presumably confident that they would continue to poll a majority of votes in legislative elections, and hence were uninterested in reducing the level of responsiveness. Missouri in 1911 thus provides an example in which vote expectations under divided government were not substantially different than under unified government – as we assume they were, at least on average, in the postwar era.

ing problem and, by the time it got around to congressional redistricting (about a month later, in early May), the strategic balance had tilted in favor of the Democrats. The court had clearly warned that all 19 House seats in Michigan would be filled at large if the legislature did not act before the 1964 election. This was a reversionary outcome that the Republicans found extremely distasteful in light of their estimates of the relative statewide strengths of the two parties in the coming (Goldwater!) election. Moreover, state law required a 90-day waiting period before any new law became effective, a requirement that could be waived only by a two-thirds vote. Consequently, because the redistricting plan had to be in place before the primary election season began (in less than 90 days) and because the Republican advantage in the state House was only 58–52 (less than two-thirds), the federal court's firm deadline and clear reversionary plan meant that concessions had to be made to the Democrats (Congressional Quarterly 1966, pp. 2066–2067). Indeed, Michigan was essentially operating under divided government during this redistricting.

The last anecdote suggests that the nature of the reversionary plan could sometimes be very important. In the next chapter, we look more systematically at the interaction between partisan control (unified or divided state government) and the nature of the reversion (automatic conservative or automatic radical).

CONCLUSION

Jurisprudentially, the Supreme Court's apportionment decisions in the period 1962–1964 were soon described as "historical landmarks" and "certain to be as historic in American constitutional history as *Marbury v. Madison*."[12] Structurally, they led to the (often substantial) redrawing of 301 of the 329 nonsouthern congressional districts during the years 1964–1970. Yet, politically, the Court's decisions are depicted as having little overall impact, either on the struggle between Democrats and Republicans or on the struggle between incumbents and challengers. This contrast between large jurisprudential and structural effects and small political effects is the puzzle that the current literature presents.

In the next part of the book, we begin to unpack this puzzle by reconsidering how one ought to model the redistricting process. Most of the literature has focused only on the issue of which party controls what

---

[12] The opinions are from Baker (1966, p. 3) and Dixon (1968, p. 99).

branches of state government, ignoring two central questions: First, what happens if the state government does not enact a new districting bill after a federal census? Second, how did the entrance of the courts into the redistricting fray affect legislators' and governors' strategies? In the next part of the book, we develop a model that incorporates answers to both of these questions. The consequence of bringing these issues more explicitly into view is to change one's view of the political impact of the Court's reapportionment decisions rather drastically.

PART II

Democrats and Republicans

3

A Model of Congressional Redistricting in the United States

In this chapter, we develop a general model of the redistricting process in the United States. We use this model to examine two features of how congressional votes translate into seats: *partisan bias* (how much larger or smaller a party's seat share is than its vote share would warrant) and *responsiveness* (how much party seat shares respond to changes in vote shares). Bias and responsiveness are standard concepts in the analysis of redistricting and will be defined more fully later. From our model, we derive specific hypotheses about how the bias and responsiveness of a redistricting plan will differ as a function of two conditions obtaining when that plan is enacted: (1) the legally defined reversionary outcome of the redistricting process and (2) which party controls the legislative branches (house, senate, and governorship) of the state. We test our hypotheses in the next chapter.

A MODEL OF CONGRESSIONAL REDISTRICTING

The literature on redistricting categorizes gerrymanders according to the varying goals that those who redraw district lines pursue. For present purposes, the most important categories are proincumbent gerrymanders (when a bipartisan alliance draws the lines to preserve the current incumbents' chances of victory) and partisan gerrymanders (when a single party draws the lines to maximize its seat share).[1] In this section, we develop a model in which these two types of gerrymander – along with a third "mixed" type – emerge endogenously as a function of partisan control of the redistricting process and the nature of the reversionary outcome.

---

[1] A third type of gerrymander, which we do not consider here, is the racial gerrymander.

The basic elements of our model are straightforward. There are two parties, the Republicans and the Democrats, in a given state. Each party likes to have more seats rather than fewer, and each is risk averse. Each makes a strategic decision regarding how much bias and how much responsiveness its ideal redistricting plan would have and then bargains with the other in an attempt to attain or approximate that ideal. The parties' relative bargaining strength is determined by two factors: partisan control of state government (unified Democratic, divided, or unified Republican) and whether the reversionary plan is an automatic conservative or an automatic radical one.[2]

In the following sections, we elaborate our model. We give the reader fair warning when we present technical details by prefacing sentences or paragraphs with the word *formally*, so that those so inclined can skip over the indicated bits without losing the line of argument. However, the argument is not much more complicated than standard discussions of bargaining in introductory microeconomics courses, so there is not too much to skip even for the mathematically disinclined.

Preliminaries

The literal output of the redistricting process is a statutory description of the boundary lines of each congressional district in the state. But parties care about who wins the various seats at stake, not about lines per se, and so districting plans are usually described in terms of their political rather than literal characteristics. One approach (see, e.g., Owen and Grofman 1988; McDonald 1999) focuses on how boundary lines affect the resultant partisan makeup of each district (measured, for example, by the number of registered Republicans and Democrats). In our approach, we think of the redistricting process as entailing two steps: first, a broad strategic decision about how much partisan bias (here denoted λ) and how much responsiveness (denoted ρ) the redistricting plan will entail; second, a particular set of lines that implement the broader strategy. We shall ignore the implementing lines and focus on the levels of partisan bias and responsiveness.[3]

---

[2] The types of reversion – conservative and radical – are defined fully in Chapter 2. Briefly, when the current plan is also the reversionary plan, we say that the reversion is conservative. Otherwise, the reversion is radical. A reversion is automatic if it is pre-specified and does not depend on the discretion of any political actor.

[3] It is possible to recast our model in terms of the allocation of voters across districts (see Cox and Katz 2001), but here we take the choice of responsiveness and bias

What are partisan bias and responsiveness? They are features of a redistricting plan that affect how votes translate into seats, hence the parties' expected seat shares. If a single party controls the redistricting process, the standard gerrymandering recipe is to pack as many of the other party's supporters in as few districts as possible (creating inefficiently safe districts) while spreading its own supporters evenly across as many districts as possible (creating winnable but not inefficiently safe districts). This strategy ensures that the "out" party pays more in votes for each seat it wins than does the redistricting party, which is the same as saying that the redistricting plan engineers *bias* in favor of the redistricting party.

It is important to note that increasing partisan bias is not the only way a redistricting party might seek to increase its expected seat share. If a party is confident that it will get a majority of votes cast in its favor over the life of a districting plan, another way to increase its expected seat share is to make every district a microcosm of the state. Compared to the packing strategy, this creates more marginal districts and will thus increase what is typically called the *responsiveness* of the system. Another way to think of the microcosm strategy is that it makes the system more like a winner-take-all election: whoever gets the most votes statewide typically gets the most votes in all the districts (which are microcosms of the state by hypothesis) and, therefore, typically wins all the seats. Given sufficient certainty about its electoral strength, a redistricting party might rationally seek to maximize its expected seat share by maximizing responsiveness rather than by engineering a bias specifically in its own favor. The high-responsiveness strategy runs the risk of giving the "out" party all the seats, should it manage an unexpectedly good electoral showing, but it does not concede any districts at all to the opposition, as the packing strategy does. Finally, note that various compromises between the pure packing and microcosm strategies are possible, yielding intermediate plans.

A given districting plan – identified with its associated bias-responsiveness pair, (ρ, λ) – determines how votes will translate into seats. In particular, it determines how big is the bonus in seats that the party winning the most votes gets (via ρ) and whether one party's votes translate at more favorable "terms of trade" into seats than the other's (via λ).

---

as primitive. This allows us to focus more clearly on the bargaining issues that arise during redistricting.

Formally, we assume that the plan parameters affect the votes-to-seats mapping according to the following formula (based on the classic "cube law" and widely used in the redistricting literature – see, e.g., King and Browning 1987; King 1989; Campagna and Grofman 1990):

$$\frac{s}{1-s} = e^{\lambda}\left(\frac{\nu}{1-\nu}\right)^{\rho} \tag{1}$$

Here s denotes the share of legislative seats that the Democrats win in some state, and ν denotes the mean share of the vote that the Democrats garner in that election across all districts.

Figure 3.1 illustrates how variations in responsiveness (ρ) affect votes-to-seats translations, given zero bias ($\lambda = 0$). For $\rho = 1$, each party can expect to get a seat share equal to its vote share – proportional representation. For $\rho = 3$, we have the classic cube law outcome in which the vote-richer party is overrepresented in terms of seats fairly substantially (for example, a party garnering 55% of the vote can expect almost 65% of the seats). Larger values of ρ lead to even larger bonuses awarded to the vote-richer party.

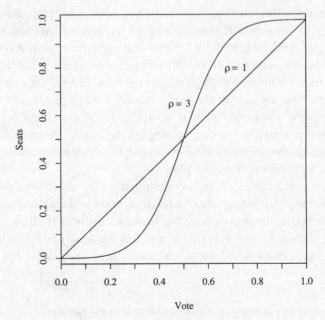

Figure 3.1 Examples of seats-vote curves for two values of ρ: 1 and 3.

What the Parties Want

Just knowing how votes turn into seats is not enough to allow parties to forecast their seat shares with certainty over the life of a districting plan, because they do not know their future vote shares with certainty. At the time a new districting plan is fashioned, however, the parties do presumably have a keen interest in their future vote shares and some well-considered ideas about their likely size.

Formally, we represent parties' beliefs about their (and their opponent's) vote shares by a cumulative probability distribution F, where $F(v)$ is the probability that the stronger party's vote share is less than or equal to v.[4] The "stronger party" is simply the one expected to get the larger vote share.[5] Note that both parties have the *same* probabilistic beliefs about the stronger party's vote share; we do not consider the case in which the parties have divergent beliefs about how well the stronger party will do.

We are now in a position to say what the parties want more precisely. We envision the stronger party as having some utility for seats, denoted by a utility function u, and choosing λ and ρ (if it controls the redistricting process) in order to maximize the expected utility of its seat share.[6] Similarly, the weaker party (the one expected to get a vote share of less than one-half) has a utility function w and chooses λ and ρ (if it controls the redistricting process) in order to maximize the expected utility of its seat share.[7]

---

[4] The vote share here can be thought of as either the statewide vote share or the simple average of the district vote shares. The latter statistic will itself be a function of the district lines drawn when malapportionment is possible. However, when malapportionment is eradicated, as we assume for purposes of the model that it was after *Baker*, then the simple average of district vote shares and the statewide vote share will be equal, regardless of the lines drawn (subject to the constraint that all districts have equal population, with all voters having equal propensities to vote). We ignore the complication posed by the dependence of the simple average on the district lines when malapportionment is present. The empirical analyses, however, are much the same whether one uses the simple average, as we do, or the statewide share, as we have also done but do not report here.

[5] Thus, letting f denote the probability density function associated with F, $E(v) = \int v f(v) dv > .5$ (the expected vote share for the stronger party exceeds one-half). If both parties are expected to get exactly half of the vote, then we would choose one arbitrarily as the "strong" party. Cases of ties do not arise naturally in our theory, however, so we assume that one party does have an expected advantage over the other.

[6] Formally, the strong party's expected utility is $\int u[s(v;\lambda,\rho)] f(v) dv$.

[7] Formally, the weak party's expected utility is $\int w[1 - s(v;\lambda,\rho)] f(v) dv$.

We assume that parties maximize a function of their seat share, rather than just the seat share, because we also assume that both parties are *risk averse*. That is, given the choice between a redistricting plan that offered the certainty of n seats and one that offered equal chances of winning either $n + 1$ or $n - 1$ seats, each would prefer the sure thing. State parties might be risk averse because congressional incumbents – who naturally value the seats the party already holds more than new ones it might win – are able to influence them.[8] Alternatively, state parties might be risk averse because congressional seniority underpins the state's ability to get a larger share of federal largesse. The more valuable congressional seniority is, the more valuable it is to keep one's own incumbents and the less valuable it is to knock off the other party's incumbents.

At this point, we can step back and focus on how the two parties view bias (λ) and responsiveness (ρ). Adopting the convention that λ denotes bias in the strong party's favor, the strong party obviously views bias as a "good," while the weak party views it as a "bad."[9] Moreover, for a class of risk-averse parties, the strong party views responsiveness as a "good," while the weak party views it as a "bad."[10] We shall focus on this case in what follows, which allows us to represent each party's preferences over bias and responsiveness much as economists represent consumer preferences over two commodities.

Note that how much each party likes responsiveness relative to bias depends on how large the strong party's expected vote advantage is. The

---

[8] Such influence might not be automatic if state legislators as a class coveted higher office and thus favored plans that would oust as many incumbents as possible. This sort of anti-congressional-incumbent sentiment is mentioned in some case histories but does not appear to have been a dominant consideration in any redistricting in our dataset.

[9] Formally: $\partial Eu/\partial\lambda > 0$ for all (ρ,λ) and $\partial Ew/\partial\lambda < 0$ for all (ρ,λ).

[10] Formally: $\partial Eu/\partial\rho > 0$ for all (ρ,λ) and $\partial Ew/\partial\rho < 0$ for all (ρ,λ). To see that there are risk-averse functions u for which responsiveness is a good, let $x = \ln(\nu/(1 - \nu))$ and note that $\partial Eu/\partial\rho = \int u'\partial s(x;\lambda,\rho)/\partial\rho g(x)dx$ by Leibnitz's rule. Now, $\partial s/\partial\rho$
$$= \frac{\exp(-\lambda + \rho x)}{(\exp(-\lambda) + \exp(\rho x))^2} x,$$ which is positive if $x > 0$ (equivalently, $\nu > .5$), zero if $x = 0$ ($\nu = .5$), and negative if $x < 0$ ($\nu < .5$). Suppose that u is risk neutral, so that u' is a constant, and also that the density g is symmetric about its mean 0. In this case, $\partial Eu/\partial\rho = 0$. Thus, any density h such that h stochastically dominates g will guarantee that $\partial Eu/\partial\rho > 0$. For a given h, there will be a range of risk-averse functions t for which $\partial Et/\partial\rho > 0$ also. In other words, there is always a risk-averse function for which ρ is a good if $E\nu > .5$ for the strong party. In essence, we are assuming that the strong parties in our sample always had expected votes strictly above .5 and were not too risk-averse.

more sure it is that it will out-poll its opponent, for example, the more bias the strong party is willing to sacrifice in order to gain an additional unit of responsiveness. Our subsequent results are all simple consequences of the trade-offs between bias and responsiveness that the parties are willing to make under different circumstances.

What the Parties Can Get

When the parties choose ρ and λ, they cannot simply pick any imaginable values. We assume that it would be impossible, for example, to draw the lines so that responsiveness was below unity (which would imply that the fewer votes a party wins, the more overrepresented it is). More generally, we assume that there exists a set of feasible plans, A, from which the redistricting party (or parties) must choose.

Substantively, we assume that the redistricting party (or parties) faces (face) a trade-off between bias and responsiveness. Even if it (they) wanted to increase one without diminishing the other, after some point it would not be possible to do so. Formally, the assumption that there is a trade-off between bias and responsiveness can be incorporated by assuming that A is a strictly convex subset of $\rho - \lambda$ space with a smooth boundary, as illustrated in Figure 3.2.

To justify the trade-off assumption, consider the set of feasible plans that yield zero bias and select from among these the one with the highest responsiveness. What might this zero-bias, high-responsiveness plan look like? If the state is almost evenly divided between the Democrats and Republicans, it might simply be a plan in which every district is a microcosm of the state, replicating the close balance in every district. Starting from such a plan, the strong party (let us suppose it controls the redistricting) could increase bias by packing one or more districts as fully as possible with the weaker parties' supporters, leaving the other districts safer – but not inefficiently safe – for its own candidates. Suppose the optimal number of such "packed" districts is three. Then, for each of the first three districts packed with opposition party supporters, bias will increase (by inefficiently concentrating the other party's supporters) and responsiveness will decrease (the packed districts are safe and the other districts are getting less marginal as well). Continuing to pack districts full of opposition supporters eventually produces excessively safe districts for the stronger party as well as the weaker party (and exhausts the number of weak-party supporters). Thus, continuing to pack districts will continue to depress responsiveness but will also depress bias.

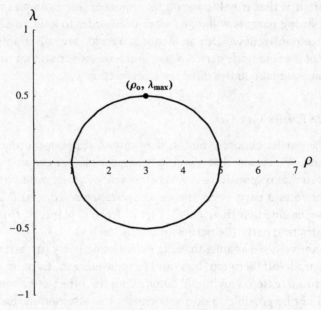

Figure 3.2 An example of a set of feasible plans, *A*.

Eventually, one arrives at something like a pure incumbent-protecting gerrymander, with half the seats safe for the opposition and half the seats safe for the redistricting party (yielding near-zero bias and very low responsiveness).

BARGAINING OVER REDISTRICTING PLANS

In this section, we consider how utility-maximizing parties might interact in the redistricting process. When there is unified government and an automatic reversion, there is no need for the party controlling redistricting (presumably the stronger party) to bargain with its opponent (presumably the weaker). However, when there is divided government, both parties have seats at the table. Their bargaining positions in this case depend on the reversionary outcome.

Three Redistricting Scenarios

To explain the importance of reversions, consider what the values of ρ and λ will be under three different constellations of partisan control and reversionary outcome: (1) the strong party enjoys unified control of the state and faces an automatic reversion (either conservative or radical); (2) there is divided government, with an automatic conservative reversion favoring the strong party; or (3) there is divided government with an automatic radical reversion. These three cases all pertain to typical prerevolutionary constellations of government control and reversion. (We shall deal with the discretionary reversions typical of the postrevolutionary period in Chapters 5 and 6.) Some direct, yet nonobvious, consequences of the assumptions made thus far are presented in propositions 1–3.

> **Proposition 1:** If a party enjoys unified control of the state government, faces an automatic reversion, and has an expected vote share greater than .5, then any new plan will exhibit high values of both bias and responsiveness.
> **Proof:** See Appendix.

Under unified control, whether an automatic reversionary plan is conservative or radical should not matter; whichever party controls the state should simply impose a plan in its own interests. Hence, we refer to these as *partisan plans*. To illustrate a partisan plan, suppose that the Republicans control the redistricting process. They would prefer a plan with larger pro-Republican bias, responsiveness held constant. They would also like higher levels of responsiveness (to exploit their larger expected vote), bias held constant. Given that the constraint set is convex, well-defined solutions to the party's maximization problem exist. In particular, since both bias and responsiveness are "goods" for the party, its choice will be somewhere on the northeast portion of the constraint set, where both bias and responsiveness are "high."[11]

> **Proposition 2:** Suppose (1) that there is divided government facing an automatic conservative reversion; (2) that the current districting plan, denoted $(\rho_{rev}, \lambda_{rev})$, was chosen by the strong party when it last enjoyed unified control; and (3) that the strong party's

---

[11] The reason the word "high" is in quotation marks is that, if the strong party has sufficiently good vote prospects, it may be willing to trade bias down to fairly low levels. For example, if it expected a vote share of .9, with a sufficiently small variance, then its optimum would be a system with near-maximal responsiveness and near-zero bias. As the strong party's vote prospects worsen, however, it prefers higher bias and lower responsiveness. Thus, the exact value of bias and responsiveness is not determined.

expected vote is now smaller (under divided government) than it was when the party designed the reversionary plan (under unified government). Then any new plan (ρ, λ) will exhibit lower responsiveness than the current plan (which is also the reversion) but higher bias: $\rho < \rho_{\text{rev}}$; $\lambda > \lambda_{\text{rev}}$.

The proof of this proposition can be given in words as follows. Note first that the strong party must agree to any new plan under divided government. Therefore, if there is a new plan, the strong party must (weakly) prefer it to the reversionary plan.

Since the strong party views both bias and responsiveness as goods, the only plans that it will weakly prefer to the reversion fall into three categories: (1) plans with both higher bias and higher responsiveness; (2) plans that compensate for lower bias with sufficiently large increases in responsiveness; and (3) plans that compensate for lower responsiveness with sufficiently large increases in bias. No plans in the first category are feasible (if there were such plans, the strong party would have chosen them when it last redistricted, since it prefers both higher bias and higher responsiveness).

Are there any feasible plans in the second and third categories? Recall that we have assumed that the strong party's expected vote is *lower* under divided government than it was when the strong party last enjoyed unified control. Intuitively, this means that the party is *less* fond of responsiveness relative to bias now than it was when it fashioned the current plan. Thus, the only feasible plans that it prefers to the current plan are those with lower responsiveness and higher bias.

To explain this last claim more fully, consider the nature of the strong party's indifference curves – that is, curves through the responsiveness-bias plane such that all plans on the curve are equally good from the party's perspective (see Figure 3.3). The key point is that because the party is now less fond of responsiveness, due to its lower expected vote share, its current indifference curves are flatter than they were when it last drew the lines (Lemma 3 in the Appendix provides a formal proof of this assertion). Thus, to reiterate, the only *feasible* plans the strong party prefers to the reversion are those with lower responsiveness and higher bias. (A discussion of the argument in terms of indifference curves is given in the Appendix.)

Proposition 2 shows that, under certain conditions, plans passed under divided government with conservative reversions will lead to lower responsiveness and, strikingly, even higher bias than entailed in the reversionary plan. Since the reversionary plan by assumption was put in force the last time the strong party enjoyed unified control, we can conclude (from Proposition 1) that the reversionary bias is high, so that the new plan's bias will also be high. Note that this conclusion does not depend on any specific theory of bargaining between the parties; any bargaining theory in which the final outcome is (weakly) preferred by the strong party to the reversion will do. We will refer to plans passed under divided government in the face of automatic conservative reversions as *mixed plans* since bias can be high (as in a partisan plan) but responsiveness is low (as in a bipartisan plan, considered next).

> **Proposition 3:** Suppose there is a divided government facing an automatic radical reversion in which bias is zero ($\lambda_{rev} = 0$) and responsiveness (ρ_{rev}) is maximal. If the slope of the constraint set A at its rightmost point is negative infinity, as in Figure 3.2, then any new plan (ρ, λ) will exhibit lower responsiveness than the reversionary plan but higher bias: $\rho < \rho_{rev}$; $\lambda > \lambda_{rev}$.

The proof of this proposition can also be given in words. If there is a new plan, the strong party must (weakly) prefer it to the reversionary plan. By definition, the radical reversion has zero bias and maximal responsiveness – which we assume puts it at the rightmost point in the constraint set, A. Since both bias and responsiveness are goods, the strong party's indifference curves have negative but *finite* slope. Thus, the slope of the indifference curve through ($\rho_{rev}, \lambda_{rev}$) will not be as steep as the slope of the constraint set at that point. This means that the only feasible plans that the strong party prefers to the reversion will have lower responsiveness and higher bias than the reversion.

This proposition is intended to apply to radical reversions before *Baker*. To see the proposition's applicability, recall that prerevolutionary radical reversions mandated that all seats be filled by at-large election. If all voters voted straight party tickets, then the resulting system would have infinitely high responsiveness: whichever party won the most votes statewide would win all the seats. If some voters could not be counted on to vote straight tickets, however, then responsiveness would be lower, similar to that obtained by creating a series of districts all of which were microcosms of the state as a whole. We believe the latter scenario is more plausible and so envision maximal but not infinite responsiveness in the reversionary plan. Given such a reversion, and given that the strong party's indifference curves are negatively sloped, if there is a new plan agreed to, it will have lower responsiveness and higher bias.

Will the bias in radical reversion cases be higher or lower than that in conservative reversion cases? If the indifference curves of the two parties have the nice convexity properties typically assumed in Edgeworth box analyses, then the level of bias in a new plan agreed to under divided government will increase with the bias of the reversionary plan (under standard bargaining solutions such as Nash's). Thus, we expect that the bias under radical reversions will not only be positive but will also be less than that observed under conservative reversions. We will refer to these relatively low-bias, low-responsiveness plans as *bipartisan plans*.

Summary

All told, our expectations regarding prerevolutionary plans are as summarized in Table 3.1. Under unified control with automatic reversion, we expect partisan gerrymanders, yielding high levels of both partisan bias and responsiveness. Under divided control with automatic radical reversion, we expect bipartisan incumbent-protecting gerrymanders, yielding lower levels of both partisan bias and responsiveness (the bias favoring the party with the larger expected vote share). Finally, under divided control with automatic conservative reversion, we expect higher levels of bias but lower levels of responsiveness – a mixed case that has features of both partisan and bipartisan gerrymanders.

We note some limitations of our classification of plans before going on to our empirical analysis in the next chapter. First, the category of mixed plans includes all those written under divided government in the face of an automatic conservative reversion. But in Proposition 2 we

Table 3.1. *Predictions for Bias and Responsiveness as a Function of Government Control and Legal Reversion*

	Automatic Conservative Reversion	Automatic Radical Reversion
Unified Control of State Government	Partisan Plan: High Bias and High Responsiveness	Partisan Plan: High Bias and High Responsiveness
Divided Control of State Government	Mixed Plan: High Bias and Low Responsiveness	Bipartisan Plan: Low Bias and Low Responsiveness

assume that the strong party is also the party that benefits under the reversion, thus excluding the somewhat different case in which the weak party benefits under the reversion. As an empirical matter, we believe that essentially all our cases of mixed plans conform to the narrower category assumed in Proposition 2, so that the prediction contained in Proposition 2 is the appropriate one. But in principle there may be some mistakes. Second, our analysis in the next chapter is confined to automatic reversions. We take up the case of discretionary reversions in Chapters 5 and 6.

CONCLUSION

In this chapter, we have developed a model of the redistricting process that highlights the importance of two factors: first, unified or divided control of state government; second, the nature of the reversionary outcome should the state legislature and governor fail to agree on a new districting plan. The importance of keeping track of which party controls the state government enacting a new districting statute is readily and widely appreciated. The importance of keeping track of which party controls the courts, and hence the power to set the reversionary outcome, has been almost entirely neglected in the scholarly literature on redistricting. In Chapters 5 and 6, we show that partisan control of reversionary outcomes systematically and substantially affected redistricting outcomes in the 1960s. In the next chapter, we focus on the impact of partisan control of state government, along with the automatic reversions that characterized redistricting before *Baker v. Carr*.

Appendix: Proofs and Illustrations

ASSUMPTIONS

Our model has two actors: a strong party and a weak party redistricting a given state. Letting v_j ($j = 1, \ldots, J$) denote the vote share of the strong party in the jth district in the state, and letting $v = 1/J \sum_j v_j$ be the party's average vote share, positive values of $x = \ln(v/(1 - v))$ indicate average vote majorities for the strong party, while negative values indicate average vote majorities for the weak party. The strong party seeks to set ρ and λ in order to maximize $E[u(s(x;\rho,\lambda))]$, where $s(x;\rho,\lambda)$ – the strong party's seat share, given x – can be derived from Equation (1) as

$$s(x;\rho,\lambda) = \frac{\exp(\rho x)}{\exp(-\lambda) + \exp(\rho x)}. \tag{2}$$

We let $\mu = E(x)$ and $\sigma^2 = \text{Var}(x)$.

Substituting, the strong party's maximization problem can be expressed as

$$\max_{(\rho,\lambda) \in A} \int_{-\infty}^{\infty} u\left(\frac{e^{\rho x}}{e^{-\lambda} + e^{\rho x}}\right) f(x)dx \tag{3a}$$

(where f represents the density governing x). The weak party, meanwhile, seeks to set ρ and λ in order to maximize $E[w(1 - s(x;\rho,\lambda))]$, or

$$\max_{(\rho,\lambda) \in A} \int_{-\infty}^{\infty} w\left(\frac{e^{-\lambda}}{e^{-\lambda} + e^{\rho x}}\right) f(x)dx. \tag{3b}$$

Both parties must choose ρ,λ from the constraint set A, which we assume is strictly convex with a smooth boundary. Given these assumptions, the upper boundary of A – that is, the portion of the boundary with non-negative values of λ – can be described by $A^{up} = \{(\rho,\lambda): \lambda = g(\rho)\}$, where $g' > 0$ at the left endpoint of A^{up}, $g' < 0$ at the right endpoint of A^{up}, and $g'' < 0$. We further assume that the slope of g at the right endpoint of A^{up} is steep: $|g'| = -\infty$. We do not use this assumption in Cox and Katz (1999), but it is convenient here. Given these conditions, there exists a unique point on A^{up} at which $g' = 0$. At this point – call it $(\rho_0, \lambda_{\max})$ – bias will be maximal and responsiveness will be strictly above the minimum attained in A (see Figure 3.2 for an illustration). We shall say that responsiveness is high if $\rho > \rho_0 = \rho_{hi}$ and that bias is high if $\lambda > 0$.

Condition C: (1) The strong party views responsiveness as a "good" ($\partial Eu/\partial\rho > 0$ for all (ρ,λ) in A). (2) The weak party views responsiveness as a "bad" ($\partial Ew/\partial\rho < 0$ for all (ρ,λ) in A).

Given condition C, the nature of new districting plans (if any) passed under various constellations of divided/unified government and conservative/radical reversion can be characterized. We do this in the first part of the Appendix. The second part then explores when condition C will hold. The third part briefly considers *whether* a new plan will be agreed to under divided government.

A Model of Congressional Redistricting

RESULTS

Lemma 1: The strong party views bias as a "good" ($\partial Eu/\partial\lambda > 0$) for all (ρ,λ). The weak party views bias as a "bad" ($\partial Ew/\partial\lambda < 0$) for all (ρ,λ).
Proof: Obvious.

Lemma 2: If $\mu > 0$ and $\lambda \geq 0$, then the slope of the strong party's indifference curves will be no less than $-\mu$.
Proof: We need to show that $d\lambda/d\rho \geq -\mu$ along any level curve of $E[u(s(x))]$. Taking the total derivative along an arbitrary level curve, one finds that $d\lambda/d\rho = (-\partial Eu/\partial\rho)/(\partial Eu/\partial\lambda)$. Now,

$$\frac{\partial Eu}{\partial\lambda} = \int u' \frac{e^{\rho x}e^{-\lambda}}{(e^{-\lambda}+e^{\rho x})^2}\varphi(x)dx = \int u's(x)[1-s(x)]\varphi(x)dx,$$

the second equality following from equation (2) and from the fact that $1 - s(x;\rho,\lambda) = (e^{-\lambda})/(e^{-\lambda} + e^{\rho x})$. Writing for convenience $s(x)$ instead of $s(x;\rho,\lambda)$, letting $z(x) = u's(x)[1 - s(x)]$, and changing variables to $\tau = x - \mu$,

$$\frac{\partial Eu}{\partial\lambda} = \int z(\mu+\tau)\varphi(\tau;0,\sigma)d\tau,$$

where $\varphi(\bullet;s,t)$ denotes the normal density with mean s and standard deviation t. Similarly,

$$\frac{\partial Eu}{\partial\rho} = \int z(\mu+\tau)(\mu+\tau)\varphi(\tau;0,\sigma)d\tau$$

$$= \mu\frac{\partial Eu}{\partial\lambda} + \int z(\mu+\tau)\tau\varphi(\tau;0,\sigma)d\tau. \tag{*}$$

Thus,

$$\frac{\partial Eu/\partial\rho}{\partial Eu/\partial\lambda} = \mu + \frac{\int z(\mu+\tau)\tau\varphi(\tau;0,\sigma)d\tau}{\partial Eu/\partial\lambda}. \tag{**}$$

Since $\partial Eu/\partial\lambda > 0$, it suffices to show that the integral I in the numerator of the second term is not positive. Taking advantage of $\varphi(\tau;0,\sigma) = \varphi(-\tau;0,\sigma)$ to rewrite,

$$I = \int_0^\infty [z(\mu+\tau) - z(\mu-\tau)]\tau\varphi(\tau;0,\sigma)d\tau.$$

45

That the term in square brackets is negative for arbitrary $\tau > 0$ can be seen as follows. First, $s(\mu + \tau) > s(\mu - \tau)$ since s is an increasing function. Second, $s(\mu + \tau) > 1 - s(\mu - \tau)$ since

$$\frac{e^{\rho(\mu+\tau)}}{e^{-\lambda} + e^{\rho(\mu+\tau)}} > 1 - \frac{e^{\rho(\mu-\tau)}}{e^{-\lambda} + e^{\rho(\mu-\tau)}} \leftrightarrow$$

$$e^{2\rho\mu} + e^{\rho(\mu+\tau)-\lambda} > e^{-2\lambda} + e^{\rho(\mu+\tau)-\lambda} \leftrightarrow \rho\mu > -\lambda,$$

which is true since $\mu > 0$ and $\lambda \geq 0$ (and $\rho \geq 1$ for all feasible plans). Thus, we have condition (i): $s(\mu + \tau) > \max\{s(\mu - \tau), 1 - s(\mu - \tau)\}$. But

(i) & $0 < s(x) < 1 \; \forall x \rightarrow$ (ii) $s(\mu + \tau)[1 - s(\mu + \tau)]$
$\qquad\qquad\qquad\qquad\qquad\qquad\qquad < s(\mu - \tau)[1 - s(\mu - \tau)]$

(i) & $u'' < 0 \rightarrow$ (iii) $u'[s(\mu + \tau)] < u'[s(\mu - \tau)]$

(ii) & (iii) $\rightarrow$ $z(\mu + \tau) < z(\mu - \tau)$.

Thus, I is negative, $(\partial Eu/\partial\rho)/(\partial Eu/\partial\lambda) \leq \mu$, and $d\lambda/d\rho \geq -\mu$. QED.

Lemma 3: Suppose that condition C(a) holds. Then the slope of the strong party's indifference curves declines (in absolute value) with declining μ.

Proof: We need to show that

$$D \equiv \frac{\partial\left(\left|\dfrac{d\lambda}{d\rho}\right|\right)}{\partial\mu} > 0.$$

Given C(a),

$$\left|\frac{d\lambda}{d\rho}\right| = \frac{\partial Eu/\partial\rho}{\partial Eu/\partial\lambda}.$$

Thus,

$$D = \frac{(\partial Eu/\partial\lambda)(\partial^2 Eu/\partial\rho\partial\mu) - (\partial Eu/\partial\rho)(\partial^2 Eu/\partial\lambda\partial\mu)}{(\partial Eu/\partial\lambda)^2}.$$

Since $\partial Eu/\partial\lambda > 0$, the sign of D equals that of the numerator on the right-hand side. $D > 0$ is equivalent to

$$E_1 \equiv \frac{\partial^2 Eu/\partial\rho\partial\mu}{\partial^2 Eu/\partial\lambda\partial\mu} > \frac{\partial Eu/\partial\rho}{\partial Eu/\partial\lambda} \equiv E_2.$$

Consider E_1 first. The denominator of E_1 is

$$\frac{\partial^2 Eu}{\partial\lambda\partial\mu} = \frac{1}{\sigma^2}\int u' \frac{e^{\rho x}e^{-\lambda}}{\left(e^{-\lambda}+e^{\rho x}\right)^2}(x-\mu)\varphi(x)dx$$

$$= \frac{1}{\sigma^2}\int u's(x)[1-s(x)](x-\mu)\varphi(x)dx$$

$$= \frac{1}{\sigma^2}\int z(\mu+\tau)\tau\varphi(\tau;0,\sigma)d\tau$$

$$= \frac{1}{\sigma^2}I < 0.$$

The third equality follows by changing the variable of integration to $\tau = x - \mu$ and using the function z defined in Lemma 2. The final inequality follows since the integral I was shown in Lemma 2 to be negative. A similar argument shows that

$$\frac{\partial^2 Eu}{\partial\lambda\partial\rho} = \frac{1}{\sigma^2}\left(\mu I + \int z(\mu+\tau)\tau^2\phi(\tau;0,\sigma)d\tau\right).$$

Thus

$$E_1 = \mu + \frac{\int z(\mu+\tau)\tau^2\phi(\tau;0,\sigma)d\tau}{I}.$$

Since $E_2 = \mu + (I/\partial Eu/\partial\lambda)$, from Lemma 2, equation (**), $E_1 > E_2$ if and only if

$$\int z(\mu+\tau)\phi(\tau;0,\sigma)d\tau\int z(\mu+\tau)\tau^2\phi(\tau;0,\sigma)d\tau$$
$$> \int z(\mu+\tau)\tau\phi(\tau;0,\sigma)d\tau\int z(\mu+\tau)\tau\phi(\tau;0,\sigma)d\tau.$$

We shall denote the preceding inequality B and compare it to other inequalities stated in terms of sums instead of integrals. Let $w(\tau) = z(\mu + \tau)\varphi(\tau;0,\sigma)$ and consider the inequality $B(d;n)$, defined as

$$\sum_{j=-n}^{n} w(\tau_j)\sum_{j=-n}^{n} w(\tau_j)\tau_j^2 > \sum_{j=-n}^{n} w(\tau_j)\tau_j \sum_{j=-n}^{n} w(\tau_j)\tau_j \leftrightarrow$$
$$\sum_{j=-n}^{n}\sum_{k=-n}^{n} w(\tau_j)w(\tau_k)\tau_k^2 > \sum_{j=-n}^{n}\sum_{k=-n}^{n} w(\tau_j)\tau_j w(\tau_k)\tau_k,$$

where $\tau_j = j/d$. Consider an arbitrary j and k. Select the terms (j,j), (j,k), (k,j), and (k,k) from both the left-hand-side sum and the right-hand-side sum. If $j = k$, then there is only one term from each sum

47

– since $(j,j) = (j,k) = (k,j) = (k,k)$ – and the corresponding terms in the two sums are equal. If $j \neq k$, then we have

$$w(\tau_j)^2 \tau_j^2 + w(\tau_j)w(\tau_k)\tau_k^2 + w(\tau_k)w(\tau_j)\tau_j^2 + w(\tau_k)^2 \tau_k^2 >$$
$$w(\tau_j)^2 \tau_j^2 + w(\tau_j)\tau_j w(\tau_k)\tau_k + w(\tau_k)\tau_k w(\tau_j)\tau_j + w(\tau_k)^2 \tau_k^2 \leftrightarrow$$
$$w(\tau_j)w(\tau_k)(\tau_k^2 + \tau_j^2) > 2w(\tau_j)w(\tau_k)\tau_k\tau_j \leftrightarrow$$
$$\tau_k^2 + \tau_j^2 - 2\tau_k\tau_j > 0 \leftrightarrow (\tau_k - \tau_j)^2 > 0.$$

The last inequality holds if $j \neq k$. Thus, the inequality $B(d;n)$ holds for all $d > 0$ and positive integers n. But as d and n approach infinity, $B(d;n)$ approaches B. QED.

Proof of Proposition 1: The constraint set is convex, with a strictly concave decreasing northeast boundary. By Lemma 2 and condition C(a), the slope of any of the strong party's indifference curves at any point in A is between 0 and $-\mu$. If (ρ^*,λ^*) is a constrained optimum, then it must lie on the boundary of A. (To see this, consider any point (ρ,λ) in the interior of A. Since (ρ,λ) is in the interior of A, there will exist a point (ρ',λ') with $\rho' > \rho$ and $\lambda' > \lambda$. But, as both responsiveness and bias are goods, (ρ',λ') will yield higher utility.) Suppose that L is a level curve of Eu that intersects only the boundary of A. Since the slope of all level curves is between $-\mu$ and 0, such a level curve must intersect the boundary only at points (ρ,λ) such that $-\mu < g'(\rho) < 0$. This is sufficient to conclude that $\rho > \rho_{hi}$ and $\lambda > 0$. QED.

UNDERLYING CONDITIONS

The following proposition identifies a condition sufficient to ensure that condition C(a) will hold.

Proposition 4: Given any $\mu > 0$, condition C(a) is satisfied for sufficiently small σ.

Proof: Repeating equation (*) from the proof of Lemma 2

$$\frac{\partial Eu}{\partial \rho} = \int z(\mu + \tau)(\mu + \tau)\varphi(\tau;0,\sigma)d\tau$$

$$= \mu \frac{\partial Eu}{\partial \lambda} + \int z(\mu + \tau)\tau\varphi(\tau;0,\sigma)d\tau.$$

(*)

But

$$\lim_{\sigma \to 0} \frac{\partial Eu}{\partial \lambda} = u'[s(\mu)]s(\mu)[1-s(\mu)] > 0$$

and

$$\lim_{\sigma \to 0} \int z(\mu + \tau)\tau\varphi(\tau;0,\sigma)d\tau = z(\mu) \times 0 = 0.$$

Thus, for any $\mu > 0$, $\partial Eu/\partial \rho > 0$ for sufficiently small σ. QED.

This provides an alternative sufficient condition to that given in footnote 10.

EXISTENCE

We have thus far said nothing about whether there will be room for a bargain between the two parties. If both parties are risk neutral – that is, pure expected seat maximizers – then the game is zero-sum and there will be no room for bargaining. Under divided government, then, and assuming condition C, there would never be a new plan that both could agree on. In the case of risk-averse parties, the game is no longer zero-

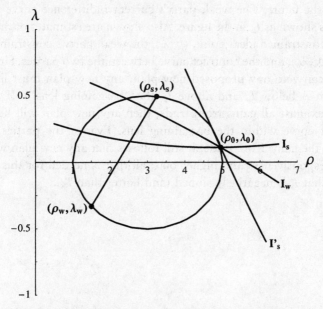

Figure 3.3 An example of bargaining under divided control with a conservative reversion.

sum and the possibility of mutually beneficial trades is opened. A sufficient condition for the generic existence of gains from trade would be that the strong party's level curves were convex to the origin, while the weak party's level curves were concave to the origin. These conditions can be shown to be satisfied for special cases. But they are merely sufficient conditions, not necessary. We prefer simply to assume that mutually beneficial trades do sometimes exist – non-zero-sumness is sufficient for this – and to characterize what trades will look like should any occur.

PART 4: ILLUSTRATION FOR PROPOSITION 2

Figure 3.3 illustrates the argument behind Proposition 2, based on numerical estimates of the case where u and w are both the natural logarithm function. When the strong party last redistricted with unified control, it chose the point (ρ_0, λ_0). Its indifference curves at that time were relatively steep. That is, it valued responsiveness relatively highly, demanding a fairly large payment in increased bias to compensate for a unit decrease in responsiveness. One of the indifference curves – the one tangent to the constraint set at (ρ_0, λ_0) – is shown as I'_s in the figure. Currently, under divided government, the strong party's indifference curves are flatter. One of them – the one that passes through (ρ_0, λ_0) – is shown as I_s in the figure. The weak party's current indifference curve through (ρ_0, λ_0) is shown as I_w in the figure. Also shown are estimates of the strong party's constrained ideal point, (ρ_s, λ_s), the weak party's constrained ideal point, (ρ_w, λ_w), and the contract curve between the two parties. Since both parties can veto any proposed new plan, any new plan must lie somewhere in A below I_w and above I_s (the "bargaining lens"). If the two parties exhaust all gains from trade, then any new plan will lie on the contract curve within the bargaining lens. Even if the parties do not exhaust the gains from trade, it still follows that any new plan will have lower responsiveness and higher bias; all that is needed for this conclusion is that I_s is negatively sloped (and flatter than I'_s).

4

The Case of the Disappearing Bias

In Chapter 3, we generated several predictions about how bias and responsiveness in a state's congressional elections should vary as a function of the political context obtaining when the state's district lines were drawn. In this chapter, we put those predictions to the test.

Substantively, we focus on how redistricting in the 1960s affected the partisan outcome of nonsouthern congressional elections. The conventional wisdom is that redistricting is unlikely in general to produce net partisan gains nationwide. Moreover, previous studies of the 1960s in particular have either found no net partisan advantage for either party or claimed that the advantage lay with the Republicans. Nonetheless, we show that nonsouthern Democrats were substantial net beneficiaries of redistricting in the 1960s. Our results explain a long-standing puzzle in the literature on congressional elections: the sudden disappearance of pro-Republican bias in the translation of votes into seats in nonsouthern elections circa 1966.

The rest of the chapter proceeds as follows. We first review work on "the case of the disappearing bias" and consider whether redistricting might help explain this mystery. We then test our theoretical expectations about redistricting – derived in Chapter 3 – against the empirical record in the 1960s. Unlike several previous studies of postwar redistricting, we find that a model in which parties are the key actors explains the data well and that control of state government typically translated into substantial redistricting gains for a party throughout the period prior to the reapportionment revolution. We also find that the legal reversion (or default outcome) of the redistricting process had a systematic and thus-far-neglected impact on how congressional votes translated into seats prior to *Baker v. Carr* and *Wesberry v. Sanders*. Substantively, our results help explain the abrupt disappearance of pro-Republican bias in nonsouthern elections in the mid-1960s.

THE CASE OF THE DISAPPEARING BIAS

Partisan bias is a standard concept in the literature on elections, intended to capture how many more (or fewer) seats a party gets than its vote share warrants. In U.S. legislative elections, bias is usually defined as the difference between two quantities: (1) the seat share that a given party gets on average when its vote share is 0.5 and (2) its "fair seat share" of 0.5 (half of the seats for half of the votes). For example, if the Democrats on average win 55% of New Jersey's state assembly seats when the party wins 50% of the vote, then the translation of votes into seats in New Jersey legislative elections exhibits a 5% pro-Democratic bias.[1]

A series of studies (e.g., Erikson 1972; Jacobson 1990a; Brady and Grofman 1991; King and Gelman 1991) show the disappearance (circa 1966) of a substantial pro-Republican bias in nonsouthern House elections. Erikson (1972, p. 1234), for example, estimated partisan bias by regressing the Democratic share of nonsouthern seats on the aggregate Democratic share of the nonsouthern vote. Over the period 1952–1964 he found that, "had the aggregate vote division been a 50–50 partisan split, the Democrats could have expected to win only about 44.6 per cent of the seats" – indicating a 5.4% pro-Republican bias. In contrast, his study found no pro-Republican bias in the translation of congressional votes into seats after 1966. Although well known and replicated with longer time series of data (by, e.g., Jacobson 1990a; Brady and Grofman 1991; King and Gelman 1991), this abrupt disappearance of partisan bias in nonsouthern House elections has not been adequately explained in the literature.

Some have suggested that the disappearing bias simply reflects the nature of malapportionment in the North. By this argument, Republicans were strongest in rural areas, which were the most heavily overrepresented. Thus, eradicating malapportionment must necessarily have lessened rural representation, thereby hurting the GOP. There is a well-

---

[1] For purposes of calculating bias, the Democrats' vote share in the New Jersey example could be defined either as their statewide vote share or as the average of their candidates' district vote shares. The difference between these two methods does not concern us here.

known problem with this story, however. As Erikson (1972, p. 1236) reports, the correlation between Democratic vote share and population in nonsouthern districts was negative prior to the mid-1960s, not positive. That is, Democrats tended to do worse in the more populous (more *under*represented) districts and better in the less populous (more *over*represented) districts. The Republicans were well aware of this, having commissioned an internal study to forecast the consequences of eradicating malapportionment in 1964 – and concluding that they would benefit (cf. Prendergast 1965).

The most prominent explanation of the disappearing bias is Erikson's (1972) and King and Gelman's (1991) suggestion that growth in the incumbency advantage explains the pro-Democratic trend in partisan bias. King and Gelman's figures on nonsouthern pro-Democratic bias (1991, p. 128) show no linear trend over the period 1946–1964, with the year-by-year estimates averaging roughly –10%; a jump from –10% in 1964 to +2% in 1966 (by far the biggest shift between consecutive years); followed by no consistent linear trend in the period 1966–1986 (with an average of about +0.5%). Their figures on the incumbency advantage can be read as showing a shallow rate of growth from 1946 to 1964, followed by a large (10%) increase between 1964 and 1966, with no linear trend thereafter. King and Gelman (1991, p. 131) thus suggest that "the explanation of the trend in bias seems to be that the incumbency advantage happened to begin its dramatic increase at a time . . . when Democrats held a majority of House seats."

The main problem with this story is that the Gelman–King measure of the incumbency advantage is vote-denominated, not seat-denominated. That is, they measure how much running an incumbent rather than a nonincumbent candidate boosts a party's expected *vote share*, not its expected *probability of victory*. If running an incumbent confers more votes on average but does not increase the probability of victory, then the efficiency with which Democratic votes were translated into Democratic seats would not be improved by the Democrats having more incumbents. Democratic incumbents would simply win their seats at a higher average cost in votes, which, other things equal, would lower pro-Democratic bias (raise pro-Republican bias). Of course, Republican incumbents would also be paying more in votes for their seats if the vote-denominated incumbency advantage increased for both parties, and so the relative efficiency of the two parties (how many seats per vote each won) remains unclear. The Erikson, King, and Gelman story line requires that the seat-denominated incumbency advantage increased, but it seems doubtful that this happened over the relevant time period (Jacobson 1987). Thus, the abrupt disappearance of pro-Republican bias outside the South remains a puzzle.

WAS REDISTRICTING THE CULPRIT?

It is natural to think of redistricting when addressing the case of the disappearing bias. However, even if the Democrats had controlled all redistricting action in the 1960s (which they didn't), it would not be a foregone conclusion that their best strategy was to design plans that produced high levels of pro-Democratic bias. If their vote prospects were good enough, they might instead have opted for highly responsive plans.

To complicate matters further, many redistrictings in the 1960s were conducted by divided state governments, in which no single party controlled both the state legislature and the governorship. In these situations, the typical expectation in the literature is that the parties will agree to protect the current band of incumbents, so that bias is little affected – and certainly not greatly increased in one party's favor (the other would not stand for this).

All told, then, it is unclear whether redistricting in the 1960s can explain the disappearance of pro-Republican bias. One would need to look at the full range of redistricting actions taken both before and after the reapportionment revolution, estimate the bias and responsiveness in the plans constructed, and see whether there was indeed a trend in bias away from the Republicans. In the next section, we embark on this task.

HOW THE REAPPORTIONMENT REVOLUTION AFFECTED BIAS AND RESPONSIVENESS

In this section, we look at how the wave of court-ordered redistrictings in the 1960s changed bias and responsiveness in nonsouthern congressional elections. Our strategy is to estimate bias and responsiveness parameters for each of six kinds of plan: partisan Republican (i.e., a plan passed under unified Republican government); mixed Republican (i.e., a plan passed under divided government and an automatic conservative reversion in which the reversionary plan favors the Republicans); bipartisan Republican (i.e., a plan passed under divided government and an automatic radical reversion in which the Republicans are the strong party);[2] bipartisan Democratic; mixed Democratic; and partisan Democratic.

Our analysis focuses on how the Democratic seat share in state j at election t varies as a function of the mean Democratic share of the vote in state j at election t.[3] As the whole point of the analysis is to study the effect of redistricting, and as redistricting happens within individual states, we do not pool votes and seats across the entire nonsouthern portion of the United States, as have most previous authors. Instead, we take as our unit of analysis the state-year: the election of a contingent of U.S. House members from a particular state in a particular year. We then estimate a version of the seats-votes curve given in the last chapter (as Equation (1)). Full estimation details are given in the Appendix.

Our data cover the years 1946 to 1970 and include all nonsouthern House elections except contests held in single-seat states (for which the responsiveness parameter is necessarily infinite and the bias parameter necessarily zero) and those held under multimember rules in four two-seat states (Hawaii 1958–1970; Arizona 1946; New Mexico 1946–1958; and North Dakota 1946–1960).[4] We stop the analysis in 1970 so that the immediate effects of the reapportionment revolution are not confounded with the effects of later redistrictings.

Naturally, correct identification of the nature of partisan control in each state at the time of each redistricting is crucial to our analysis, as is the correct assignment of each election in each state to a particular plan. Fortunately, Martis (1982) lists the date of passage of each redistricting plan in all 50 states. We have used various sources to identify the partisan composition of each house of the state legislature and the partisanship of the governor at the time of each redistricting, taking account when necessary of the fact that some states allow overrides of

---

[2] In practice, we assume that the party that last had unified control of the state is the strong party.

[3] Using the statewide Democratic share of the vote instead of the mean Democratic share affects the level of bias because Democrats tend to win seats in lower-turnout races (Campbell 1996). But it does not much affect estimates of how bias responded to 1960s redistricting. This gibes with previous results in the literature using the overall vote (e.g., Tufte 1973; Jacobson 1990a), which show a change in bias in the pro-Democratic direction in 1966–1970 similar to that found in studies using the mean district vote.

[4] Recall that we classify Tennessee and Maryland as southern because both were even less competitive than at least one southern state; they are thus excluded from the analysis. Our data, including our identification of the plan types for each state, can be found at http://jkatz.caltech.edu.

Table 4.1. *Responsiveness Under Eight Different Districting Plans in 32 Nonsouthern States, 1946–1970*

Plan Type	Prerevolutionary	Postrevolutionary
Partisan: Republican	3.54	4.44
	(0.30)	(0.60)
Mixed: Republican	2.17	—
	(0.80)	
Bipartisan: Republican	2.06	2.02
	(0.28)	(0.51)
Bipartisan: Democratic	—	1.16
		(0.71)
Mixed: Democratic	—	—
Partisan: Democratic	3.50	5.32
	(0.37)	(0.76)

Notes: Standard errors are in parentheses. Full estimation notes are in the appendix.

gubernatorial vetoes with less than a two-thirds vote by the legislature or in which the governor did not possess a veto.[5]

Our results are displayed in Tables 4.1 (which gives estimates of responsiveness) and 4.2 (which gives estimates of bias). Consider the responsiveness results first.

Responsiveness

For prerevolutionary plans, we expect significantly lower responsiveness for plans adopted under divided government – that is, for bipartisan and mixed plans. Somewhat similar expectations are derived for postrevolutionary plans in the next chapter. Consistent with these expectations, the four lowest responsiveness values in the table are observed for such plan types. Indeed, one can reject neither the null hypothesis that the responsiveness values in all the divided control plans are the same nor the null hypothesis that the responsiveness values in all the partisan plans are the

---

[5] A special case is worth noting: Michigan. Michigan was under unified Republican control. Yet, a Democratic court had imposed a strict time limit on the state's deliberations, effectively forcing the Republicans to deal with the Democrats, as described in Chapter 2. In this chapter, we classify the Michigan 1964 plan as bipartisan. In the next chapter, when the role of the courts is explicitly controlled for, we classify it as unified Republican facing a Democratic court and let the data sort out the relative impact of state and court control.

same – but one can reject the null hypothesis that these two responsiveness levels are the same.

Substantively, the partisan plans all produce responsiveness levels above the classic cube law expectation of 3, ranging as high as 5.32. In contrast, the bipartisan and mixed plans all fall below the cube-law benchmark, consistent with the notion that incumbents are protected under such plans.[6]

If one examines specific plans enacted under divided government, it is not always obvious that incumbent protection has carried the day. But in some cases, it is abundantly clear. Consider, for example, the 1962 redistricting in Massachusetts. Initially, the Democratic state legislature had considered a partisan gerrymander, despite threats of a veto from the Republican governor. Ultimately, however, a bipartisan group of congressional incumbents (led by Tip O'Neill) proposed a plan to protect as many incumbents as possible from the consequences of the state's loss of two seats. The incumbents met with state legislators and the governor, even enlisting the White House to lobby a few powerful legislative dissidents rumored to have an eye on running for Congress themselves (and therefore favoring the less predictable reversionary outcome). One dissident "attacked the state's U.S. House delegation for 'dictating a freeze-in for themselves' and as 'vultures sweeping down over the State House to preserve their own jobs'" (Congressional Quarterly 1962, p. 1643). But in the end the deed was done.

Partisan Bias

Consider next the results on partisan bias, displayed in Table 4.2 (which adopts the convention that positive bias is pro-Democratic, negative bias pro-Republican). How well do these results tally with our three main expectations about bias?

First, we expect pre-*Wesberry* partisan plans to produce significant levels of bias in favor of the redistricting party. As can be seen, they do: partisan Republican plans produced a pro-Republican bias of 8.27%, while partisan Democratic plans produced a pro-Democratic bias of 5.43%.

Second, we expect that mixed plans – plans enacted under divided government when the reversionary outcome was automatic conservative – should have largely maintained, perhaps even increased, any

---

[6] If incumbents are made safer, then necessarily responsiveness will decline.

Table 4.2. *Partisan Bias Under Eight Different Districting Plans in 32 Nonsouthern States, 1946–1970*

Plan Type	Prerevolutionary	Postrevolutionary
Partisan: Republican	−8.27	−1.15
	(1.08)	(2.68)
Mixed: Republican	−8.35	—
	(1.98)	
Bipartisan: Republican	−5.33	−2.16
	(1.25)	(2.24)
Bipartisan: Democratic	—	1.52
		(2.92)
Mixed: Democratic	—	—
Partisan: Democratic	5.43	8.70
	(2.10)	(3.73)

Notes: Standard errors are in parentheses. Full estimation notes are in the appendix. Empty cells had no data.

preexisting partisan bias. As all postrevolutionary reversions were radical, we can only test this expectation by comparing prerevolutionary plans. As can be seen in Table 4.2, mixed Republican plans do show a slightly higher bias than partisan Republican plans, although the difference is statistically indiscernible from zero. (There were no mixed Democratic plans in our dataset, so we cannot test the hypothesis that such plans produced higher levels of pro-Democratic bias.)

Our results show that the continuation of pro-Republican bias outside the South was consequentially aided by the nature of legal reversions prior to the reapportionment revolution. High levels of pro-Republican bias established in a given state could survive episodes of divided government in that state if the reversion was an automatic conservative one (that is, if the state did not lose seats at the reapportionment).

Third, we expect bias under bipartisan Republican (Democratic) plans to be negative (positive) but not as markedly negative (positive) as under mixed and partisan Republican (Democratic) plans.[7] This is basically the pattern that we find.

[7] The reason for this prediction is that we assume that whichever party last drew the lines is more likely to be the strong party in a state drawing new lines under divided government and facing a radical reversion. Since a radical reversion corresponds to the rightmost point in the constraint set, *A* (see Figure 3.2), the strong party's indifference curves are negatively sloped, and the strong party must assent to any plan

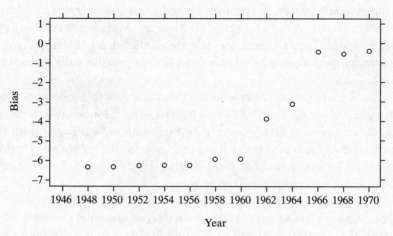

Figure 4.1 Estimates of overall bias in 32 nonsouthern states, 1946–1970.

The most puzzling result in Table 4.2 is the divergence between partisan plans in the postrevolutionary period: postrevolutionary Democratic plans produced a pro-Democratic bias of 8.70%, but postrevolutionary Republican plans produced a small and insignificant bias. We return to this anemic Republican showing in the next chapter.

The Net Partisan Effect of 1960s Redistrictings

Overall, how much did the reapportionment revolution hurt the Republicans? Some light is shed on this question in Figure 4.1, which displays the overall partisan bias in the nonsouthern districts under study here for each year from 1946 to 1970. The overall bias is calculated by taking the proportion of the districts that fell into each plan type in each year, multiplying by the estimated average partisan bias for that plan type (using the estimates in Table 4.2), and summing across all plan types.

As can be seen, bias in the North was, by our estimates, running between 6.0% and 6.4% pro-Republican in every year from 1946 to 1960 inclusive (worth about 20 seats). Our estimates largely conform to previous figures (e.g., Erikson 1972), although our estimation procedure

adopted under divided government, we can conclude that bias will be pro-Republican under bipartisan Republican plans but pro-Democratic under bipartisan Democratic plans.

is substantially different and we imposed no requirement or constraint on the analysis to match previous estimates. Aggregate bias in 1946–1960 is *stable* because there was relatively little consequential redistricting in that period; it is *pro-Republican* simply because most plans were Republican-favoring.

The Republican advantage in the North begins to erode noticeably in 1962, when California, Massachusetts, and Pennsylvania replaced Republican plans with Democratic or bipartisan/radical plans. With the entry of the courts into the redistricting process, the number of Democratic and bipartisan/radical plans further increased and, by 1966, the Republican advantage was largely gone.

The decline in pro-Republican bias, from about 6.0% in 1960 to about 0.7% in 1966–1970, is due both to compositional change – there were fewer partisan and mixed Republican plans and more bipartisan and partisan-Democratic plans – and to changes in plan effects – the estimated bias for partisan Republican, bipartisan Republican, and partisan Democratic plan types all shifted in a pro-Democratic direction after the reapportionment revolution. (There is no evidence of any shift in plan effects prior to 1964.)[8] If one calculates the decline that would have been observed had the distribution of plans changed as it actually did, while the old plan effects continued at their previous levels, one still finds a substantial decline: to about 3.1%. By this calculation, about 55% of the total decline can be attributed to compositional change, with the other 45% due to shifts in plan effects.

The shift in the composition of plans is in large part a direct consequence of the reapportionment decisions in combination with Republican losses in the 1964 elections. Are the shifts in plan effects also attributable to judicial entry into the redistricting process? In the next chapter, we show that Democrats dominated the federal courts that heard redistricting cases, and that which party had a majority on the court hearing a case systematically affected the levels of bias attained by the corresponding plan, even if the court itself did not impose the plan. In other words, the shift in plan effects in the pro-Democratic direction appears also to have been due to judicial entry.

[8] We examined whether any plan effect differed significantly in 1962–1964 from that in previous years. The likelihood ratio test statistic was 1.69, with two degrees of freedom, far from any critical values. That is, we could not reject the null hypothesis that the plan effects were the same in 1962–1964 as they had been previously.

CONCLUSION

The Supreme Court's landmark apportionment decisions, beginning with *Baker v. Carr*, led to the abrupt eradication of malapportionment in state legislative and congressional districts. On the face of it, eradicating malapportionment would appear to be the single most important change in the conduct of elections in the United States since the Nineteenth Amendment gave women the vote in 1920. Yet, although legal scholars were quick to recognize the enormous jurisprudential importance of the decisions, hailing them as nothing less than a "reapportionment revolution," political scientists have not found that the decisions produced sweeping consequences – other than the immediate consequence of redistricting itself.

In this chapter, we show that the nature of a redistricting plan – in terms of bias and responsiveness in the elections held under that plan – is a function of both partisan control of state government and the legally defined default outcomes of the redistricting process. That partisan control matters may not strike some as particularly surprising, but it runs counter to most of the literature, which finds only modest differences between partisan and bipartisan plans. That reversionary outcomes matter has not previously been demonstrated.

In addition to properly identifying the effects of various kinds of plan, our work provides clear evidence that the reapportionment revolution substantially affected an important macrofeature of postwar congressional elections. In particular, we show that the well-known disappearance circa 1966 of what had been a long-time pro-Republican bias of about 6% in nonsouthern congressional elections can be explained by the courts' entry. More than half of the disappearing act results simply from the shift in the composition of nonsouthern redistricting plans away from categories more favorable to Republicans, with this compositional shift due mostly to the combination of Republican losses in the 1964 elections and the wave of court-supervised redistricting in the 1960s. The rest of the disappearance results from shifts in the impact of different sorts of plan, which we show in the next two chapters were due largely to the courts' increased involvement in redistricting.

Appendix: Estimation Details

In this appendix we consider estimation of Equation (1) given in chapter 3. As written the equation is deterministic and cannot be used directly to estimate the parameters of interest from observed data. However, if we assume a stochastic model – following King and Browning (1987; see also King 1990) – then Equation (1) defines the expected portion of seats in a state i in election t going to the Democrats as

$$
\begin{aligned}
E[s_{i,t}] &= \left[1 + e^{\lambda}\left(\frac{\nu_{i,t}}{1-\nu_{i,t}}\right)^{\rho}\right]^{-1} \\
&= \left[1 + \exp\left(-\lambda - \rho\ln\left(\frac{\nu_{i,t}}{1-\nu_{i,t}}\right)\right)\right]^{-1}.
\end{aligned}
\tag{A1}
$$

The second expression for the expected seat proportion is same as the mean function for the standard logit model for grouped data with a constant, λ, and a single independent variable, $\ln(\nu_{i,t}/1 - \nu_{i,t})$. If we were further to assume that the probability of the Democrats winning a district is independently and identically distributed, we could model the process with a binomial distribution. The binomial assumption and Equation (A1) then set up a standard grouped logit model that we could estimate either via maximum likelihood (as in King and Browning 1987) or two-step minimum chi-square methods (see Greene 1993, pp. 653–657 or Maddala 1983, pp. 28–34). However, we suspect that there is still some unmodeled heterogeneity – beyond that being picked up by the logistic of the vote shares – and possibly some correlation in the probabilities across districts. In fact, an optimal partisan gerrymander would require such heterogeneity across districts. Assuming that there were not enough partisan voters for the dominant party to win every district, there would be two types of districts in the state: a handful that the minority party wins overwhelmingly, plus the remaining districts in which the dominant party wins but not by huge margins. In order to handle this heterogeneity we assume that the seat shares follow an extended beta-binomial instead of a standard binomial distribution. The extended beta-binomial is generated by assuming that the probability (from a binomial model) that a district is won by the Democrats varies according to a beta distribution (see King 1989, pp. 45–48 for a complete derivation of the extended beta-binomial distribution). Let $S_{i,t}$ be the number of seats the Democrats win in state i in election t and let N_i be the total number of districts in state i. The extended beta-binomial can then be written as

$$
f(s_{i,t}|\pi_i,\gamma) = \frac{N_i!}{S_{i,t}!(N_i - S_{i,t})!} \frac{\prod_{j=0}^{S_{i,t}-1}(\pi_i + \gamma j)\prod_{j=0}^{N_i-S_{i,t}-1}(1 - \pi_i + \gamma j)}{\prod_{j=0}^{N_i-1}(1+\gamma j)},
$$

where we adopt the convention that if any of the constituent products are negative, then the term is set to 1. Note that, since we are explicitly conditioning on N_i, the model incorporates the heteroskedasticity caused by the varying number of districts across states in our sample.

The parameter π_i is the average probability that a given district in state i is won by the Democrats. Thus,

$$\pi_i = \frac{E[S_{i,t}]}{N_i} = E[s_{i,t}].$$

So we can use Equation (A1) to model the systematic variation in the underlying probability. The parameter γ captures the amount that π_i varies over the districts or the correlation across districts. If γ is zero, then the extended beta-binomial is just the binomial, and districts are identically and independently distributed. If $\gamma > 0$ there is positive correlation between districts, and when $\gamma < 0$ there is negative correlation between districts.

The log likelihood is straightforward to derive assuming independence across states. The contribution of each state i, ignoring terms that do not depend on the parameters, is

$$L_i(\pi_i, \gamma | S_{i,t}, N_i) \propto \sum_{j=0}^{S_{i,t}-1} (\pi_i + \gamma j) + \sum_{j=0}^{N_i - S_{i,t}-1} (1\pi_i + \gamma j) - \sum_{j=0}^{N_i-1} (1 + \gamma j).$$

We then substitute Equation (A1) for π_i to get $L_i(\lambda, \rho, \gamma \mid S_{i,t}, N_i, v_{i,t})$. The likelihood for the entire sample is found by summing the L_i across the states. In our actual estimation we allow λ and ρ to vary over plan types, but we will assume a common γ to ensure a comparable scale of the coefficients.

The raw results can be found in Table 4A.1. These serve as the basis of Tables 4.1 and 4.2. Responsiveness can be read directly off the estimation results. However, to calculate the partisan bias, we need to transform the estimated λ values. This is a consistent estimate of partisan bias, since maximum likelihood is invariant to reparamaterization. However, in order to calculate the standard errors for the estimate, we need to use the Delta method (Greene 1993, p. 297). If $\hat{\theta}$ is a maximum likelihood estimate, then the standard error of $f(\hat{\theta})$ is

$$\text{var}[f(\hat{\theta})] = \left(\frac{df(\hat{\theta})}{d\hat{\theta}} \right)^2 \text{var}[\hat{\theta}].$$

Table 4A.1. *Untransformed Estimates of Partisan
Bias and Responsiveness by Plan Type in 32
Nonsouthern States, 1946–1970*

Plan Type	λ	ρ
Prerevolutionary Plans		
Partisan: Republican	−0.33	3.54
	(0.04)	(0.30)
Mixed: Republican	−0.34	2.17
	(0.08)	(0.80)
Bipartisan: Republican	−0.21	2.06
	(0.05)	(0.28)
Partisan: Democratic	0.22	3.50
	(0.08)	(0.37)
Postrevolutionary Plans		
Partisan: Republican	−0.05	4.43
	(0.11)	(0.60)
Bipartisan: Republican	−0.09	2.02
	(0.09)	(0.51)
Bipartisan: Democratic	0.06	1.16
	(0.12)	(0.71)
Partisan: Democratic	0.35	5.32
	(0.15)	(0.76)
γ	−0.012	
	(0.002)	
N	400	
Log likelihood	−2459.6	

The square root of this variance is reported in Table 4.2 as the estimate of the standard error of the partisan bias estimate.

As Table 4A.1 shows, the estimate of γ is negative and significantly different from zero, as expected given an optimal gerrymander. Unfortunately, the maximization for the extended beta-binomial likelihood is not straightforward since γ has a lower bound that depends on the true, but unknown, π. Therefore to confirm our results, we estimated our model using a binomial model – that is, fixing $\gamma = 0$ – both via maximum likelihood methods and via a two-stage minimum chi-square method with the seat logits smoothed, as suggested by Cox (1970, p. 33). Although both techniques assume independent and identically distributed data, they are still consistent – but inefficient – if this assumption fails (Gourieroux, Monfort, and Trongon 1984). The results from all three estimations are similar, boosting our confidence in the findings. As a further test of the robustness of our findings, we ran our model allowing year effects and then allowing responsiveness to vary by the number of districts in the state. While these changed the exact numeric results, the underlying pattern of results remained the same.

5

The Role of the Courts in the 1960s Redistricting Process

In the previous chapter, we focused on redistricting plans drawn prior to the courts' entry into the redistricting process. During this precourt period, reversionary plans – that is, the plans that would stand in force should the state legislature and governor be unable to agree on a new plan – were automatic. Both their content and the conditions under which they would come into force were prespecified and did not depend on the decisions of any strategic actor. In contrast, after the Supreme Court's reapportionment decisions, individual courts decided both the content of the reversionary plan and, to some degree, the conditions under which it would be invoked. In this chapter, we begin to consider the political consequences of this change from automatic to discretionary reversions.

The first two sections consider how the partisan complexion of the courts supervising (or potentially supervising) redistricting actions in the 1960s might in theory have affected the plans ultimately used. Based on an extension of the model developed in the previous chapter, we argue that one should expect court partisanship to affect the partisan bias and responsiveness embodied in the implemented plan, even if the court did not impose a plan and even though bias and responsiveness were not justiciable.

The third section provides qualitative evidence that each court's partisan complexion did affect its decisions. The fourth section provides quantitative evidence that each court's partisan complexion, relative to that of the plan it was judging, affected the level of malapportionment it was prepared to tolerate. The final section concludes.

JUDICIAL INFLUENCE OVER REDISTRICTING: PREMISES

After *Wesberry*, the potential for court involvement in the redistricting process was a constant and should have been recognized by state legislators. The judiciary's potential involvement was obvious when the state redistricted after ordered to do so by a specific court. Clearly, state legislators would have considered what the court would and would not accept in these instances. Even when a state decided to redistrict with no suit in the offing, prudent legislators would have considered whether any new plan they produced would provoke a suit and, if so, what court would hear the case. In some cases, the answers may have been so clear – for example, the opposition would file a suit before a court with a majority of opposition jurists – that the politics of redistricting were little different than if the suit had already been filed and the court had already entered.

In this section, we consider how anticipation by the political parties of the partisan inclinations of the supervising court ought in theory to have affected the bias, responsiveness, and malapportionment of the districting plan that a state produced. We argue that the courts could have influence, even though bias and responsiveness were not justiciable at this time.

Most of the courts hearing redistricting cases in the 1960s were federal. Although several state courts heard cases as well, there were not enough to sustain an analysis of whether state and federal courts differed in their handling of the issues at stake. Thus, in what follows, we talk of supervising courts without systematically distinguishing between state and federal panels.[1]

Judges' Preferences

When evaluating redistricting plans, we assume that judges cared both about the plans' partisan electoral consequences (embodied in their responsiveness and bias levels) and about their jurisprudentially relevant characteristics (viz., malapportionment levels). To simplify the

---

[1] Beiser (1968), in a study that covered mostly state legislative districting cases, found little or no significant difference in how state and federal judges handled *Baker v. Carr*. Such a difference may have become more important after Beiser's study, as an accumulation of cases at both the state and federal levels could have driven a larger wedge between the jurisprudential issues the two sorts of court had to consider.

discussion, we shall suppose that the courts in the 1960s had agreed on a particular measure of malapportionment.[2] As most contemporary discussions focused on the maximum allowable deviation that a district could exhibit from the average population of all districts in the state, we shall talk as if this was the agreed-upon measure of malapportionment, denoting it by D.[3]

We shall also suppose that there was a clear maximum allowable deviation, established by precedent, denoted D_{max}. In the immediate aftermath of *Wesberry*, notions about the acceptable amount of malapportionment were varied. The Court itself had only required that districts be "as nearly as is practicable" of equal population. Voices in Congress argued for a lax interpretation of what was practicable – one allowing deviations as large as 15%.[4] It was not until *Kirkpatrick v. Preisler* (1969; 394 U.S. 526) that the Supreme Court clarified the standard, allowing "only the limited population variances which are unavoidable despite a good-faith effort to achieve absolute equality, or for which justification is shown." In terms of the model, the court set D_{max} substantially closer to zero (with *Karcher v. Daggett* [1983; 462 U.S. 725] further specifying and narrowing the grounds on which deviations could be justified).

We assume that a judge's preferences concerning bias and responsiveness were *separable* from his or her preferences concerning malapportionment. This allows us to express the utility that a particular judge derived from a particular plan as a weighted sum of terms reflecting the partisan electoral consequences of the plan, on the one hand, and the jurisprudential consequences (i.e., those related to malapportionment), on the other. We also assume that judges face an opportunity cost of overturning state plans.

To sum up: in our model, judges care both about the partisan electoral consequences of their decisions and about the jurisprudential consequences. We place virtually no restriction (see the Appendix) on *how much* they care about these things. If the weight placed on partisan electoral consequences is near unity, then the model is one of "judges as

---

[2] To the extent that a standard had not been agreed to, judicial discretion and influence should have been greater than our model would suggest.

[3] For example, a state with three districts with populations of 90,000, 100,000, and 110,000 would have a D of 10%.

[4] This had been the standard suggested by Emmanuel Celler, chair of the House Judiciary Committee since the 82nd Congress.

partisan hacks." Alternatively, if the weight on jurisprudential consequences is near unity, then the model is one of "impartial jurists with very slight partisan inclinations." We do not propose to choose among the many possibilities on a priori grounds. Although we believe that the weight on partisan electoral values was nontrivial, the empirical analysis to come will speak to how heavy this weight might have been.

When Can Judges Accept and Reject Plans?

Virtually all of our data concern redistricting plans adopted prior to *Preisler*, and in this period lower courts potentially had substantial discretion in accepting and rejecting state plans. We assume that all courts were constrained to reject plans with high malapportionment, that is, those with $D > D_{max}$. We also assume that courts were constrained to accept plans with perfect apportionment, that is, those with $D = 0$.

Between these extremes, however, lower courts could exercise some discretion. They could allow a state to meet a "pragmatic" standard of population equality, with a maximum deviation, D, close to or even above the 15% that congresspersons and state politicians were asking for in the immediate aftermath of *Wesberry*. For example, the California Supreme Court, dominated by Democrats, allowed the state to continue using a Democratic plan in 1965, although the plan's maximum deviation was 29.1%.[5] Similarly, a three-judge panel drawn from a federal district court, with a 2–1 Republican majority, allowed Republican Kansas to continue using its plan in 1964, despite a maximum deviation of 23.8%.[6] Alternatively, lower courts could demand more exact population equality, anticipating the position eventually articulated in *Preisler*. For example, in 1965 a Democratic district court judged Republican Montana's plan, with a maximum deviation of 15.8%, invalid.[7]

---

[5] *Silver v. Reagan*, 63 Cal 2d 270 (1965).

[6] *Meeks v. Anderson*, 229 F. Supp. 271 (1964). Both the Kansas court and the California court, it should be noted, declared the plans unconstitutional. Both, nonetheless, allowed the plans to be used in the next election. Neither was constrained to do so, as either could have ordered all at-large elections, as Michigan's court had threatened to do. We provide further evidence on the contrast between accepting plans in principle (declaring them constitutionally valid) and accepting them in practice (allowing them to be used in the next election) later.

[7] *Roberts v. Babcock*, 246 F. Supp. 396 (1965).

Discretionary Reversions

We assume that courts also had substantial discretion in determining what the reversionary plan would be in case the state failed to produce an acceptable plan. In particular, we assume that the court could pick whatever plan it wished, subject to two constraints. First, the court's plan had to exhibit a degree of malapportionment sufficiently low to pass muster with existing precedent. Second, the court's plan had to be no more malapportioned than the state plan it overturned (given that the only justiciable basis at this time for overturning a plan was its degree of malapportionment, we assume that a court faced prohibitive costs in overturning a plan only to replace it with one that was even more malapportioned).

More formally, our assumption can be stated as follows. After rejecting a state plan with deviation D_{state}, the court could impose any reversionary plan, with deviation D_{rev}, such that $D_{rev} \leq D_{state}$ and $D_{rev} \leq D_{max}$.

Feasible Plans

In the previous chapter, we introduced the concept of a feasible set of redistricting plans, A. Defined formally as a subset of $\rho - \lambda$ space, the feasible set reflected the fact that there were responsiveness and bias values so extreme that it would be technically impossible to draw a redistricting plan to implement them.

In this chapter, we shall denote the feasible set of plans as a function of D, $A(D)$; we assume that the feasible set shrinks uniformly and continuously as D decreases. The notion is that, as a more and more demanding constraint on malapportionment is imposed, the set of attainable plans (in terms of bias and responsiveness) shrinks. Note that we do not assume that the feasible set necessarily shrinks by a substantively significant amount. We merely admit the possibility.

What the Parties Knew About the Courts

The simplest way to model court-supervised redistricting in the 1960s is to assume that both parties knew the preferences of the supervising court well and could thus accurately and precisely anticipate its reactions to the various possible plans that the state might submit. In particular, we assume that each party could correctly forecast which plans the court would accept and reject; and, in case the court rejected the state plan, each party could correctly anticipate what plan the court would impose in its stead. In a state under the unified control of a single party, the controlling party could thus choose the best plan among all those that it knew the court would accept.

While this account certainly overstates the precision with which a party could anticipate the behavior of a court, it does allow us to focus on what we believe is the primary issue – what the court would accept, what it would impose in case it did not accept, and how parties' anticipation of the court's reactions colored their behavior. Introducing risk to the model would not change the basic predictions regarding whether states facing "hostile" courts might have produced systematically different plans than those facing "friendly" courts.

Another issue is whether state politicians knew which court would ultimately judge their handiwork. In addition to 4 cases in which the court imposed its own plan, there were 14 cases in our dataset – where by a *case* we mean an instance of state politicians drawing new district lines under court supervision. In seven of these cases, only a single court was ever involved in the litigation – and thus state politicians should have known the identity of the supervising court without difficulty. In five other cases, one or more lower courts were involved but the U.S. Supreme Court entered the process *before* the state had to redraw. We assume that state politicians in these cases viewed the Supreme Court as the supervising court. Finally, in two cases, the state acted before the Supreme Court had entered the process. In these cases, we assume that the district court hearing the case was viewed as the supervising court (as it turns out, there was a Democratic partisan majority on both the district court and the Supreme Court, so that recoding these observations to make the Supreme Court the supervising court does not affect the analysis).

Appeals

If lower courts had some discretion in deciding how much malapportionment was too much, did their influence disappear because of the possibility of appeal? If appeals had been costless (to plaintiffs, defendants, and courts), then lower courts might indeed have had no influence. However, appeals were not costless. For plaintiffs and defendants, appeals entailed legal costs. For the higher courts, appeals entailed opportunity costs. Thus, so long as the lower courts did not stray too far from what the relevant higher courts would tolerate, the transactions costs of appeals provided them some room to maneuver.[8] Relying on this argument, we ignore the possibility of appeal in the formal model (exposited in the Appendix).

Summary

Our model applies most straightforwardly, but not only, when a state redistricts after ordered to do so by a specific court. In any event, we assume that the state acts knowing the preferences of the judges on the supervising court; the costs to the judges of overturning the state's plan; and the jurisprudential constraints the judges face (what plans they can reject or accept; what plans they could impose if they reject).

JUDICIAL INFLUENCE OVER REDISTRICTING: PREDICTIONS

Court Influence When the State Is Under Unified Control

We first consider the case of a strong party enjoying unified control of state government (recall that a party is strong if its expected vote share in the next election exceeds that of its adversary). Under the automatic reversions of the prerevolutionary period, such a party needed only to enact a redistricting statute. The reversionary plan came into force only if it failed in this endeavor. Under the discretionary reversions of the postrevolutionary period, in contrast, a strong party enjoying unified control may still have worried that the court that had ordered the state to redistrict would invalidate its plan unless it created districts with exactly equal populations. Creating more equally populated districts, however, was costly.[9] Worry over potential judicial intervention thus gave the redistricting party an incentive to accommodate the court's preferences in the plan that it enacted in order to forestall actual intervention.

In terms of our model, a state under unified control facing a favorable court could typically submit a plan with the maximum allowable

---

[8] This is a fairly standard argument. Similar arguments can be found, for example, in Murphy (1964), O'Brien (1984), and McCubbins, Noll, and Weingast (1995).

[9] In the model, this cost appears in the shrinking of $A(D)$ as D declines: the levels of attainable bias and responsiveness were lower for lower levels of malapportionment. However, it is plausible that there were other costs to lowering malapportionment in terms of splitting counties and other natural local political jurisdictions. We do not represent these costs formally in the model but note their existence.

malapportionment and its (the state's) ideal combination of bias and responsiveness (which coincided with the court's) and expect the court to accept it. In contrast, a state facing a hostile court might have thought along the following lines. If it produced a plan with the maximum allowable deviation and its ideal combination of bias and responsiveness, the court could reject the plan and substitute one that was substantially better for it (the court) both in jurisprudential terms (less malapportionment) and in partisan electoral terms (better values of bias and responsiveness). Rather than accept this outcome, the state could reduce bias, responsiveness, and malapportionment – all things the other-party judges would like – until the court was just willing to accept the plan. The precise combination of reductions in bias, responsiveness, and malapportionment that was best would depend formally on the model's details. The assumptions we have adopted suffice to ensure that the typical result is a reduction in all three parameters rather than in just one. (For a more elaborate discussion, see the Appendix.)

Thus, our predictions in the case of unified government can be stated as follows. First, *plans drawn under the supervision of Democratic courts should have exhibited more pro-Democratic bias than plans drawn under the supervision of Republican courts, holding constant which party controlled the state government.* Second, responsiveness should have been lower in states under divided control than in states under unified control for the reasons articulated in the previous chapter. But *within the class of unified states, responsiveness should have been lower where the court was controlled by the opposite party than where the state and court were both under the same party's control.* (To see the intuition behind this claim, recall that parties enjoying unified control are presumed to have good vote expectations, and hence to favor higher levels of responsiveness. When the court is in enemy hands, it is not disposed to allow the state to enact the plan it most prefers, and hence the state settles for somewhat lower responsiveness.) Third, *malapportionment should have been higher in unified states facing friendly courts than in those facing hostile courts.*

The tendencies just identified, it should be stressed, can be quite weak under our model. Indeed, if one assumes that the courts placed no weight at all on partisan electoral considerations ($w = 0$), then there is no reason under the model to expect any of these patterns. It is only if the weight placed by jurists on electoral payoffs was sufficiently high that these predictions will have much punch. We leave it to the data to sort out which assumption about judicial preferences is better supported.

Court Influence When the State Is Under Divided Control

Now consider a plan drawn under conditions of divided government. The difference between having a Democratic or a Republican court supervising redistricting should have been mostly a difference in expected bias, with pro-Democratic bias higher under more Democratic courts, lower under more Republican courts. As the state is under divided control by assumption, and we assume that strong parties in divided states expect lower vote shares than do strong parties in unified states, even the strong party should prefer relatively low levels of responsiveness. Thus, whether or not the court was on the strong party's side would matter little as far as responsiveness is concerned. Similarly, there is no clear prediction regarding the level of malapportionment, as we make no assumption that Republican jurists valued the reduction of malapportionment less (or more) than Democratic jurists.

Court Influence After Preisler

If one assumes that judges' ability to influence state plans depended significantly on their ability to exercise discretion regarding the level of malapportionment they would allow in the range below D_{max}, then one must also believe that judicial influence declined substantially after the Supreme Court's decision in *Preisler* reduced D_{max} to nearly zero. In contrast, if one believes that judges still had substantial discretion after *Preisler* – in setting tough or lax deadlines, in requiring that more recent state census population figures be used instead of less recent federal census figures, in setting harsh or favorable reversions, and perhaps elsewhere – then one might expect judicial influence to continue.

We cannot arbitrate empirically between these contending views here, lacking the post-1960s dataset that would be required to investigate the matter. We can, however, note two sorts of evidence that suggests that partisanship continued to influence congressional reapportionment decisions.

First, Lloyd (1995) finds – in a study of 44 state redistricting cases from 1964 to 1983 – that federal judges were substantially more likely to rule against plans drawn by the other party than they were to rule against plans drawn by their own party. Because state legislative districts were never subject to the stringent *Preisler* requirements, Lloyd's study, while it certainly jibes with the results we report later, cannot shed too much light on the continued vibrancy of partisanship in congressional redistricting cases after *Preisler*.

Circumstantial and anecdotal evidence of such vibrancy certainly exists, however. Karlan (1993, p. 1730) notes that the Republican governor of Alabama induced fellow Republicans to sue him in order to give control of Alabama's congressional redistricting to judges rather than the Democratic state legislature. In California, the plaintiffs in *Badham v. March Fong Eu*, 568 F. Supp. 156 (1983) sought a state court rather than the federal district court, apparently in light of the differing partisan complexion of the two. In Texas, then-Governor George W. Bush "refused to call the Democratic-controlled state legislature into session, apparently calculating that fellow Republicans would be better served by a remedial plan drawn by the district court composed of three Republican-appointed judges, one of whom . . . had previously served as general counsel for the Texas Republican Party" (Fisher 1997, p. 1406, no. 19). More generally, Grofman (1993, footnotes 53 and 54) suggests that, after the 1990 census, the Republican National Committee advised states under divided control to favor a litigation strategy, rather than compromising with the Democrats, partly because of the heavily conservative federal bench at that time. To the extent that this sort of venue shopping was widespread (see also Solimine 2001), it suggests that plaintiffs believed the partisanship of the court hearing the case still mattered, even after *Preisler* (and *Karcher*). How much it mattered, and whether it mattered less than it did in the 1960s, is of course not illuminated by these anecdotes and remains a topic for future investigation.

JUDICIAL INFLUENCE OVER REDISTRICTING: QUALITATIVE EVIDENCE

In this section, we briefly consider some of the court cases that will figure in the statistical analyses to come. Our purpose is to provide circumstantial evidence that court partisanship was relevant in 1960s redistricting decisions rather than to defend this thesis carefully by close scrutiny of any one case.

We can begin by noting that there are 44 separate court cases reflected in our dataset, arising out of the redistricting process in 13 separate states. Of these 44 decisions, 8 (18%) were handed down on straight party-line votes. In two other cases (New York 1967, Indiana 1968), the only dissent(s) on the court were from the minority party on the panel, but at least one minority jurist also concurred with the majority opinion.

In Illinois, two courts were involved – one a federal panel with a 2–1 Democratic majority, one the state supreme court with a 4–2 Republican majority. There were also two plans submitted – the Democrats' and the Republicans'. In the end, the court(s) stapled together the Democrats' plan for Cook County (11 districts) with the Republicans' plan for downstate (13 districts) and called it a day.

Another quintet of cases are interesting because they were appealed all the way to the Supreme Court. These cases involved two of the largest Republican states in the sample – New York (1968 and 1970) and Ohio (1968) – plus Missouri (1968 and 1970). The decisions rendered seem to have favored the Democrats. The Supreme Court reversed decisions made by lower courts with Republican majorities in New York (1970) and Ohio (1968). In the latter case, the (Republican) Ohio Supreme Court had approved a plan drawn up by the Republican state government, but the (Democractic) U.S. Supreme Court reversed that decision and remanded the case to a federal panel. In New York, the Supreme Court affirmed a finding that the existing plan was invalid but reversed the (Republican) lower court's decision to allow the invalid plan to be used in the 1970 election. In Missouri, a federal court with a Democratic majority ruled the Democrats' 1965 plan unconstitutional but allowed it to be used in 1966. The same federal panel ruled the plan the state Democrats enacted in 1967 also unconstitutional but again allowed it to be used in the next election (1968). The Supreme Court affirmed the lower court's decision to allow the 1967 plan's use in the 1968 election, unlike its decision in New York, then later declared the plan unconstitutional and gave the state another opportunity to redraw. The state did so, producing what the Republican Senate minority leader called a "very scientific and magnificent gerrymander," one that created the most population-equal districts in the nation, and – finally! – passed judicial muster (Congressional Quarterly 1969, p. 1644). Counterbalancing these cases in which the partisan effect of the Supreme Court's decisions seemed to favor the Democrats was the Court's *per curiam* order in Indiana, requiring a district court to review its decision to approve a Democratic plan in that state.

A final interesting case occurred in New Jersey. The state supreme court, with a 6–1 Democratic edge, was reported as saying that partisan considerations were beyond its jurisdiction (Congressional Quarterly 1968, p. 829). However, if one looks at the Republican plan that was being challenged, one finds that it sought to change a preexisting Democratic plan that had been hailed as an act to preserve freshly minted Democratic incumbents elected in Lyndon Baines Johnson's landslide victory. How much did the Republicans seek to change what they had previously described as a notorious gerrymander? They sought to change only 2 of New Jersey's 15 congressional districts, those in Bergen County, by making the dividing line run north/south instead of east/west. Although the apparent objective was to target a Democratic incumbent, the plan can hardly be called ambitious. Were the Republicans worried that the Democratic Supreme Court's judicial forbearance might have limits?

The survey just given cannot do justice to the full complexity of the cases. It can serve, however, to show that partisanship of one sort or another seems to insert itself into the judicial handling of many cases. Sometimes the judges voted on party lines or, as in Illinois, there were two courts seemingly split on party lines. Sometimes partisanship seems plausible in the pattern of cases that were appealed to the Supreme Court. Why would it have been worthwhile to appeal the Ohio Supreme Court's decision to the U.S. Supreme Court but not the California Supreme Court's or the New Jersey Supreme Court's? Perhaps because the Ohio Supreme Court was Republican, and Ohio's disappointed Democrats reckoned that they might get a better deal at the U.S. Supreme Court. In contrast, the supreme courts in California and New Jersey were Democratic, and both had evidently succeeded in convincing largely Republican state governments to take half a loaf or less; there were no disappointed Democrats to appeal the case further, and the Republicans knew better. Finally, sometimes partisanship seems plausible in the pattern of reversions and timetables. Why did the court in Michigan 1964 (on which see Chapter 4) give the state so little time to act, whereas in Missouri the state was allowed ample time and even got to use its first two (unconstitutional) tries at getting things right at the ensuing elections? It certainly seems as if the Democratic court in Michigan was attempting, rather successfully, to force the Republicans to cut a deal with the state Democrats. Meanwhile, in solidly Democratic Missouri, timetables were relaxed and reversions turned out to be whatever the state had just produced.

MALAPPORTIONMENT AND COURT PARTISANSHIP

In this section, we investigate the levels of malapportionment that courts in the 1960s were prepared to tolerate. Our model predicts that unified states in the 1960s facing friendly courts should have (1) anticipated more lenient enforcement of standards from friendly than from hostile courts and hence (2) produced plans with higher levels of malapportionment than did otherwise similar unified states facing hostile courts.

We test a version of the first prediction by asking whether courts in the 1960s were more likely to accept plans produced by state governments of the same partisanship than plans produced by state governments of opposite partisanship, malapportionment held constant. The unit of analysis is simply a court deciding on a plan (in the 1960s). However, we do not include all court decisions in the analysis. Only those cases, 30 in all, in which the plan is clearly partisan and we can clearly identify the partisanship of the court are included. (We identify the partisan cast of the plan with that of the state government originally enacting the plan, while the partisanship of the court depends on the majority affiliation of the jurists on the panel.)[10] The analysis focuses on the probability that a plan will be accepted, given its degree of malapportionment and the friendly or hostile partisan character of the court (relative to the plan being judged).

In order to proceed, we must first define more carefully what we mean by a court accepting a plan. There are two senses of the word *accept* that we distinguish. First, a court may judge that a plan meets the constitutional requirements set forth by the Supreme Court: it accepts the plan in principle (as constitutionally valid). Second, a court may allow a plan to be used in the next election: it accepts the plan in practice.

Following these two senses in which a court can accept a plan, we define two dependent variables. First, the variable *Validated* takes on the value of 1 if the court accepts the plan in principle (and 0 otherwise). Second, the variable *Allowed* takes on the value of 1 if the court allows the plan to be used at the next election (and 0 otherwise). All plans accepted in principle were also accepted in practice. However, of the 20 plans rejected in principle, 8 were accepted in practice (i.e., allowed for use at the next election).

[10] In determining the partisanship of a plan, we proceeded as follows. First, if the plan had been enacted by a unified state government, then its partisanship was that of the enacting government. Second, if the plan had been enacted by a divided state government, then we investigated whether that divided government had adopted its plan under a conservative or a radical reversion. If the former (a conservative reversion), then we know from Chapter 3 that any preexisting partisan cast of the districting plans in the state will have been preserved. Thus, we look past the divided government to the next previous plan. If the next previous plan was enacted by a unified partisan government, we take that government as the "originally enacting" government.

The two main independent variables in our analysis are *Deviation*, defined as the maximum deviation from the average district population that the plan entails, and *Friendly Court*, defined as 1 if the court was of the same partisanship as the state government that originally enacted the plan and −1 if the court was of the opposite partisanship. Our expectation is that, among plans with a given level of malapportionment, those judged by a friendly rather than a hostile court will be more likely to be accepted (both in principle and in practice).

We now turn to the analysis. To begin with, consider some simple bivariate comparisons. In the 20 cases involving a friendly court, the plan was validated in 7 cases and allowed in 14. In the 10 cases involving a hostile court, the plan was validated in 3 cases and allowed in 4. Thus, friendly courts were slightly more likely to accept plans in principle (accepting 35% versus 30% for the hostile courts) and considerably more likely to accept them in practice (allowing 70% versus 40% for the hostile courts).

Now consider the controlled analyses presented in Table 5.1. Plans were more likely to be validated, malapportionment held constant, if the court was friendly – but the effect is substantively trivial and statistically indiscernible from zero. Plans were also more likely to be allowed, malapportionment held constant, if the court was friendly – and here the

Table 5.1. *Court Acceptance of Redistricting Plans, 1964–1970*

Independent Variables	Dependent Variable = Validated	Dependent Variable = Allowed
Constant	0.070	1.007**
	(0.424)	(0.469)
Deviation	−0.045	−0.068**
	(0.031)	(0.031)
Friendly Court	0.113	0.521*
	(0.263)	(0.276)
Number of observations	30	30
Pseudo-R^2	.074	.231

Notes: Cell entries give the estimated coefficients, with the standard error in parentheses below. *Deviation* is the maximum deviation from the average district population in the state that the plan entails. *Friendly Court* equals 1 if the supervising court is controlled by the same party that fashioned the plan being judged, 0 otherwise.
* = significant at the .05 level in a one-tailed test.
** = significant at the .05 level in a two-tailed test.

effect is statistically significant (in a one-tailed test, appropriate given our hypothesis, at the .05 level). To see the substantive size of this effect, consider an example of two plans, both with a maximum deviation of 12.8%. If such a plan were reviewed by a friendly court, the estimated probability of acceptance would be 0.75. In contrast, if such a plan were reviewed by a hostile court, the estimated probability of acceptance would be 0.35. Thus, there was quite a difference in the probability of a plan being allowed for use at the next election in the 1960s, depending on whether the court was friendly or hostile.

There is something in our results both for those who emphasize the constraining force of precedent and for those who stress judicial discretion. On the one hand, the courts did not differ discernibly in their judgments of constitutional validity. Holding constant a plan's malapportionment, a friendly court was not significantly more likely to accept it in principle than a hostile court. On the other hand, the courts did exercise discretion regarding the more practical issue of whether a plan would be *used* or not. Moreover, their discretion appears to have been exercised systematically for partisan effect, with courts more likely to accept a plan with a given level of malapportionment, if that plan had been enacted by a state of the same partisanship as the court.[11]

CONCLUSION

In this chapter, we have argued that the whole congressional redistricting game changed fundamentally after the Supreme Court's decision in *Wesberry*. Even in a state in which one party enjoyed unified control, it could no longer gerrymander to its partisan heart's content, as it could prior to the reapportionment revolution. Instead, the party needed to ask a few questions: Will the other party bring suit against the plan? If so, in which court will the suit be brought? Conditional on a suit being brought in a particular court, what are the chances that the plan will be voided and another put in its place? And so on.

State parties' anticipations of what the supervising court would tolerate in turn affected what the states offered to begin with. We generate,

---

[11] We can also report the following. Regressing a plan's deviation on whether the court was friendly and whether the plan was allowed reveals that plans submitted to friendly courts tended to have higher malapportionment. This difference (about 2.9%) is of the expected sign but misses standard levels of significance (although it is significant at the .10 level in a one-tailed test).

in particular, three predictions: (1) bias should be more pro-Republican if the supervising court was Republican rather than Democratic (partisanship of state held constant); (2) in unified states, the responsiveness of the plan adopted should have been higher if the supervising court was friendly than if it was hostile; (3) in unified states, the malapportionment of the plan offered should have been higher if the supervising court was friendly than if it was hostile.

In this chapter, we have tested a version of the last of these predictions, finding that friendly courts were no more likely to accept a plan as *constitutionally valid* than hostile courts but were more likely to *allow a plan to be used at the next election*. This propensity of courts to deal more leniently with states controlled by the same party jibes with part of our model. In particular, it provides evidence in favor of one specific mechanism by which we think the courts may have influenced the states: if unified states anticipated that hostile courts would hold them to a more demanding standard on malapportionment, they had an incentive to bid for the courts' acceptance not just with lower malapportionment but also with lower bias and responsiveness. We do not wish to say that this was the only avenue of court influence. However, it is one plausible such avenue, and there is some evidence that it was traveled.

Our model suggests an answer to a puzzle we noted in Chapter 3 concerning the Republicans' poor showing at partisan gerrymandering in the 1960s. As it turns out, the highest courts supervising redistricting action in the largest Republican-controlled states – Michigan 1964, Ohio 1968, New Jersey 1968, and New York 1968–1970 – all had Democratic majorities. Perhaps Republican politicians in these states worried that, if they passed a plan without perfectly equal-population districts, the court would invalidate it – especially if the enacted plan produced heavy pro-Republican bias. To the extent that achieving the equal-population standard was costly, in order to get Democratic courts to accept some population discrepancies, Republicans in these states might have reduced the level of bias in their plans. In the next chapter, we test this notion more systematically across the full range of observations for which we have data.

Appendix: A Model of Redistricting Under Court Supervision

In this Appendix, we state more formally the reasoning that lies behind our predictions in the case of unified partisan control of the state government. The main prediction is that malapportionment, bias, and responsiveness will all be lower when there is a hostile court than when there is a friendly court.

To clarify our assumptions about judges' preferences, suppose that a state under unified Republican control submits a plan with responsiveness, bias, and malapportionment represented by (ρ,λ,D). Consider the reaction to this plan of a particular jurist (the *focal judge*).

If the court accepts the state's plan and the focal judge is in the majority, his or her payoff is $wu(\rho,\lambda) + (1 - w)v(D)$. The term $u(\rho,\lambda)$ represents how much the judge likes the partisan electoral consequences (responsiveness and bias) of the plan. We assume that each judge's preferences regarding bias and responsiveness were identical to state politicians' preferences of the same party. (Our theory does not require that *all* judges had partisan preferences in this sense, but it is easier to exposit for this pure case, and so we defer a more nuanced discussion until the next chapter.) The term $v(D)$ represents the plan's jurisprudential value (which depends on its level of malapportionment). The terms w and $1 - w$ reflect the weights attached by the focal judge to the partisan electoral payoff $u(\rho,\lambda)$ and the jurisprudential payoff $v(D)$, respectively. We assume that $0 < w < 1$.

If the court rejects the state's plan and imposes an alternative plan $(\rho_{rev},\lambda_{rev};D_{rev})$, the focal judge's payoff is $wu(\rho_{rev},\lambda_{rev}) + (1 - w)v(D_{rev}) - c$. (We again assume that the focal judge is in the majority.) The first term again represents the (weighted) partisan electoral payoff of the plan, this time the court's reversionary plan. The second term again represents the (weighted) jurisprudential payoff of the plan. The third term, c, represents the opportunity cost of overturning the state's plan. (We ignore any collective action problems that arise in writing majority opinions and assume that each member of the majority must "pay" some of the fixed cost, even if he or she does not write the opinion.)

To simplify matters, we assume that the majority judges on each type of court (friendly, hostile) have identical preferences, so that we can speak of the court as a unitary actor in what follows. The favorable court and the hostile court are assumed to be identical as regards the value they place on malapportionment. Formally, the weight w is identical for both courts; the function $v(\bullet)$ is identical for both courts; and the cost c is identical for both courts. The only difference between the two courts lies in their evaluation of the partisan electoral consequences of each redistricting plan, represented by the utility functions u_f (for the favorable court) and u_h (for the hostile court).

Figure 5A.1 illustrates the basic elements of the model in $\rho - \lambda$ space. First, the ellipse pictured, along with its interior, represents the largest possible feasible set, $A(D_{max})$. Given our assumptions, smaller levels of malapportionment, $D < D_{max}$, would entail smaller feasible sets, $A(D) \subset A(D_{max})$. Indeed, we assume that $A(D)$ is simply a scaled-down version of the ellipse $A(D_{max})$. Second, the point S (on the upper right side of the ellipse) represents the constrained ideal point of the state. A few of the state's indifference curves (those that bow away from the origin) are also pictured. Third, the point S also represents the ideal point of a favorable court, given a level of malapportionment D_{max}. This identity of constrained ideal points follows because we have assumed that (1) judges' preferences concerning bias and responsiveness were identical to those of their copartisans in the state and (2) judges' preferences concerning bias and responsiveness were separable from their preferences concerning malapportionment. These same assumptions also imply that the entire indifference curve map of the friendly court coincides with that of the state. Fourth, the point H (on the lower left side of the ellipse) represents the constrained ideal point of a hostile court. Also pictured are a few of this court's ideal curves. Fifth, the curve connecting H and S is the *contract curve* between the state and the hostile court.

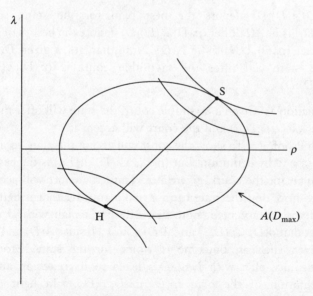

Figure 5A.1 An example of bargaining over a redistricting plan under court supervision.

To sketch the main formal result, we need some notation. We consider first what the courts will accept, then what the state will offer a favorable court, then finally what the state will offer a hostile court.

WHAT THE COURTS WILL ACCEPT

Let $W_j(D) = \max\{wu_j(\rho_{rev},\lambda_{rev}) + (1 - w)v(D_{rev}) - c: (\rho_{rev},\lambda_{rev}) \in A(D_{rev})$ and $D_{rev} \leq D\}$ be the best possible payoff for a court of type j ($j \in \{f,h\}$), if it rejects a state plan with malapportionment D. The court accepts the state plan $(\rho,\lambda;D)$ if and only if $wu_j(\rho,\lambda) + (1 - w)v(D) \geq W_j(D)$.

Let $B_j(D) = \{(\rho,\lambda)$: a court of type j will accept the plan $(\rho,\lambda;D)\}$. We assume (call this the *monotonicity assumption*) that there exists a $D_{crit} \in (0,D_{max}]$ such that $B_f(D_{crit}) \neq \varnothing$ and $B_f(D) = \varnothing$ for all $D > D_{crit}$. That is, there is a critical value of malapportionment, D_{crit}, such that the favorable court will accept some plans with $D \leq D_{crit}$ but will reject all plans with $D > D_{crit}$. This might follow, for example, if $v(\bullet)$ is convex decreasing in D, while increases in D lead to linear increases in the electoral payoff for the court.

WHAT THE STATE WILL OFFER TO
THE FAVORABLE COURT

Let $(\rho(D),\lambda(D);D)$ denote the best plan for the state, such that $(\rho(D),\lambda(D))$ is in $A(D)$. Let $(\rho_j(D),\lambda_j(D);D)$ denote the best plan for court j, such that $(\rho_j(D),\lambda_j(D))$ is in $A(D)$. Note that, for a given D, the best plan the state can offer the favorable court is $(\rho_j(D),\lambda_j(D);D) = (\rho(D),\lambda(D);D)$.

Proposition 1: Given a favorable court, the state will offer the plan $(\rho(D_{crit}),\lambda(D_{crit});D_{crit})$ and the court will accept it.
Sketch Proof: (1) To show the court will accept the plan, recall that $B_f(D_{crit}) \neq \varnothing$ by definition. But $(\rho(D_{crit}),\lambda(D_{crit});D_{crit})$ is the best possible plan for the court, given D_{crit}. Thus, the court will accept it. (2) To show that the state cannot make an offer that is better for it and will be accepted, note that offering a plan with $D < D_{crit}$ implies that $\rho(D) < \rho(D_{crit})$ and $\lambda(D) < \lambda(D_{crit})$, since $A(D) \subset A(D_{crit})$. However, such an outcome is worse for the state. Moreover, offering any plan with $D > D_{crit}$ leads to its rejection and implementation of the plan $(\rho(D_{rev}),\lambda(D_{rev});D_{rev})$. In light of the monotonicity assumption, $D_{rev} \leq D_{crit}$. [If not, then $B_f(D_{rev}) = \varnothing$,

which implies that $wu_f(\rho(D_{rev}),\lambda(D_{rev})) + (1 - w)v(D_{rev}) < W_f(D_{rev})$, which in turn implies that D_{rev} is not the court's optimal plan.] Hence, $(\rho(D_{rev}),\lambda(D_{rev});D_{rev})$ is no better for the state than $(\rho(D_{crit}),\lambda(D_{crit});D_{crit})$ and may be worse. (To put things technically correctly, we assume that the state prefers to have its offer accepted, all else equal.)

WHAT THE STATE WILL OFFER TO THE HOSTILE COURT

Let CC denote the contract curve between the state and the hostile court. Given our assumptions about the utility functions of the parties and courts, this curve will be a well-behaved one running from southwest to northeast, as pictured in Figure 5A.1.

Lemma 1: Suppose that the state must offer a plan with malapportionment D and that $A(D) \not\subset B_h(D)$. The state's optimal offer to the hostile court in this case is given by the intersection of CC and the boundary of $B_h(D)$.

Sketch Proof: Given our assumptions, $B_h(D)$ is always one of the hostile court's upper contour sets. The best element for the state from such a set is given by the intersection of its boundary with the contract curve, CC.

We assume that $\max\{D: (\rho,\lambda;D)$ is acceptable to the hostile court$\} = D_{crit,h} \le D_{crit}$ and that the hostile court also satisfies the monotonicity condition (with $D_{crit,h}$ in place of D_{crit}). That is, the most malapportioned plan that the hostile court will accept is no more malapportioned than the most malapportioned plan that the favorable court will accept. The most natural thing in terms of preserving the symmetry of the courts is to assume equality earlier – and we do so subsequently – but the results will follow a fortiori otherwise.

Lemma 2: If $D_1 < D_2$, then $B_h(D_1) \supset B_h(D_2)$.

Proposition 4: Given a hostile court, the state will offer a plan $(\rho,\lambda;D)$ such that $D < D_{crit}$, $\rho < \rho(D_{crit})$ and $\lambda < \lambda(D_{crit})$. The court will accept the offer.

Sketch Proof: By assumption, the largest malapportionment that the hostile court will accept is D_{crit}, the same as for the favorable court. There exist plans with lower malapportionment that the hostile court will accept by the monotonicity assumption. Some of these plans will have higher bias and responsiveness in light of Lemma 2. Since the state prefers higher bias and responsiveness, it will offer a plan with $D < D_{crit}$. If $D < D_{crit}$, however, then $\rho \leq \rho(D)$ $< \rho(D_{crit})$ and $\lambda \leq \lambda(D) < \lambda(D_{crit})$. The first (weak) inequalities follow in light of Lemma 1. The second (strict) inequalities follow because $A(D) \subset A(D_{crit})$ and CC runs from the southwest to the northeast.

6

Bias, Responsiveness, and the Courts

In the previous chapter, we presented a model of the role of the courts in the 1960s redistricting process. In this chapter we test two of the key predictions of that model, those regarding bias and responsiveness.

The first section deals with the operational details of our tests. The second section shows that Democratic courts supervised plans that had more pro-Democratic bias, while Republican courts supervised plans that had more pro-Republican bias, controlling for partisan control of state government. It also shows that responsiveness tended to be higher in plans written by unified states facing friendly rather than hostile courts. Both of the bias-responsiveness predictions articulated in the previous chapter, in other words, are supported by the data.

The third section shows that there were many more Democratic than Republican courts with jurisdiction over congressional redistricting cases in the 1960s – part of the legacy of Democratic hegemony in the New Deal era. Putting the predominance of Democratic courts together with the impact of court partisanship on plan bias helps explain why Republican partisan gerrymanders in the 1960s produced such low levels of pro-Republican bias; why bipartisan Republican plans in the 1960s produced lower levels of pro-Republican bias than they had earlier; and thus why what had been about a 6% pro-Republican bias outside the South abruptly disappeared.

The fourth and fifth sections consider the extent to which judges appear to have pursued partisan interests and the role – dynamic or constrained – of the judiciary. The sixth section concludes.

OPERATIONAL MATTERS

Obviously, the Democratic seat share in a state should increase as the Democratic vote share in that state increases. The model we estimate in this chapter, like that in Chapter 4, addresses two features of *how* this votes-to-seats translation occurs. First, is there a seat bonus for the party winning more votes statewide and, if so, how large is it? This is a question of responsiveness, as explained in Chapter 3. Second, does one party get a seat bonus above and beyond what would be expected on the basis of its vote share and the responsiveness of the system? This is a question of bias.

The analysis in this chapter differs from that in Chapter 4 in three main ways. First, we measure state control (i.e., which party controls state government) in terms of the number of branches of state government (lower house, upper house, and governorship) that each party controls, rather than simply distinguishing unified and divided cases. We also consider, later in the chapter, alternative codings of state control, including that used in Chapter 4. Precise variable definitions are given in the Appendix.

Second, we model bias and responsiveness as functions of state control and court control (i.e., which party controls the court supervising the state's redistricting action), rather than as functions of state control and the legally defined default outcome of the redistricting process. For the post-*Wesberry* period we study, the legally defined default does not vary – in all cases, it is up to the supervising court to determine. However, the partisanship of the supervising court does vary.

Third, we consider three different specifications of how control of state governments and supervising courts affected the responsiveness of districting plans. Our first specification allows only one common level of responsiveness for all states, as is common practice in the previous literature. Our second specification allows two levels of responsiveness – one for unified states facing favorable courts and one for all other states (divided or unified facing a hostile court). Our third specification allows three levels of responsiveness – one for divided states, one for unified states facing hostile courts, and one for unified states facing favorable courts. The expectation is that responsiveness will be lowest in the first category (divided), highest in the last category (unified/favorable), and intermediate in the middle category (unified/hostile).[1]

---

[1] In this chapter, bias and responsiveness vary as functions of two regressors indicating state and court control. Relative to the analysis in Chapter 4, therefore, we

Data

Our dataset draws from all 37 nonsouthern state elections in the period 1964–1970 that were held under districting plans constructed under the supervision of a specific court.[2] For each supervising court, we have identified the partisan affiliation of each judge.[3] All elections took place in 14 states – Arizona, California, Illinois, Indiana, Kansas, Kentucky, Massachusetts, Michigan, Missouri, Montana, Nebraska, New Jersey, New York, and Ohio – that among them accounted for 214 of the 329 nonsouthern congressional districts.

Some states that did have ongoing litigation in a particular year nonetheless used in their election an old, prerevolutionary plan that

---

impose some parametric constraints. (Essentially that analysis separately estimated each cell in the two-way classification of our regressors in this chapter.) We do so partly because these constraints appear plausible but also to help with degrees-of-freedom issues.

[2] The two exceptions to this rule are Kentucky 1966–1970 and Illinois 1966–1970. The Kentucky legislature adopted a plan in 1966 after a federal judge hinted that he would intervene otherwise; there was not a case before the judge at that time, however, nor was there later. Thus, we are assuming that the judge's hint was credible (someone could have been found to file a suit) and that the plan drawn was the same as it would have been had the court already had a suit before it. Our results change very little – and without affecting any conclusion – if we simply drop Kentucky 1966–1970 from the analysis. The Illinois exception arises because there were two courts quarreling over the matter. We have more to say about Illinois later.

[3] The sources used to identify the partisanship of most federal judges were Chase, Krislov, Boyum, and Clark (1976) and *Judges of the United States*, put out by the Bicentennial Committee of The Judicial Conference of the United States (1983). The latter source provides thumbnail biographies of all federal judges up to the time of publication. For most, it explicitly says "Democrat" or "Republican." For all, it at least gives the year of appointment, which tells one the partisanship of the appointing president. It often also refers to past political activity, which can provide useful clues: appointive positions can be cross-referenced with the party of the appointing president or governor. In some cases, there is a consistent pattern to these clues; in others, there is not. For judges whose partisanship was not clearly stated in the main sources, we (or, more precisely, our enterprising research assistant, Chris Den Hartog) looked elsewhere – e.g., the *New York Times Index*, the *San Francisco Chronicle Index*, the *Reader's Guide* – looking for any articles that might refer to the judges' partisanship. In the end, each judge's partisanship was coded as "definitely," "probably," or "maybe" a Democrat or a Republican. Definite classifications were based on explicit references to partisan affiliation; probable classifications were based on consistent clues; "maybe" classifications were based on a single clue or a preponderance of clues. For purposes of analysis, we collapsed our "definite," "probable," and "maybe" categories into two partisan classifications – Republican and Democrat. There were only 9 judges out of 64 coded who fell into the "maybe" category.

could not have been affected by anticipations of judicial reactions. These states' elections are not included in the analysis (until such time as they adopted a plan under court supervision and then used it).[4] There is no significant difference in the average degree of malapportionment, between the states included and those excluded from the analysis.[5]

In exploring the impact of court partisanship on redistricting plans, we would ideally consider all postrevolutionary redistrictings. In practice, however, we have little chance of identifying what state politicians perceived as the relevant courts in those cases where suits had not been filed. The politicians in state X in 1966 may all have understood which court was the potential supervisor of their redistricting shenanigans, but we don't know.

Accordingly, *we confine our attention in what follows to those cases in which suits were filed and courts did enter.* This has the tremendous advantage of allowing us to identify the partisanship of the jurists on each involved court. We can thus ask whether plans produced under the supervision of Democratic courts differed systematically from plans produced under the supervision of Republican courts, partisan control of state government held constant.

Selection Bias

Confining our attention to cases in which a suit had been filed also has a potential cost, which goes under the technical name of *selection bias*. If suits were brought by plaintiffs who sought to change the likely bias and responsiveness of the redistricting plan in their state, then the court effect we find in the cases that make it into our dataset will probably be

---

[4] For example, we exclude Kansas 1964. There, a Republican court invalidated the Republicans' 1961 plan but allowed it to be used in 1964; thus, as the plan in force in 1964 was written without regard to judicial reactions (it was before *Baker v. Carr*), we exclude the Kansas 1964 election from our analysis. It is for this sort of reason that our dataset does not reflect all cases of court involvement.

[5] We note this in response to a query from an anonymous reviewer. He or she wondered whether the states in which litigation was launched tended to be more severely malapportioned – which would lend credence to a picture of the courts as simply enforcing the new "one person, one vote" rule. The state-years not included in our analysis are a mixture of those in which no suit was brought and those in which a suit was brought but the court allowed the old plan to continue in use. The average similarity score (see Chapter 2 for a definition) in states included in our analysis was 74, versus 75 for states not included. Thus, the actual creation of new court-supervised plans bears no relation to the preexisting severity of malapportionment.

larger than it would be in the whole universe of cases (where court entry would not have much impact, the courts are not called in).

There are two preliminary points to make about this line of criticism. First, even if selection bias is more serious than we think (see the subsequent discussion), our work will still provide a clear indication of the nature of judicial influence over redistricting in an important subset of cases, one entailing roughly two-thirds of all nonsouthern districts.

Second, in order to criticize our results as suffering from selection bias, one must essentially accept the main conclusion of our analysis. In particular, it is only if plaintiffs in the 1960s thought that supervising courts would influence the bias and responsiveness of the plans they supervised in a partisan fashion that one might worry about the selection bias issue just raised.

With these two points in mind, we can simply add that we do not believe that selection bias is a substantial problem for two reasons. First, there is a plausible alternative theory about what motivated plaintiffs to bring suit, which does not entail that only cases with large court effects on bias and responsiveness make it into our sample. The alternative theory about these early post-*Baker* suits is that many were brought simply to prod the state into action by those primarily interested in how *malapportionment* affected the balance of urban and rural forces in a particular state. If prodding states into action so that malapportionment would be eradicated was the main motivation for filing suits at this time, however, then there would be relatively little selection bias to worry about on the bias/responsiveness side of the equation.

Second, there is some evidence that bears on these two competing theories about what plaintiffs were after in the 1960s. For the purpose of producing a different bias and responsiveness in the next redistricting plan, plaintiffs needed to find a court with different preferences on these matters than the state government. Thus, one expects that unified Republican states would typically have faced suits that ended up in Democratic courts, while unified Democratic states would typically have faced suits that ended up in Republican courts. For the purpose of forcing a state to take action, in contrast, any court sufficed since the Supreme Court's precedent on malapportionment was sufficiently clear that no court could ignore it with impunity. Under this theory, one does not expect a strong tendency toward courts of different partisanship from the states they supervise.

Looking at the actual data, we find almost no relationship between which party controls the state and which controls the court. Of the five unified Republican cases in the dataset, three were supervised by Democratic courts and two by Republican courts. Of the four unified Democratic cases in the dataset, two were supervised by Republican courts and two by Democratic courts. The evidence thus does not support the notion that plaintiffs were venue-shopping in an effort to find courts of a different partisan stripe than the states they were suing.

RESULTS

Bias

Our results, given in Table 6.1, show that a plan's bias was systematically related to partisan control of both the state government and the supervising court. Pro-Democratic bias increased as the number of branches of state government controlled by the Democrats increased. More importantly for present purposes, the more Democratic jurists and the fewer Republican jurists there were on the supervising court, the higher was the estimated pro-Democratic bias in the resulting plan, partisan control of state government held constant. Indeed, *all three models' results suggest that a party's getting one more judge on the supervising panel affected the bias of the resulting plan roughly as much as its getting one more branch of government.* This is a dramatic indication of how much the courts mattered in determining the characteristics of the plan ultimately implemented.

To help interpret how important controlling the state government and the supervising court was, consider a state in which the Democrats won 50% of the vote (that is, the simple average of the Democratic vote percentage across all districts in the state was 50%).[6] In such a state, what was the Democrat's expected seat share? Table 6.2 provides the answer (based on Model 2) as a function of two variables: the number of branches of state government controlled by each party and the number of judges on the supervising court who were affiliated with either party.

As can be seen, the Democrats in a dead-heat state could have expected 23.4% of the seats, if the districting plan had been drawn up by a unified Republican state supervised by a completely Republican court, but 67.7% of the seats, if the districting plan had been drawn up by a unified Democratic state supervised by a completely Democratic

---

[6] Given this outcome, $\ln[DV/(1 - DV)] = 0$, and so all terms involving $\ln[DV/(1 - DV)]$ also equal zero.

Table 6.1. *Judicial Influence on the Bias and Responsiveness of Redistricting Plans in the 1960s*

Independent Variables	Model 1 Coefficient Estimates	Model 2 Coefficient Estimates	Model 3 Coefficient Estimates
Constant	−.315**	−.222	−.203
	(.138)	(.149)	(.154)
Branches	.229***	.173**	.155*
	(.064)	(.071)	(.091)
Judges	.204***	.148**	.172**
	(.065)	(.072)	(.080)
Unified/Favorable	—	—	−.025
			(.423)
Unified/Hostile	—	—	−.073
			(.259)
Baseline	2.096***	1.78***	.876
responsiveness[a]	(.549)	(.568)	(.795)
How much larger	—	3.53*	4.44**
responsiveness is		(1.93)	(2.03)
in unified states			
supervised by a			
friendly court[b]			
How much larger	—	—	2.196*
responsiveness is			(1.30)
in unified states			
supervised by a			
hostile court[c]			
Number of observations	532	532	532
Wald χ^2	53.73	57.70	60.60
	($p = .0000$)	($p = .0000$)	($p = .0000$)

[a] The independent variable here is $\ln[DV/(1 - DV)]$, where ln is the natural logarithm and DV is the Democratic share of the vote in the state. In Model 1, baseline responsiveness is the level across all cases. In Model 2, baseline responsiveness is the level in divided states plus unified states supervised by hostile courts. In Model 3, baseline responsiveness is the level in divided states.

[b] The independent variable here is $\ln[DV/(1 - DV)] \times$ *Unified/Favorable*.

[c] The independent variable here is $\ln[DV/(1 - DV)] \times$ *Unified/Hostile*.

* = significant at the .10 level in a two-tailed test; ** = significant at the .05 level in a two-tailed test; *** = significant at the .01 level in a two-tailed test.

Table 6.2. *Expected Democratic Seat Share in a State in Which the Democrats Win 50% of the Vote, as a Function of Branches and Judges*

Branches	Judges (Three-Judge Panel Assumed)	Expected Democratic Seat Share
Unified Republican control (*Branches* = −3)	All three judges Republican (*Judges* = −3)	.234
Unified Republican control (*Branches* = −3)	Two of three judges Republican (*Judges* = −1)	.291
Democrats control two of three branches (*Branches* = +1)	Two of three judges Republican (*Judges* = −1)	.451
Democrats control one branch (*Branches* = −1)	Two of three judges Democratic (*Judges* = +1)	.439
Democrats control two of three branches (*Branches* = +1)	Two of three judges Democratic (*Judges* = +1)	.525
Unified Democratic control (*Branches* = +3)	Two of three judges Democratic (*Judges* = +1)	.609
Unified Democratic control (*Branches* = +3)	All judges Democratic (*Judges* = +3)	.677

Note: Estimates calculated from Model 2, Table 6.1.

court. This is a large difference, one that suggests that the parties wanted to and did gerrymander in the 1960s. The difference, moreover, reflects differences in bias between the various plans, not differences in responsiveness – recall that a 50% Democratic vote share is assumed throughout, which translates into a 50% seat share if bias is nil.

Although the difference between 67.7% and 23.4% is striking, it should be noted that it reflects an extrapolation to hypothetical cases: there was only one court case in which a panel had judges all from a single party and the state in question – Massachusetts – was under divided government at the time. Thus, there are no actual data in the top and bottom rows of Table 6.2; the table shows by extrapolation what the expected outcome would have been in such states.

The table also shows the expected seat share for intermediate levels of partisan control where neither party had all the branches and judges. As can be seen, the levels of bias here are smaller but still substantively significant. In a state redistricted under unified Republican control and the supervision of a court on which two of three judges were also Republican – such as Kansas – the Democrats could expect to get 29.1% of the seats for 50% of the vote. In contrast, in a state where the roles were reversed (unified Democratic state, two of three judges Democratic), such as Arizona or New Jersey in 1966, the Democrats could expect to get 60.9% of the seats for 50% of the vote. This is still a very considerable difference in outcomes.[7] Although bias was not itself justiciable at this time (not until *Davis v. Bandemer*, 478 U.S. 109, decided on 30 June 1986), states acted as if they expected the courts to be partisan.

Responsiveness

What about the effect of the courts on the responsiveness of plans? Model 2 shows that the level of responsiveness is significantly higher in unified states facing favorable courts than in the other cases. When the unified states are further split into unified facing a hostile court and unified facing a favorable court, one finds (see Model 3) the expected pattern: the divided states have the lowest responsiveness, followed by the unified/hostile states and then the unified/favorable states. The difference between divided and unified/hostile states is statistically discernible from zero (in a one-tailed test at the .05 level), as is that between divided and unified/favorable states. But the difference between unified/hostile and unified/favorable states is statistically insignificant. These results provide some support, albeit weak, for the notion that courts were allowing higher responsiveness in states their party controlled while reining it in somewhat in states the other party controlled.[8]

---

[7] As a final note, the impact of judicial partisanship on estimated bias does not vary significantly as between states where the court actually imposed a plan and those where it did not.

[8] After running Model 3, we tested the joint hypothesis that *Unified/Favorable*, *Unified/Hostile*, and *ln[DV/(1 − DV)]*Unified/Hostile* were all zero, finding that we could not reject it. This is why we also present the simpler Model 2, in which these restrictions are applied.

Alternative Measures of Court and State Partisanship

The results we have reported do not change if we employ different plausible measures of court and state partisanship. As explained in the Appendix, we have also classified court partisanship simply by whether a majority of the jurists on the supervising panel were Republican or Democratic, and also augmented this to identify larger-than-bare majorities in favor of either party. As regards state partisanship, we have measured this with a simple Unified Republican/Divided/Unified Democratic classification and also with two separate variables tracking each party's control of the chambers of the state legislature and the governorship. Our findings remain qualitatively similar regardless of what variables we use.

Robustness of Results

In order to further examine the robustness of our results, we re-ran Models 1 and 2 in Table 6.1 after deleting, one at a time, each of the 14 states in the analysis. In other words, we first reran the analyses deleting all observations from Arizona, then all observations from California, and so on through all the states in the analysis. Note that, for large states with multiple elections, this procedure removed a substantial number of observations. Removing California, for example, reduced the total number of observations by 76. Even with such wholesale removal of observations, our results always yield the same qualitative story, regardless of which state one removes. This shows that no single state "drives" our results. The gerrymandering tendencies we have uncovered appear to have been widespread in the states examined.

DEMOCRATIC DOMINANCE OF THE FEDERAL JUDICIARY

The previous section showed that, the more Democratic jurists and the fewer Republican jurists a court had, the higher the level of pro-Democratic bias in the redistricting plan it supervised. Or, to put the matter the other way around, the more Republican jurists and the fewer Democratic jurists a court had, the higher the level of pro-Republican bias in the plan it supervised.

Had the (mostly federal) courts that heard redistricting suits in the 1960s been evenly balanced between Democratic and Republican jurists, the effects of judicial partisanship might well have canceled out, with the increased pro-Democratic bias of Democratic-majority courts balancing the increased pro-Republican bias of Republican-majority courts. However, the federal judiciary had a clear preponderance of Democratic jurists by the mid-1960s due to Democratic dominance of the presidency from 1932 to 1952 and from 1960 to 1964. Moreover, this general preponderance was reflected in the specific courts that heard redistricting suits. Of the 37 state elections and 532 district elections involved in the previous section's analysis, Democratic-majority courts had supervised the redistricting plan used in 24 of the state elections (65%) and 396 of the district elections (74%). The Republicans did not have clear control of the remaining cases, however, as three elections in Illinois were held under a plan devised under the supervision of two quarreling courts, one with a Democratic majority and one with a Republican majority. Thus, Republican-majority courts supervised only 10 state elections (27%). As the states involved were generally smaller, only 64 districts, or 12% of the total, held elections under plans supervised by Republican courts. Probably the clearest indication of Democratic dominance in our court cases is the number of districts redrawn under the supervision of Democratic as opposed to Republican courts: 396 (or 74%) versus 64 (or 12%).

In Chapter 4, we found that plans drawn under unified Republican control of the state government in the prerevolutionary period generated a healthy 8.27% pro-Republican bias, while similar plans in the postrevolutionary period puzzlingly generated an anemic and insignificant 0.9% pro-Republican bias. We are now in a position to say why Republican control of state government mattered so much less in the 1960s than it had previously: the three largest Republican-held states, Ohio, New Jersey and New York, faced Democratic courts, and their redistricting plans appear to have been seriously affected by this for-the-Republicans-unfortunate situation.[9]

---

[9] Michigan 1964 was another large Republican state adversely affected by a Democratic court's decisions. However, as described in Chapter 2, the adverse effect in this case was so large that we reclassified Michigan as a divided state for purposes of Chapter 4's analysis. So the Michigan case is not contributing to the poor Republican performance cited in the paragraph (which reports Chapter 4's results). As noted in footnote 2, we classify Michigan as unified Republican in *this* chapter's analysis – since here we wish to separate judicial influence from that of the elected branches of government.

JUDGES' MOTIVATIONS

Having presented our results in the previous sections, let us now return to the issue of what motivated judges sitting on redistricting cases in the 1960s. Our assumption was that (1) these judges had the same preferences concerning bias and responsiveness as did their copartisans holding elective state offices but that (2) they also valued reducing malapportionment. The first part of this assumption might seem descriptively inaccurate to some readers, especially those inclined to view judges as nonpartisan arbiters heavily constrained by jurisprudential norms and the necessity of conforming to judicial precedent.

One route to justifying our assumption would be to examine the personal histories and statements of the judges involved. By such a procedure we might unearth a longtime machine pol incongruously placed on the federal bench via an arrogant boss's influence. But it is unlikely that many such cases would be found. Most would involve jurists with solid professional credentials. The task of tarring them with the brush of partisanship would be difficult and the result probably unconvincing.

So consider a second, instrumentalist route to justifying the assumption of judicial partisanship. There are four steps to the argument.

First, just as there is reason to be skeptical of circumstantial evidence that a particular judge is partisan, so there is also reason to be skeptical of judges' presentations of self as nonpartisan. So far as we know, the idea that judges are ethically obliged to be robust partisans is not currently in fashion and was not in the 1960s. Indeed, just the reverse was true. All respected legal theorists urged judges to be above partisanship. Thus, it is unlikely that one would find many judges willing to admit their partisan inclinations straightforwardly – perhaps even to themselves. In other words, this is one of those cases where actors' accounts of what they are up to are likely to be uninformative, so that analysts must rely on actions to speak louder than words.

Second, in the present context, unlike most others where debates about judicial partisanship rage, there is a very clear standard by which to gauge whether actions count as partisan. Those actions that promote outcomes – that is districting plans – with high levels of bias in favor of the judge's own party are partisan. So are those actions that promote plans with high levels of responsiveness in cases where the judge's party has good electoral prospects.

Third, in the present context, again unlike many others, the constraint on judges from precedent was minimal, for the simple reason that there were so few cases that had been decided previously in this new area of jurisprudence. The only clear constraint on judges' decisions was that the districts in any approved plan be of equal population. Even here, however, the maximum allowable amount of deviation from exact equality was relatively large until the *Preisler* decision in 1969. Moreover, even if a state produced a plan with, say, a maximum deviation of 10%, might the court not insist on an even stricter standard of equality? The decision itself could be framed in terms of a more exact compliance with the "one person, one vote" principle, even if the reason for doing so was to reject a plan with unpleasant partisan implications.

Fourth, the first three points together amount to saying that the Friedmanite instrumentalist argument carries considerable weight in our study (Friedman 1953). It is particularly difficult to provide credible evidence one way or another about judges' partisanship; but we know they were less constrained by precedent than in other areas; and there are clear predictions about the actions and outcomes expected under the assumption that they were partisan. We cannot systematically observe the actions, such as setting time deadlines and reversions, but we can systematically observe the outcomes – whether the plans constructed under each court's supervision had the expected bias and responsiveness. As it turns out, the outcomes are very much as one would predict on the assumption that judges were partisan.

Were Judges Strict Partisans?

A workable departure from the assumption that judges' preferences concerning outcomes were strictly partisan is to assume that each judge had a probability q of having such preferences and a probability $1 - q$ of having nonpartisan preferences. For $q = 1$, one has the original assumption that all judges were partisans. For $q < 1$, there is a chance that some judges were nonpartisan.

What would nonpartisan judges' preferences concerning districting plans be? We assume that such judges wish to promote plans with zero bias and are willing to split the difference between the two parties' preferences as regards responsiveness: halfway between the relatively high responsiveness preferred by the strong party and the relatively low responsiveness preferred by the weak party. With some symmetry assumptions, this assumption amounts to assuming that nonpartisan judges' ideal plans are those with zero bias ($\lambda = 0$) and proportional representation ($\rho = 1$).

To explore the possibility that some fraction of judges were nonpartisan, we measured the partisanship of the supervising court by a variable *Court(q)*, equal to the probability of a partisan Democratic majority less the probability of a Republican partisan majority. We calculated the probabilities on the assumption that each judge had an *independent* probability q of being a partisan (in favor of his or her own party). For example, on a three-judge panel with two Democrats and one Republican, $Court(q) = q^2 - 0 = q^2$.[10] When $q = 1$, *Court(q)* becomes a simple indicator of which party has a majority on the court.[11] When $q < 1$, however, this is no longer true. If one of the two Democrats turns out to be nonpartisan, there is no partisan majority for either party. *Court(q)* for $q < 1$ thus reflects not just the existence but also the size of the majority for a party.

Now one can ask: which value of q works best in the sense of maximizing the overall fit of the model? To investigate this question, we simply ran Model 1 from Table 6.1, substituting for our original variable (*Judges*) the variables *Court(q)* for $q = 1$, .975, .95, .925, .9, and so forth. The value of q for which the Wald χ^2 goodness-of-fit statistic was highest turned out to be .9. Although our method is lacking in that it does not provide an estimate of q's standard error, this result does indicate that the best assumption as far as the data are concerned is that judges were very likely to be partisans in the area of redistricting – about 90% of the time.

THE COURTS: CONSTRAINED OR DYNAMIC?

There has been a perennial debate regarding the influence of the courts. Rosenberg (1991) frames the debate as being between the "Constrained Court" view (those who see the Supreme Court as limited in its ability to effect change unilaterally) and the "Dynamic Court" view (those who see the Court as more powerful). The former view traces its roots to Hamilton's famous labeling of the courts as "the least dangerous branch" (*Federalist 78*); Rosenberg's is the most recent, thorough, and explicit exposition of this view. The Dynamic Court view, stemming largely from

---

[10] The only way for a partisan Democratic majority to arise is if both Democrats turn out to be partisan, the probability of which is q^2. There is no way for a Republican majority to arise, so the probability of that occurrence is zero.

[11] When $q = 1$, $Court(1) = Court\ Majority$ (the latter variable defined in the Appendix).

the perceived influence of the Warren Court, is so widely held that it is often an implicit premise of legal scholarship (for instance, heated political debates about judicial activism versus judicial restraint turn largely on questions of whether activist judges abuse the inherent power of the Court). An explicit example of the Dynamic Court view is Aronow (1980).

Our findings bear on this debate in two ways. First, they show clear judicial impact on an important shift in congressional elections (with further implications to be discussed in the next part of the book). That is, they provide one bit of evidence for the Dynamic Court viewpoint. Weber (1995) provides additional evidence of judicial activism in the redistricting arena for the 1990s.

Second, we have suggested some of the conditions that opened up room for judicial discretion and influence in our case. There were few constraining precedents. In particular, the maximum allowable population deviation was unclear, and individual courts could either accept any plan that squeaked in under this limit or enforce a more demanding standard of equality. Moreover, the courts were empowered to set deadlines, wholly outside the process of writing down decisions but freighted with political implications. At one extreme, a Democratic court might give a Republican state 90 days to redraw its lines (Michigan 1964). At the other extreme, a Republican court might let a Republican state continue to use the existing plan, despite having declared it unconstitutional (e.g., Kansas 1964). Finally, the courts were also empowered to impose their own plans if the state failed to produce an acceptable one, and there were few clear constraints on these "reversionary plans."

CONCLUSION

Many of the redistricting actions prompted by *Wesberry* were taken under the supervision of a specific court. By identifying the partisanship of each jurist participating in 35 redistricting decisions during the 1960s, we have been able to show that the partisan balance on the supervising courts systematically affected the level of partisan bias in the resulting plans. Indeed, as we have noted, having more judges on the supervising court seems to have been more important than controlling more branches of state government in terms of generating partisan bias in one's favor.

Given these results, we can explain the "case of the disappearing bias" introduced in the previous chapter almost completely as a consequence of redistricting actions in the 1960s, especially those taken after the

Supreme Court's reapportionment decisions. About half of the disappearance was due to a shift away from unified Republican control of nonsouthern state governments toward divided or Democratic control, as shown in the previous chapter.[12] The other half of the disappearance was due to the shift from automatic reversions to discretionary reversions brought on by the Supreme Court's reapportionment decisions. Once courts established the reversionary plans that would stand in force should the state fail to produce a satisfactory plan, Democratic preponderance on the federal courts translated into another impetus away from the solidly Republican districting plans that had characterized the nonsouthern states throughout the twentieth century. All told, Republican bias disappeared due to two main factors: first, the Republicans lost some key states in the round of redistricting before the 1962 elections; second, Republican weakness in both state governments and the federal judiciary, just when the Supreme Court's decisions unleashed a wave of redistricting under (actual or potential) court supervision, meant that they fared poorly in many other states' redistricting actions. Combined, these factors produced a fairly abrupt decline from what had been a steady 6% pro-Republican bias outside the South (1946–1960) to essentially a level playing field (by 1968–1970).

Why was this abrupt decline preserved? Why did the bias not change back in a pro-Republican direction or shift further toward the Democrats in the redistricting actions of 1972–1974, 1982, and 1992? In our view, there are two main conditions that must be met before one can expect redistricting to produce a substantial change in bias at the national aggregate level: first, the existing array of plans must differ substantially from the existing pattern of partisan control in the states; second, the pattern of legal reversions must facilitate rather than hinder adjustment of the plans toward the new partisan reality.

In the 1960s, both of these conditions were met. First, the existing plans were mostly Republican, in part due to the conservative reversions that had obtained prior to *Baker*, while the existing pattern of partisan control in the nonsouthern states was considerably more favorable to the Democrats than it had historically been. Second, Democratic dominance of the federal judiciary, combined with court discretion in deciding which plans were adequate in terms of malapportionment, meant that the pattern of reversions greatly facilitated, indeed pushed, the adjustment of plans in a pro-Democratic direction.

---

[12] For clarification of this point, see the later discussion.

After 1970, in contrast, the first condition was not met. The existing array of plans (established in the 1960s) more or less matched the pattern of partisan control in the states (which did not change dramatically but did drift toward more divided government). Moreover, the courts' influence was (if anything) lessened, so that the general trend toward an increasingly Republican judiciary could not have had as much impact on redistricting, at least until bias and responsiveness themselves became justiciable in the 1980s. (Although we have not investigated the matter, our approach would suggest that judicial influence was potentially stronger in the 1992 redistricting actions than in 1972 or 1982. Perhaps this is part of the reason that redistricting in the South had the effect that it had, contributing to the Republicans' markedly improved fortunes in that region, although both this region and this time are beyond the scope of our study.)

As neither the 1970s redistrictings (Squire 1985; Glazer, Grofman, and Robbins 1987) nor the 1980s redistrictings (Campagna and Grofman 1990) much affected the net partisan balance, Democratic gains in 1964–1970 were preserved for some time. In the next chapter, we further bolster our story by examining district-level responses to redistricting.

Appendix: Defining the Variables We Use to Measure State and Court Partisanship

Branches is equal to the number of branches of state government controlled by the Democrats less the number controlled by the Republicans. Thus, for example, a state under unified Democratic control scores a $3 - 0 = +3$; a state with two Democratic legislative chambers but a Republican governor scores $2 - 1 = +1$; and a state under unified Republican control scores a $0 - 3 = -3$. The notion is that the more branches of a state's government a party controls, the greater will be the bias in its favor in the resulting districting plan.

We ignore two cases of impotent governors. Specifically, although New York's governor cannot veto redistricting legislation, and although New Jersey's legislature had large enough Republican majorities to override the Democratic governor's veto, we nonetheless coded New York and New Jersey as we did all the others – merely looking to which party held which branches. In the case of New York, the state was under unified Republican control in any event, so recoding would make no difference. In the case of New Jersey, if one recodes *Branches* to equal -3, indicating complete Republican control of the legislative process, none of our substantive claims are affected. We should also note that we code Michigan 1964 as a −3 – denoting unified Republican control – although, as explained in the previous chapter, the court's forceful entry had in a sense converted it into a case of divided control. In Chapter 4, which did not control specifically for court variables, we preferred to classify Michigan's plan as bipartisan. In this chapter, we code state and court control separately; hence it is appropriately classified as unified Republican.

Judges is equal to the number of Democratic jurists on the supervising court less the number of Republican jurists. (The supervising court is defined as the highest court hearing the case; see Chapter 5.) Thus, positive values of *Judges* indicate Democratic majorities, negative values indicate Republican majorities, and a value of zero indicates that neither party held a majority. (In our data, the only case of divided court control occurs in Illinois, where two courts – one Republican, one Democratic – fought for jurisdiction.) The motivation behind this variable is that a party should do better the larger its net advantage on the supervising court is. Assuming that jurists were less reliable partisans than state legislators, having a bare partisan majority on a supervising court would have translated into strong pressure for bias favoring the court-majority party only if the state legislators were confident that the court majority would hold together in support of a substantial level of bias. With a larger majority on the supervising court, a party could afford to "lose" a jurist and still have a majority in favor of an appropriately biased plan.

In order to explore the robustness of our findings to alternative measures of court partisanship, we reran our analysis substituting for our original variable (*Judges*) the following variables: (1) *Court Majority*, a dummy variable taking values −1 (for courts on which the Republicans had a majority), 0 (for tied courts), and +1 (for courts on which the Democrats had a majority) and (2) *Court Majority 2*, a variable equal to *Court Majority* in all cases except those in which the Democrats had more than a bare majority, which were coded as +2 (in practice, the larger-than-bare Democratic majorities were all just one judge larger than bare and there were no larger-than-bare Republican majorities).

All Model 1 results are qualitatively similar using either alternative measure. Model 2 results are also qualitatively similar using *Court Majority 2*. However, the coefficient on *Court Majority* in Model 2 is statistically insignificant. We interpret this as showing that the size of the judicial majority – something to which both *Judges* and *Court Majority 2* are sensitive but *Court Majority* is not – matters.

Another question about our results concerns the measurement of state partisanship. We have tried the following measures in place of our original variable (*Branches*): (1) *Unified*, a variable equal to −1 for unified Republican states, 0 for divided states, and +1 for unified Democratic states (this is the variable we used implicitly in defining the plan types in Chapter 4) and (2) a combination of *Chambers* (equal to −2 if both chambers of the state legislature are Republican, 0 if the chambers are split, +2 if both are Democratic) and *Governor* (equal to −1 for states with Republican governors, +1 for states with Democratic governors). *Unified* contains less information than *Branches*, as it neglects the difference between divided governments in which the Republicans control one branch and divided governments in which they control two. The combination of *Chambers* and *Governor* contains more information than *Branches*: knowing the first two, one can compute the third: *Branches = Chambers + Governor*; but knowing just *Branches*, one cannot deduce the first two. Using the two variables instead of just one simply removes an implicit linear restriction in the model, according to which governors and legislative chambers are about equally valuable.

Our results for both Model 1 and Model 2 are qualitatively similar when we replace *Branches* with the measures just described. We do find some evidence that governors are more influential in the congressional redistricting process than are state legislative chambers. However, both chambers and governors are useful things to have on one's side and, as we are not here interested in these institutions' relative powers, we continue to focus on the results using *Branches*.

7

Redistricting's Differing Impact on Democratic and Republican Incumbents

In Chapters 4–6, we argued that pro-Republican bias in nonsouthern congressional elections disappeared in the mid-1960s as a consequence of (1) a change in partisan control of state governments away from unified Republican control, (2) a change in the legal reversion to the redistricting process, and (3) the role of the largely Democratic federal judiciary in supervising the redistricting actions of the states. If our account is correct, redistricting during the 1960s should have affected Democratic and Republican incumbents differently.

Perhaps the simplest way to state our expectations is by contrasting them with Edward Tufte's well-known hypothesis that the wave of 1960s redistricting was mostly an exercise in incumbent protection – a position that fit well with then-emerging evidence that incumbents' margins of victory were increasing. Our thesis is that the wave of 1960s redistricting had a distinct anti-Republican cast to it, making most districting plans less Republican-friendly than their predecessors. In this chapter, we investigate whether the partisan differences we expect appear in the empirical record.

The first purpose of this chapter, then, is to provide further (albeit indirect) evidence for the main thesis of this part of the book. The second purpose is to reconsider some alternative hypotheses about the case of the disappearing bias. The final purpose is to begin to introduce the topic of the next part of the book: how redistricting affected the electoral performance of incumbents and the much-debated rise of the incumbency advantage.

We state our predictions regarding how redistricting should have affected district-level vote shares in the first section. We then test them in the second section, finding that redistricting had a systematically different impact on the two parties' electoral fortunes. After a technical aside, we recap the full range of evidence in favor of our theory of bias, in contrast to alternative theories, and then conclude.

GERRYMANDERING AND DISTRICT-LEVEL
VOTE SHARES: PREDICTIONS

We have argued that most of the changes in districting plans that occurred in the 1960s were from more Republican-friendly to less Republican-friendly. To clarify the district-level consequences that such a shift in redistricting plans might have had, consider the incumbents in a state that has a Republican gerrymander at election $t - 1$ and converts to a Democratic gerrymander at election t. This is the most extreme possible change along the continuum from more to less Republican-friendly and illustrates the effects that can be expected.

Suppose that the Democrats, in redrawing the district lines in our hypothetical state, follow the classic partisan gerrymandering recipe. In particular, they (1) *pack* some of the Republican incumbents' districts with more Republican voters; (2) *crack* some of the Republican incumbents' districts – that is, greatly reduce the number of Republican voters in them, sending the excised voters into the first category of packed districts; and (3) *pare* or *trim* some of the Democratic incumbents' districts – that is, remove some (but not too many) Democratic voters, shifting the surplus into the subset of cracked Republican districts to create new, winnable Democratic districts.

Now suppose that we try to predict the Democratic vote share in each district in our hypothetical state, in a larger analysis that includes some states that did not redistrict. Following standard practice, we could predict the Democratic vote share in district j, election t, based mainly on the Democratic vote share in the previous election in that district (the model would also account for whether the year is generally a good or bad one for Democrats and for the partisan affiliation of the incumbent, if there is one). How well would such a baseline model predict the patterns in our redistricted state?

Consider first the districts that had been won by the Democrats in the previous election. Most of these districts will have had inefficiently large concentrations of Democrats under the old Republican gerrymander and will experience a net loss of Democratic voters under the new plan.[1] The

---

[1] We are assuming that one can construct a one-to-one mapping between the old and the new districts. That is, for each new district, it is clear which old district is

baseline prediction rests primarily on the lagged vote share in these districts (our proxy for the "normal vote"). The lagged vote, however, will reflect the old partisan balance in the district, when the proportion of Democratic identifiers was higher. Thus, the baseline model will tend to *overstate* the Democratic vote share in previously Democratic districts, because it does not reflect the net exportation of Democratic identifiers entailed by the new districting plan.

Consider next the districts that had been won by the Republicans in the previous election. Most of these districts will have had efficient concentrations of Republicans under the old Republican gerrymander but will have been packed with more Republicans under the new Democratic gerrymander. The baseline model will thus again tend to *overstate* the Democratic vote share in the current election, because it does not reflect the net importation of Republican identifiers entailed by the new districting plan.

Some subset of the Republican-held seats will not be packed, however. Instead they will be cracked, entailing a substantial reduction in the proportion of Republican identifiers. The baseline model will tend to *underestimate* the Democratic vote share in these districts.

Now consider how vote shares change in districts that were won by the Republicans at election $t - 1$. Because redrawn Republican districts were either packed or cracked, we should find two things. First, redrawn districts should tend to have a lower Democratic vote share at t than would be expected from the baseline predictors. The more numerous packed Republican districts drive this result; the less numerous cracked districts work against it. Second, redrawn districts should tend also to be less predictable – to have higher variance around the baseline prediction. This second result follows because of the marked difference between the packed and cracked Republican-held districts, a source of variance that does not arise in the control group of districts – those Republican-held districts that were left untouched.

Now consider the districts won by the Democrats at election $t - 1$. The redrawn districts in this category should mostly have been pared (i.e., had their supply of Democratic identifiers trimmed).[2] Thus, as in the case of Republican-held districts, redrawn districts should tend to

"closest" to it and should be viewed as its predecessor. In practice, of course, identifying parent districts can sometimes be quite difficult – as we discovered in conducting the research for Chapter 2.

[2] Our thesis is not that *no* Democratic districts were packed or cracked, just that relatively few were compared to the percentages on the Republican side.

have a lower Democratic vote share at t than would be expected from the baseline predictors. Contrary to the expectation in Republican-held districts, however, there is little reason to expect that redistricting made vote shares less predictable – because relatively few Democratic districts were either packed or cracked.

Having spelled out our predictions in the extreme case of changing from a Republican to a Democratic gerrymander, we next note that many of the same predictions follow if one believes that redistricting plans were generally moving from more Republican-friendly to less Republican-friendly. In particular, suppose that one believes the following *anti-Republican redistricting hypothesis*: states generally tended either to pack or to crack Republican-held districts while trimming Democrat-held districts, with relatively fewer contrary changes (packing/cracking Democratic districts or trimming Republican districts). This redistricting pattern could arise with a change in plan type from Republican gerrymander to Democratic gerrymander, as noted previously. It could also arise even holding constant the plan type: an old Republican gerrymander fashioned without court supervision, for example, may have been markedly more effective for the Republicans than a new plan fashioned under the supervision of a Democratic court.

The anti-Republican redistricting hypothesis is plausible as a first-order approximation, partly because of the shift in plan types documented in Chapter 2, which reflected the erosion of Republican control in the nonsouthern states, and partly because of the largely Democratic cast of the supervising courts in the 1960s. For the moment, we wish simply to point out the hypothesis's consequences, were one to accept it (returning to alternative hypotheses later).

Given the anti-Republican hypothesis, one expects the following patterns in the 1960s. First, there should have been a general decline in pro-Republican bias. We have already seen that there was. Second, the Democratic vote share in redrawn districts should have been on average lower than it was in otherwise identical untouched districts; and this should have been true in both Republican-held and Democrat-held districts. Third, the Democratic vote share should have been less predictable (in the sense of having a higher variance around the baseline prediction) in redrawn Republican-held districts but not in redrawn Democrat-held districts.

In the next few sections, we test the second and third of these predictions. In doing so, we also revisit three related issues raised in the previous literature: whether redistricting reduced the number of "marginal" districts (i.e., those won by small margins); whether redistricting affected the swing to incumbents; and whether redistricting affected the probability of an incumbent securing reelection. In each case, the character of the results found in the original studies changes substantially when one considers the two parties separately.

GERRYMANDERING DISMISSED?

In a widely cited article, Edward Tufte suggested that congressional incumbents hijacked the redistricting process in the 1960s in order to further their own electoral interests (Tufte 1973). Such a suggestion fit well with the increase in incumbents' vote margins documented by Tufte's colleague, David Mayhew (1974). But Tufte's argument had other implications: if redistricting was the key factor in boosting incumbents' vote margins, then one ought to have seen substantial differences between incumbents whose districts had been redrawn and those whose districts had been left intact.

Ferejohn (1977) investigated whether nonsouthern incumbents were more likely to win by a comfortable margin if their districts had been redrawn: they were not. Cover (1977) investigated whether incumbents enjoyed larger vote swings if their districts had been redrawn: they did not. Bullock (1975) investigated whether incumbents were more likely to win if their districts had been redrawn: they were not.

If the anti-Republican redistricting hypothesis is correct, however, then each of these null results may hide partisan differences. Regarding marginal districts, redistricting should generally have reduced Democratic vote shares, producing *more* safe districts for Republican incumbents but *fewer* for Democratic incumbents relative to the frequencies in untouched districts. Thus, the vanishing of Republican marginal districts should have been accelerated by redistricting, while the vanishing of Democratic marginal districts should have been decelerated by redistricting.

Regarding incumbent vote swings (i.e., incumbent vote share at t less incumbent vote share at $t - 1$), redistricting should have produced larger swings for Republican incumbents but smaller swings for Democratic incumbents. To explain, note that a redistricted Democrat generally lost Democratic identifiers in the process, whereas an untouched Democrat did not (if our hypothesis is correct). Thus, a redistricted Democrat's time t vote share tended to be a bit lower than his or her time $t - 1$ vote share, producing smaller swings than experienced by otherwise similar Democrats whose districts were untouched. The story for Republican incumbents is more complicated because some will have been packed (producing larger vote swings) while others will have been cracked (producing lower swings). However, as we assume that packed districts substantially outnumbered cracked ones, we expect that Republican incumbents' swings will have been on average larger.

Regarding probabilities of victory, redistricting should generally have slightly decreased Democratic incumbents' chances of reelection. As the whole point would be to pare only *excess* supporters from the district, however, this effect would be minimal. In contrast, redistricting should have slightly helped most Republican incumbents (those whose districts were packed with excess supporters) while grievously hurting the chances of a few (those whose districts were cracked). All told, the serious damage done to the few (cracked) should have outweighed the trivial improvements of the many (packed), so that on average, being redistricted was a bad signal for a Republican.

Let us turn now to the evidence. In the next three subsections, we reconsider the studies of Ferejohn (1977), Cover (1977), and Bullock (1975) with an eye to partisan differences. Along the way, we also present our own analysis of how district-level vote shares responded in the 1960s to redistricting.

Marginal Districts: Ferejohn (1977)

Outside the South, the percentage of marginal districts does decline in both redistricted and unredistricted states in the 1960s, as Ferejohn (1977) reported. But, if one looks at Republicans and Democrats separately, one finds that Republican marginals vanish substantially more quickly in redrawn than in unaltered districts.

Following Ferejohn, we compare districts in nonsouthern states that were and were not redistricted between November 1962 and November 1966.[3] As can be seen in Table 7.1, Panel A, the percentage of districts that fell into the marginal category (a two-party Democratic vote share between 40% and 60%) fell 9.7% in the 187 districts that were redrawn but only 6.3% in the 142 districts that were unaltered. It should be noted

---

[3] In this analysis, our definition of nonsouthern matches that of Ferejohn (1977).

Table 7.1. *Competitive Seats and Redistricting in Nonsouthern House Elections, 1962–1966*

Panel A: Percentage of All Districts Marginal, by Redistricting Status

Year	Redrawn Between November 1962 and November 1966	Not Redrawn
1962	50.3	40.1
	(187)	(142)
1966	40.6	33.8
	(187)	(142)

Panel B: Percentage of Incumbent-Defended Districts Marginal, by Redistricting Status

Year	Redrawn Between November 1962 and November 1966	Not Redrawn
1962	47.5	35.5
	(162)	(121)
1966	37.9	32.1
	(174)	(137)

Panel C: Percentage of Incumbent-Defended Districts That Were Democratic Marginals, by Redistricting Status

Year	Redrawn Between November 1962 and November 1966	Not Redrawn
1962	21.6	15.7
	(162)	(121)
1966	24.7	19.7
	(174)	(137)

Panel D: Percentage of Incumbent-Defended Districts That Were Republican Marginals, by Redistricting Status

Year	Redrawn Between November 1962 and November 1966	Not Redrawn
1962	25.9	19.8
	(162)	(121)
1966	13.2	12.4
	(174)	(137)

Notes: Panel A is our attempt to replicate Ferejohn's original findings. The cell entries give the percentage of the districts that were marginal (Democratic vote percentage between 40% and 60%). The number of observations is given in parentheses. Democratic marginals are those with Democratic vote percentages between 50% and 60%, while Republican marginals are those with Democratic vote percentages between 40% and 50%.

that these figures show the marginals vanishing slightly more markedly in redistricted than in unredistricted states, contrary to Ferejohn's original findings.[4]

We know that open seats continued to be hotly contested, hence marginal. As Mayhew (1974) first noted, it is the incumbent-defended districts that increasingly fall outside the marginal category. Thus, there is some interest in refining Ferejohn's orginal analysis by restricting attention to incumbent-defended districts. If one does this, one finds – see Panel B – that the difference between states that redrew and those that did not is even larger. The incidence of marginals falls 9.6% in redrawn states but only 3.4% in untouched states.

The main point, however, is that the overall figures on marginal districts are a mixture of somewhat different results for the two parties. First, as shown in Panel C, Democratic marginals (a two-party Democratic vote share between 50% and 60%) *increase* as a percentage of all incumbent-defended districts. This increase in Democratic marginals would be expected in light of the large swing against the Democrats in 1966. More important, there is little difference between the redrawn and unaltered districts, although competitiveness in the former does increase less. Second, as shown in Panel D, Republican marginals (a two-party Democratic vote share between 40% and 50%) decrease by 12.7% in redrawn districts but only by 7.4% in unaltered districts. The decline in Republican marginals is, again, expected in light of the large swing against the Democrats in 1966. But the 5.3% difference in the amount of decline produced by redistricting is not expected by conventional accounts.

That the Republican marginals appear to vanish more quickly among redrawn districts is suggestive. In the next subsection, we consider whether vote shares also change in the way the anti-Republican redistricting hypothesis would suggest.

---

[4] This difference, we believe, is due in part to a better identification of which states redistricted. In any event, scholars who wish to double-check our numbers can access our dataset and do so. Our electoral data were provided by Gary Jacobson. We identify redistricting actions based on Martis (1982). The following nonsouthern states redistricted between November 1962 and November 1966: Arizona, Colorado, Connecticut, Idaho, Illinois, Indiana, Kansas, Kentucky, Maryland, Michigan, Missouri, Montana, New Jersey, Ohio, Oregon, Pennsylvania, Rhode Island, South Dakota, Utah, and Wisconsin. (One oddity in Ferejohn's analysis concerns the number of cases: his Table 1 includes 314 districts, but there are 329 nonsouthern districts. We believe he excluded districts with two incumbents from the analysis but are not sure.)

Incumbents' Vote Swings: Cover (1977)

Incumbents' vote swings, controlling for national tides, are indeed largely unaffected by redistricting in the 1960s, as Cover (1977) reported. But if one examines Republicans and Democrats separately, one finds that Republican incumbents' vote swings increased while Democratic incumbents' vote swings decreased if their districts were redrawn. The two effects cancel in Cover's analysis.

In order to show how Republicans' and Democrats' vote shares responded to redistricting in the 1966–1970 period, we regress the Democratic percentage of the two-party vote in the *j*th congressional district at time *t* on a dummy variable indicating whether the district was redrawn immediately prior to the election in question. The analysis controls for the lagged Democratic vote, current and lagged incumbency status, current and lagged challenger elective experience, and year effects. The control variables capture the "normal vote" that can be expected in each district, based largely on the Democratic vote share received in the previous election, but with due consideration given to whether an incumbent ran last time and whether the challengers had held previous elective office. The analysis is confined to districts that were actually contested at both $t - 1$ and t. Finally, the model allows the effect of redistricting to differ between seats won by the Democrats at $t - 1$ (the reference group) and seats won by the Republicans. (All variables are described more fully in the notes to Table 7.2.)

Because the anti-Republican redistricting hypothesis entails shifts in both the vote level and the vote variance (around the baseline prediction), the model estimates both the mean and the variance of the dependent variable (Democratic vote share). We find plausible results for all control variables and a coefficient of −1.94 on the redistricting dummy. In other words, the Democratic vote share was 1.94 percentage points lower in Democratic districts (i.e., those won by the Democrats in the previous election) that had been redrawn than in otherwise similar districts left untouched. Moreover, redistricting's impact was similar in seats held by the Republicans.[5] Thus, *the expected Democratic vote share in seats the Democrats held declined if the district was redrawn, while the*

---

[5] This follows because the coefficient on $Redist_{it} \times Repseat_{it}$ is statistically insignificant, showing that the impact of redistricting on Republican seats did not differ from that on Democratic seats. The impact of redistricting in Republican districts is, however, statistically discernible from zero (at the .10 level in a two-tailed test).

Table 7.2. *The Effect of Redistricting on the*
Distribution of the Democratic Vote Share,
1966–1970

Independent Variables	Estimated Coefficients
Mean effects	
Constant	4.99***
	(1.85)
Year 1968	6.77***
	(0.51)
Year 1970	9.49***
	(0.51)
Republican-held seat	4.46***
	(1.60)
Lagged Democratic Vote	0.74***
	(0.03)
Lagged Incumbency Status	−1.71***
	(0.42)
Incumbency Status	6.79***
	(0.79)
Lagged Democratic Quality	−0.54
Advantage	(0.42)
Democratic Quality	3.06***
Advantage	(0.42)
Redrawn District	−1.94***
	(0.55)
Redrawn District ×	0.74
Republican-held seat	(0.84)
Variance effects	
Constant	5.35***
	(0.27)
Year 1968	0.08
	(0.34)
Year 1970	0.89***
	(0.34)
Republican-held seat	−0.40
	(0.33)
Redrawn District	0.01
	(0.39)
Redrawn District ×	1.31**
Republican-held seat	(0.61)
Wald χ^2	6369.23
N	911

(continued)

Table 7.2 *(cont.)*

Notes: Standard errors are given in parentheses below the coefficient estimates. Two asterisks (**) indicate significance at the .05 level. Three asterisks (***) indicate significance at the .01 level. The dependent variable is the Democratic share of the two-party vote in district *j* at election *t*. The estimation method is heteroscedastic ordinary least squares via maximum likelihood. There were 329 nonsouthern districts in the 1960s. Since there are three years in the analysis – 1966, 1968, and 1970 – that means a total of $3 \times 329 = 987$ possible observations. We lose 76 of these potential observations, mostly due to the district being uncontested at *t* or *t* − 1, but a handful due to such oddities as two incumbents running in the same district. Our variables are defined as follows:

Year 1968 = a dummy variable equal to 1 if *t* = 1968.
Year 1970 = a dummy variable equal to 1 if *t* = 1970.
Republican-held seat = a dummy variable equal to 1 if district *j* was won by the Republicans at *t* − 1.
Lagged Democratic Vote = Democratic share of the two-party vote in district *j*, election *t* − 1.
Incumbency Status = +1 for Democratic incumbent, 0 for open seat, −1 for Republican incumbent.
Democratic Quality Advantage = +1 if the Democrat but not the Republican has held previous elective office, 0 if neither or both have held previous elective office, −1 if the Republican but not the Democrat has held previous elective office.
Redrawn District = a dummy variable equal to 1 if district *j* was redrawn before election *t*.

expected Republican vote share in seats the Republicans held increased if the district was redrawn. This comports with the anti-Republican redistricting hypothesis.

It may seem surprising that redistricting diminished the expected Democratic vote share in all states. As we shall see, however, controlling for the type of state (Republican-controlled? Democratic court?) makes little difference, partly because the Republicans' position in most nonsouthern state governments eroded or stayed constant, and partly because most redistricting actions were conducted under the supervision of Democratic courts (even in those states that remained under solid Republican control).

Incumbents' Reelection Rates: Bullock (1975)

Incumbents' reelection rates during the 1960s were indeed about the same in unredistricted and redistricted states, as Bullock (1975) noted. But if one calculates reelection rates for Republican and Democratic incumbents separately, one finds that Democratic incumbents slightly benefited from redistricting, while Republican incumbents slightly suffered. The two effects cancel in Bullock's analysis.

Table 7.3. *Incumbent Reelection Rates, by Party*

Year	Republican Incumbents, Unredrawn	Republican Incumbents, Redrawn	Democratic Incumbents, Unredrawn	Democratic Incumbents, Redrawn
1962	98.7 (76)	94.1 (68)	94.0 (116)	98.3 (115)
1964	78.0 (141)	57.9 (19)	99.0 (200)	90.3 (31)
1966	100.0 (68)	98.4 (61)	83.1 (148)	88.9 (126)
1968	100.0 (102)	100.0 (69)	97.4 (116)	98.2 (110)
1970	94.7 (150)	94.7 (19)	99.5 (187)	97.4 (38)

Note: Entries are the percentage of incumbents who won reelection. (The total number of incumbents is given in parentheses.) Thus, for example, in 1962, there were 76 Republican incumbents running for reelection, of whom 98.7% won. This analysis is not restricted to the nonsouthern states, as most analyses in the book have been, because Bullock's original analysis included the South.

As can be seen in Table 7.3, in three of the five election years from 1962 to 1970, Democratic incumbents posted higher reelection rates if their districts were redrawn. The two years that show the opposite pattern have the smallest numbers of redistricted incumbents (31 and 38). In contrast, Republican incumbents never did better if their district was redrawn and in three years did worse.

The effects shown in Table 7.3 are merely suggestive, and we make no claims regarding their statistical significance.[6] Our analysis in Table 7.2 provides a fuller set of controls and can be used to address the probability of an incumbent securing reelection.[7] Based on this analysis, we

---

[6] If one pools across all years, the difference between the parties is entirely unimpressive. Note, however, that such pooling removes the one control that Table 7.3 affords, that for year effects. Rather than head in the direction of less controlled comparisons, we stake most of our claims on the more controlled analysis in Table 7.2, per the discussion in the text to follow.

[7] A more familiar approach is to run a probit regression in which the dependent variable is coded 1 when the Democratic candidate won the seat and 0 when the Republican won. Such an analysis, however, ignores the fact that we know the vote shares obtained by each candidate. Probit analysis is usually conducted when there is an unobserved or latent variable that is believed to generate the observed categorical outcomes (won, lost). But in this case, we observe the "underlying" continuous variable – Democratic vote share in the district – that determines the classification. Since our model assumes that DV_{jt} is normally distributed, one can then compute the probability of a Republican victory directly from the model's results. The probability is $\Pr[DV_{jt} < 0.5] = \Phi[(.5 - \mu)/\sigma]$, where μ is the estimated mean, σ is the estimated standard deviation, and Φ is the cumulative distribution function of the standard normal.

found that redistricting lowered Republican incumbents' probabilities of victory but raised Democratic incumbents' chances. For example, a Republican incumbent who would expect a 60% vote share absent redistricting had an estimated probability of victory of .979. If this incumbent's district were redrawn, her estimated vote share would *increase* to 61.1% but, because of the increased variance in the vote share, her estimated probability of victory would *decline* by about .015. In contrast, a typical Democratic incumbent's probability of victory increased in similar circumstances.

How can redistricting depress Democratic vote shares on average while, if anything, raising the probability of Democratic victory? The most intelligible answer is the one suggested by the anti-Republican redistricting hypothesis and relates in particular to the variance effects we predicted. Consider Republican-held districts first. These will either have been packed, raising the incumbent's expected vote share and probability of victory, or cracked, lowering both expected votes and chances of reelection. Since the typical untouched Republican incumbent will already have had a high probability of reelection, packing will have produced a mere fillip in the probability of victory, whereas cracking will have been catastrophic, on balance producing the slight decline observed. Consider Democrat-held districts next. These will mostly have been pared, leaving expected votes a bit lower but only slightly lowering the probability of reelection. All told, redistricting will mostly have been a bad signal for Republicans (a mix of slightly good news with very bad news) but a neutral signal for Democrats (excess votes pared).

A more direct test of our predictions than is entailed in looking at probabilities of victory thus concerns the variance of the predicted vote shares for Republican-held and Democrat-held districts. The anti-Republican redistricting hypothesis predicts that redistricting will increase the variance of vote shares in Republican districts (due to the contrast between packing and cracking) but not in Democratic districts (most of which will have been pared). Looking just at the zero-order figures, redistricting did decrease the standard deviation of incumbent Democrats' vote shares by over a percentage point while increasing the standard deviation of incumbent Republicans' vote shares by almost a percentage point. Turning to the controlled analysis in Table 7.2, which provides a more appropriate test, one finds similar results: while there is no difference in the estimated variance of vote share as between redrawn and untouched Democrat-held seats, redrawn Republican-held districts had significantly higher vote share variances than did untouched

Republican-held districts.[8] This is consistent with the notion that Republican incumbents' districts were more often cracked or packed, while Democratic incumbents' districts were mostly pared.

TECHNICAL NOTE: LOOKING AT PLAN TRANSITIONS MORE CLOSELY

Should one expect that redistricting would have the effects hypothesized, regardless of the state in which the district lies? As it turns out, there are three groups of states in our dataset. For the two largest, one does expect such a change, but for the third things are not so clear a priori. In this section, we explain these three groupings and investigate whether separating out the third group improves the performance of the model.

The first and largest group of states are those in which the old districting plan was favorable to the Republicans in the sense that the expected pro-Republican bias, based on our analysis in Chapter 4, was positive and significantly different than zero. In all these states, as it turns out, the new expected level of pro-Republican bias was lower (due either to a shift in control of state government or to court influence). In these states, where we know that the expected level of Republican bias declines, we believe that preexisting Republican gerrymanders are being undone to some degree. In other words, we expect the anti-Republican redistricting hypothesis to hold up.

The second group of states had Democratic partisan gerrymanders both before and after the reapportionment revolution. In these states, we know from our results in Chapter 4 that the expected level of pro-Democratic bias increased. One possible reason for this is that, prior to the reapportionment revolution, Democrats in these states could rely to some extent on malapportionment, whereas afterward they had to get the results they wanted solely through gerrymandering – and could get such results because the Democratic courts let them.[9] In any event, because the level of pro-Democratic bias increases in these states, our expectations are similar to those for the first group.

---

[8] Note that the sum of the estimated coefficients for $Redist_{jt}$ and $Redist_{jt} \times Repseat_{jt}$ is positive and significant for the variance effects; this shows that redistricting in Republican seats increased the variance significantly.

[9] Another possible reason for the increase in pro-Democratic bias is that prerevolutionary plans in the border states were sometimes more concerned with factional fights within the Democratic party than with the Republicans.

The third group of states had Democratic partisan gerrymanders before but bipartisan or Republican plans after the reapportionment revolution. In these states, one expects that any change would be undoing preexisting Democratic gerrymanders. That is, the direction of change should be opposite to that predicted for the first two groups. As it turns out, however, the only states in which a plan drawn up by a unified Democratic state government was replaced by one drawn up by a unified Republican state government were Arizona (three districts) and Idaho (two districts), and in both of these states the supervising court was Democratic. Moreover, the change in Arizona did not happen until 1970, after a previous post-*Wesberry* redistricting in 1966. Thus, there are only 9 district-years (out of 911 total) in which one strongly expects a move counter to that expected in the first two groups.[10]

Our discussion of the three groups of states shows that the implicit assumption underlying the model in Table 7.2 – that redistricting plans became uniformly less favorable to Republicans outside the South in the 1960s – is largely justified. The assumption is acceptable partly due to changes in partisan control of state government and partly due to Democratic dominance of the supervising courts. Indeed, if one thinks that any redistricting case could have been appealed all the way to the Supreme Court, then the Democrats essentially supervised *all* redistricting action in the 1960s. Even short of this extreme, however, we know from Chapter 5 that their dominance was heavy at lower levels in the federal judiciary.

For completeness' sake, we reran the analysis in Table 7.2 allowing the effect of redistricting to vary between the baseline set of states and those in which the previous plan was a Democratic gerrymander.[11] We found that the effect of redistricting did not differ significantly between the two sets of states.

ALTERNATIVE HYPOTHESES

In Chapter 3, we discussed and rejected the most prominent hypothesis about why pro-Republican bias abruptly disappeared in the mid-1960s. This hypothesis held that the increase in the incumbency advantage, at

[10] There were no states in which the old plan was "not very Republican" (a bipartisan Republican plan) and the new plan was a Republican gerrymander.

[11] We did this by including two additional variables: a dummy variable D, equal to 1 if the previous plan in a state was a Democratic gerrymander, while the new plan was not; and an interaction term, $Redist_{it} \times D$.

a point when the Democrats possessed a majority of seats, explained the disappearing pro-Republican bias. However, as we noted, an increase in the incumbency advantage would simply have increased the price in votes that Democrats paid for each seat won by their incumbents – which would not have increased the efficiency of the votes-to-seats translation for the Democrats. Hence, this idea cannot provide an explanation.

In this section, we compare the anti-Republican redistricting hypothesis – the thesis that most redistricting actions in the 1960s were either undoing previous Republican gerrymanders or constructing new Democratic ones, with relatively few countervailing actions – with two other hypotheses: first, Erikson's natural gerrymander thesis; second, McDonald's dealignment thesis. Both of these ideas concern how dealignment in the 1960s might have affected either the effect of a given districting plan or the process of redistricting.

Erikson's Natural Gerrymander Thesis

First, consider Erikson's (1972) natural gerrymander thesis. The basic idea is that there were large concentrations of Democratic voters in the big cities, so that it was difficult to draw metropolitan districts that did not "waste" Democratic votes (i.e., have inefficiently large expected Democratic vote shares). Thus, throughout the nonsouthern states, there was something of a "natural gerrymander" against the Democrats in the pre-*Wesberry* period. In the 1960s, this did not change. What did change, however, were voters' attachments to the parties – they weakened substantially (cf., e.g., Wattenberg 1984). The decay of party loyalties, in turn, diluted the natural pro-Republican gerrymander – independently of any changes in the level or partisan direction of deliberate gerrymandering.

McDonald's Dealignment Thesis

Another way in which partisan decay might have mattered was through altering redistricters' optimal strategies. McDonald (1999) shows that the optimal partisan gerrymander becomes more like an incumbent-protecting gerrymander when voter loyalties decay. That is, when the parties recognize that the typical registered Republican (Democrat) is somewhat less likely to vote Republican (Democrat) than previously, the optimal strategy in a Republican (Democratic) gerrymander is to put more registered Republicans (Democrats) in the districts they wish to make winnable. The consequence of each party's putting more of its own partisans in its winnable districts, however, would be a decline in the overall level of bias attainable in its plans.[12]

Comments

Although we believe the decay of party loyalties is important to the redistricting story, note that neither the direct effects of dealignment (weakening the natural gerrymander) nor the indirect effects (altering the optimal gerrymander) explains the full range of phenomena that occurred. First, neither account explains why the disappearance of bias should correlate, state by state, with partisan control of the state government and of the supervising court. Second, neither explains why redistricting tended to increase both the mean and the variance of the Republican vote share in Republican-held districts while decreasing the mean and leaving the variance little changed in Democrat-held districts.

CONCLUSION

The best-known thesis about the wave of 1960s redistrictings is Tufte's claim that most of them were incumbent-protecting. Overall, the evidence against Tufte's thesis is consistent and persuasive. Studies by Ferejohn (1977), Cover (1977), and Bullock (1975) showed that redistricting had no effect on incumbents per se.

We have offered an alternative characterization of 1960s redistrictings: most of them were undoing previous Republican gerrymanders or constructing more effective Democratic gerrymanders, with relatively few countervailing moves. There is evidence for this anti-Republican redistricting hypothesis at the regional level, the state level, and the district level. At the regional level, we expect what others had previously found: a substantial and sudden drop in pro-Republican bias in the non-southern states in the mid-1960s. At the state level, we expect and find that the partisan bias of a state's plan correlates with both partisan control of state government and partisan control of the supervising court. At the district level, we expect and find that the Democratic vote share in Republican-held districts that were redrawn tended to decrease in

---

[12] McDonald's work focused on the direct implication of his theory – that a party gerrymandering a state would begin to put more of its own partisans in its winnable districts – and was not concerned with the implication we note here.

mean but increase in variance, while the Democratic vote share in Democrat-held districts that were redrawn tended to decrease in mean but to show little change in variance. This is a sufficiently intricate set of corroborating findings, at very different levels of analysis, that we have some confidence that our thesis is a useful way of thinking about what happened in the 1960s wave of redistricting. In the next part of the book, we consider whether our basic view of electoral politics in the 1960s might help explain other puzzles in the literature, those centering on the increasingly good electoral fortunes of incumbents.

PART III

Incumbents and Challengers

8

The Growth of the Incumbency Advantage

In the previous part of the book, we focused on why pro-Republican bias in nonsouthern congressional elections abruptly disappeared in the 1960s. In this part of the book, we turn to an even more famous pair of puzzles in the literature: why incumbents' margins of victory increased abruptly in 1966, and why the so-called incumbency advantage increased – again abruptly, again in 1966.

In this chapter, we set the stage for the analyses to come in three ways. First, we explain the two incumbency-related puzzles in more detail. Second, we articulate the principles behind our investigation in this part of the book, sketching the connections between incumbents' electoral fortunes and the reapportionment revolution. Third, we show that there are previously unnoticed partisan differences associated with each puzzle: the Republican marginals vanished more than did the Democratic marginals, and the Republican incumbency advantage increased more than did the Democratic incumbency advantage. We thus add two more items to the list of explananda that a complete model of postwar congressional elections must address.

INCUMBENTS' MARGINS AND ADVANTAGES

The Vanishing Marginals

A *marginal* district is one that is not firmly held by either major party. Operationally, marginal districts are usually defined as those in which the winner garners 50–55% (or sometimes 50–60%) of the two-party vote, the idea being that such a slim margin of victory might well be overcome in the next election.

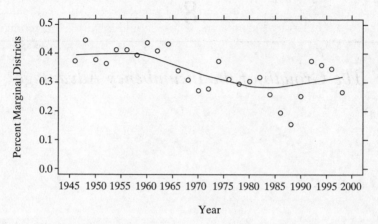

Figure 8.1 Fraction of marginal districts, 1946–1998. Note: the line in the graph is a localized (or nonparametric) regression called a *loess line*, similar to a running average.

In a famous article, Mayhew (1974) showed that marginal districts (defined by the 50–55% criterion) were fairly common in early postwar elections but rather abruptly less common after 1966. Moreover, open seats showed no trend in marginality; only districts defended by incumbents became less often marginal.

Figure 8.1 plots the percentage of all 435 congressional districts that were marginal in each year from 1946 to 1998. To complement Mayhew's analysis, we use a different definition of marginal (a two-party percentage of 50–60% for the winner). We view the figure as showing no trend in marginality in the period 1946–1964, followed by an abrupt drop to a new regime in 1966–1998, during which there is also no trend (but higher variance).[1] This impression is only strengthened if one focuses just on districts that were defended by an incumbent.

Redistricting as an Explanation of the Vanishing Marginals

In principle, post-*Wesberry* redistricting might explain the case of the vanishing marginals just described. We know from Chapter 3 that there was an increase in the fraction of nonsouthern redistricting plans that were drawn under conditions of divided government and a radical reversion, resulting in more bipartisan or incumbent-protecting gerrymanders. A

---

[1] If one regresses the percentage of districts that are marginal on a time trend and a dummy variable indicating the years 1966 and after, the time trend is insignificant and the dummy is significant.

classical incumbent-protecting gerrymander, however, will create safe districts for both parties' incumbents, which should lower the percentage of marginal districts (and the responsiveness of seat shares to vote shares).

The relationship between redistricting and marginality is more complicated than that, however. Even a partisan gerrymander will create some safe districts for the opposition. Moreover, the lower the level of party loyalty in the electorate, the more variable each party's vote will be in each district – which means that the redistricting party will want to engineer higher expected votes even in the districts it intends to win in order to insure its incumbents against the larger vote swings it now expects. Thus, even partisan gerrymandering may reduce the fraction of marginal districts if it is conducted under conditions of declining voter attachment to the parties (McDonald 1999). As the post-*Wesberry* redistrictings were conducted under such conditions, it is likely that even some of the partisan gerrymanders may have contributed to the reduction in marginal districts.

There is some evidence that both incumbent-protecting and partisan gerrymanders after *Wesberry* helped to increase incumbents' margins. First, as noted in Chapter 7, the frequency of marginal districts did increase more markedly in redrawn than in untouched states (between 1962 and 1966), especially in incumbent-held districts. Second, at an aggregate level, the large drop in pro-Republican bias and the significant drop in responsiveness that we found in Chapter 4 both coincide with Mayhew's vanishing marginals. The correlation between our estimates of nonsouthern responsiveness and the nonsouthern percentage of marginal districts in each year is positive (+.71) and significant over the period 1946–1970 for which we estimate responsiveness (see Chapter 4). The correlation between our estimates of nonsouthern pro-Republican bias and the nonsouthern percentage of marginal districts in each year is also positive (+.88) and significant over the period 1946–1970. We cannot disentangle these correlations, because pro-Republican bias, responsiveness, and the percentage of marginal districts all drop at the same time. However, this coincidence does suggest that redistricting – which clearly drove the changes in bias and responsiveness – may also have had a hand in causing the marginals to vanish.

The Incumbency Advantage

In another famous pair of articles, Erikson (1971, 1972) computed the first measures of the *incumbency advantage*, defined as the gain in votes that a party can expect when it defends one of the seats it holds with an incumbent rather than a nonincumbent candidate. His and other early work assessed the incumbency advantage by estimating two statistics: the sophomore surge, equal to the gain in votes that a party can expect when a first-time winner at election t runs for reelection as an incumbent at election $t + 1$, and the retirement slump, equal to the loss in votes that a party can expect when an incumbent does not seek reelection, so that the party must defend the seat with a nonincumbent. The literature found an abrupt increase in the incumbency advantage so measured beginning in 1966.

Later techniques used to measure the incumbency advantage have corroborated the early findings. The state-of-the-art measure, due to Gelman and King (1991), is based on a regression of the Democratic vote share in district j, year t, on three independent variables: the Democratic vote share in district j in the previous election (year $t - 2$); a seat status variable indicating which party won the seat in the last election; and an incumbency status variable (-1 if the Republicans field an incumbent, 0 if the seat is open, and $+1$ if the Democrats field an incumbent). In order to ensure that the lagged vote share is meaningful, the analysis is restricted to those districts that were not redrawn between years t and $t - 2$. The coefficient on the incumbency status variable provides a measure of how much larger the incumbent party's vote share is with an incumbent rather than a nonincumbent candidate defending the district. The analysis assumes that the value of incumbency is the same for both parties. We shall relax this assumption later.

Gelman and King estimate the value of incumbency in each year. As noted in Chapter 4, their year-by-year estimates (both for the entire nation and for the nonsouthern portion) show a sharp increase in 1966, with a shallow trend before and no trend after.

If the incumbency advantage increased abruptly in 1966, with little trend before or after, then we may as well measure the average value of incumbency in two periods: before (1946–1964) and after (1966–1998). This can be done by adapting Gelman and King's approach.[2]

---

[2] We ran the basic Gelman–King regression with four wrinkles: first, we excluded the South; second, we included all years 1946–1998 in one analysis; third, we allowed for national partisan tides via the inclusion of separate "year effects"; fourth, we allowed the slope coefficients on the three main independent variables – lagged Democratic vote, seat status, and incumbency status – to shift from the pre-1966 to the post-1966 periods.

Table 8.1. *Estimating the Incumbency Advantage for Nonsouthern Representatives Before and After 1966 (1946–1998)*

Independent Variables	Estimated Coefficients
Lagged Democratic vote share	0.81***
	(0.02)
Seat status	−0.25
	(0.42)
Incumbency status	2.40***
	(0.40)
After 1966	10.72***
	(2.59)
After 1966 × Lagged Democratic vote share	−.12***
	(0.02)
After 1966 × Seat status	−2.48***
	(0.56)
After 1966 × Incumbency status	5.90***
	(0.53)
R^2	.85
N	6194

Notes: The dependent variable is the Democratic share of the two-party vote in district *j*, year *t*. Only nonsouthern districts that had not been redistricted between years *t* − 2 and *t* were included in the analysis. The independent variables are defined as follows. The *Lagged Democratic vote share* is simply the Democratic share of the two-party vote in district *j*, year *t* − 2. *Seat status* is coded −1 for Republican-held seats, +1 for Democrat-held seats. *Incumbency status* is coded −1 for districts with a Republican incumbent seeking reelection, 0 for districts with no incumbent seeking reelection, and +1 for districts with a Democratic incumbent seeking reelection. The dummy variable, *After 1966*, equals 1 for all observations in 1966 and after, 0 for all other observations. Finally, the model allows a separate constant term for each year (not reported). Standard errors are noted in parentheses below the coefficient estimates. Three asterisks (***) indicate significance at the .01 level or better.

The results of our before/after analysis are displayed in Table 8.1. The main points to be drawn are as follows. First, the estimated incumbency advantage outside the South in the period 1946–1964 was 2.40. That is, a party defending one of its seats with an incumbent could expect a vote percentage 2.40 points higher than it could expect had it defended with a nonincumbent, all else equal. This figure, statistically significant at conventional levels, represents an average value of incumbency over the entire 1946–1964 period. Second, the estimated incumbency advantage in the period 1966–1998 was 5.90 points higher than it had been before. In other words, the incumbency advantage is estimated to have increased from 2.40 percentage points to 2.40 + 5.90 = 8.29 percentage points (note the rounding error). This more than tripling of the incumbency advantage is the first major explanandum of this part of the book.

Redistricting as an Explanation of Growth in the Incumbency Advantage

Can redistricting explain why the incumbency advantage increased? The answer is "no" if we look only at the *proximal* effects of redistricting. Reshuffling partisans among districts (the main proximal effect of redistricting relevant here) simply changes each district's normal vote – that is, the vote that could generally be expected in that district, given two candidates of average quality for each party. However, the approaches based on Gelman–King control for the normal vote (via the previous vote share) in each district. Thus, there is no reason to expect an increase (or decrease) in the incumbency advantage due to partisan redistricting.

As our focus in this part of the book is primarily on the incumbency advantage, rather than the vanishing marginals, it behooves us to explain how redistricting might have *indirectly* affected incumbents' performance advantage over nonincumbents. We do this after reviewing another issue – the size of margins and the value of incumbency for each party's incumbents.

MARGINS AND INCUMBENCY ADVANTAGES BY PARTY

The literature has uniformly assumed that the incumbency advantage is of the same size for both Democrats and Republicans. In the next two sections, we show that both incumbents' margins of victory over challengers from the other party and their performance advantage over nonincumbents from their own party increased in quite different ways for the two parties.

Margins by Party

Consider first a pair of hypothetical Democratic incumbents, one running before 1966, one after. Assume that both won by the same margin in their last election and benefit (or suffer) from an identical partisan swing. Above and beyond the effects of past margins and partisan swings, the post-1966 incumbent is estimated to have a margin of victory 2.17 percentage points larger than that of the pre-1966 incumbent, a statistically significant boost.[3]

Now consider a pair of hypothetical Republican incumbents before and after 1966, again matched in terms of prior margin and the size of the partisan swing they face. The post-1966 incumbent is estimated to have a margin of victory 3.53 percentage points larger than that of the pre-1966 incumbent, the difference being statistically significant. Moreover, the Republican boost (3.53) is 1.37 points larger than the Democratic boost (2.17), a statistically discernible difference at conventional levels of significance.

Thus, by one simple analysis, it is Republican incumbents who gain the most after the reapportionment revolution. In the next section, we explore party differences further.

Incumbency Advantages by Party

What did the incumbency advantage look like for each party over the postwar period? We estimate this by adapting the year-by-year regression advocated by Gelman and King (1991). Their equation forces the value of running an incumbent to be equal for the two major parties. Our adaptation simply removes this restriction.

Figure 8.2 shows a whisker plot of our results. The dots in the figure indicate our estimates of how much larger the Republican incumbency advantage was in a given year than the Democratic incumbency advantage. Positive values indicate that the Republican incumbency advantage was larger, while negative values indicate that the Democratic incumbency advantage was larger. The "whiskers" in the plot show the 95% confidence interval for our estimates. Intuitively, the whiskers grow longer as the level of uncertainty about the estimated difference grows. When the dot and its whiskers lie entirely on one side of zero, as they do in 1976, one can reject the null hypothesis that the two parties had identical incumbency advantages in the indicated year.

---

[3] This result comes from a regression in which the dependent variable is an incumbent's margin of victory; the main independent variables are the incumbent's previous margin and the national swing to his or her party; Republican and Democratic incumbents are allowed to have separate intercept terms; and all effects are allowed to shift in 1966. All House races in the period 1946–1992, southern and nonsouthern, that had an incumbent running for reelection were included. The results are very similar if the period 1946–1998 is analyzed.

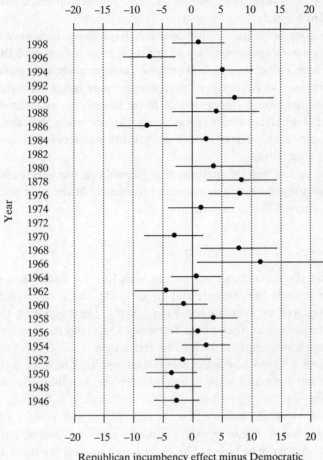

Figure 8.2 Whisker plot of estimated partisan difference in the incumbency advantage, 1946–1998. Note: reading horizontally across the graph for each year, the dot represents the point estimate of how much greater the Republican incumbency advantage was than the Democratic incumbency advantage, while the "whiskers" emerging from the dot cover the 95% confidence interval. Positive values thus correspond to a larger incumbency advantage for the Republicans, while negative values indicate a larger advantage for the Democrats.

Figure 8.2 shows that the nature of partisan differences in the incumbency advantage changed abruptly in 1966. We stress three features of the whisker plots in particular that show this.

First, the estimated difference between the Republican and Democratic incumbency advantages simply becomes bigger in absolute value. Before

1966, this difference is never greater than five percentage points. After 1966 (inclusive), the difference is greater than five percentage points in 8 of 14 years.

Second, our estimates become abruptly less certain. Prior to 1966, the 95% confidence interval (the length from the left whisker tip to the right whisker tip in a given year) is less than 10 percentage points in 9 of 10 years. After 1966 (inclusive), the confidence interval is greater than 10 percentage points in all but two years.

Third, our estimates suggest a shift toward larger Republican incumbency advantages. Prior to 1966, there does not appear to be any consistent difference between the parties. In the period 1966–1994, the pattern is quite different, with the Republican incumbency advantage larger in 10 of 12 years. The Republican advantage seems to outdistance the Democratic advantage especially after Republican electoral disasters – see 1966–1968 (after the 1964 landslide) and 1976–1978 (after the Watergate election of 1974). After the Republican takeover of the House in 1994, meanwhile, we see that the Democrats exhibit a significantly larger incumbency advantage in 1996, this being only the second such event in the period examined.

The second approach to estimating the incumbency advantage separately for each party is to include all years in a single regression, adapting the analysis presented in Table 8.1. The results of such an analysis (not reported) again show a larger increase for the Republicans (7.2) than for the Democrats (4.2) – the difference being statistically significant.[4]

WHY WOULD THE INCUMBENCY ADVANTAGE BE LARGER FOR REPUBLICANS?

The results just presented raise the question: why would the incumbency advantage be larger for the Republicans than for the Democrats? In search of an answer, let us consider some explanations in the literature concerning why the overall incumbency advantage grew.

---

[4] As a further check on our results, we acquired the data from Jackman (2000), an analysis of the full postwar period, and repeated the two analyses suggested by Jackman for the period 1966–1998. The first analysis, an ordinary replication of the Gelman–King model with year effects and normal errors, again showed that Republicans had a significantly higher incumbency advantage in this period. The second analysis, a replication based on errors following the Student's T distribution, and estimated via Markov Chain Monte Carlo, again found the Republicans with a higher incumbency advantage, with the difference significant at the .10 level. Problems in the convergence of the Markov Chain Monte Carlo results lead us to prefer the first analysis on statistical grounds.

Casework

Suppose – following Fiorina (1977) – that the incumbency advantage increased because the staff and other resources available to members of Congress grew, and they performed more casework for grateful constituents. One might think that the only partisan differences that would make sense here would favor the Democrats: they were the majority party and controlled the lion's share of committee staff (which might free up their personal staff for more casework), and they were (and are) reputed to be more enthusiastic caseworkers.[5]

But perhaps the Democrats' reputation for casework actually diminished the size of their incumbents' advantage. If everyone expects Democrats to be good at casework, then incumbent Democrats do not have a reputational advantage over nonincumbent Democrats. Whatever increment to a candidate's vote share comes from the expectation that she or he will be an expert caseworker would accrue to incumbent and nonincumbent Democrats alike. In contrast, perhaps few expect Republicans to do casework. Such an expectation would allow those Republican incumbents who actually do casework to distance themselves from their party's overall reputation; they would thus be able to build up an advantage over nonincumbent Republicans.

While this line of thought might in the abstract drive a wedge between the parties, it suffers from a substantial defect. In order to explain the observed pattern – no difference between the parties before the mid-1960s, a statistically discernible difference thereafter – one would have to believe that the posited reputational difference between the parties sprang into existence suddenly in the mid-1960s. There is, however, no evidence of such a sudden change in reputation. Thus, even if one accepts the casework hypothesis – and it is hard to provide direct evidence for it (see Fiorina 1989) – it is unlikely to explain the partisan differences we have uncovered.

Incumbency as a Voting Cue

Suppose – following Burnham (1974), Mayhew (1974), and Ferejohn (1977) – that the incumbency advantage increased because voters

---

[5] Nonetheless, Lockerbie (1999) finds little difference between the parties in terms of voters' perceptions of their incumbents' performance of casework and general helpfulness.

dealigning from the parties began using incumbency per se as a cue. Suppose also that more Democrats dealign than Republicans. In this case, Republican incumbents would be able to gather more stray Democrats into their column by hard work of one sort or another (casework, position-taking, advertising). When these Republicans retired, the stray Democrats would be up for grabs, and thus the nonincumbent Republican defending the seat would expect to do less well than the former incumbent. The same story plays out for Democratic incumbents and nonincumbents but is less consequential because, by the hypothesis, there are fewer stray Republicans.

As far as we know, there is no evidence that the probability of a Republican voter straying in a congressional election was lower than the probability of an otherwise comparable Democrat straying. Certainly the literature on dealignment makes relatively little of partisan differences, depicting both parties as suffering similar difficulties in holding on to their partisans. Accordingly, we do not find this possibility a likely one to pursue, but we note its existence.

Candidate Quality and Recruitment

Suppose – following Jacobson (1987, 1990a) and Cox and Katz (1996) – that the incumbency advantage increased because candidate quality became a more important determinant of electoral outcomes beginning in the 1960s. By this line of thinking, the party with the larger incumbency advantage will be the one that has greater trouble finding (1) electorally experienced nonincumbents to defend its districts after its incumbents retire and (2) electorally experienced challengers to attack districts vacated by the other party's incumbents. Such a party will more often find, after its incumbents retire, that it has fielded an inexperienced defender, or faces an experienced challenger, or both. Its average vote share accordingly will drop rather precipitously, especially if candidate characteristics matter more in determining outcomes. The party that is better at recruiting candidates, in contrast, will more often find that it has fielded an experienced defender, or faces an inexperienced challenger, or both, after its incumbents retire. Its vote share will thus hold up better.

The argument just sketched is related to one we propose to pursue in later chapters. As several scholars have noted, the Republicans had considerable and persistent difficulty in fielding high-quality candidates during the 1970s and 1980s (e.g., Gilmour and Rothstein 1993;

Ansolabehere and Gerber 1997). What we add to this observation is an explanation of how the Republicans' recruitment difficulties were rooted in congressional redistricting.

CONCLUSION

In this chapter, we have reviewed two central puzzles of postwar congressional elections: not only did incumbents begin winning by larger margins in the 1960s, but they also began to do better relative to their party's nonincumbent candidates. We also showed that Republican incumbents' margins increased more than did Democratic incumbents' margins, and that Republican incumbents' performance advantage over Republican nonincumbents increased more than did the corresponding Democratic incumbency advantage. These partisan differences have not been noticed in the previous literature and are incompatible with the best-known explanations of the incumbency advantage's growth.

In the next four chapters, we seek to explain not just the increase in the incumbency advantage but also why there are partisan differences. We shall argue that much of the incumbency advantage, as currently measured, is not a real advantage but rather a statistical artifact generated by strategic entry. If we are correct, the direction of causality is (to a substantial extent) the reverse of that posited as dominant in previous studies: it is the anticipation of (low) vote shares for their parties that drives incumbents out of the race, rather than the presence of incumbents that drives their parties' vote shares up.

This perspective prompts us to explain the apparent increase in the incumbency advantage in terms of systematic changes in entry stimulated by the reapportionment revolution, not changes in the perquisites of office or the value of incumbency as a cue. It also prompts us to explain differences between the parties in the value and over-time development of the incumbency advantage in terms of systematic differences in career calculations (when to enter, when to exit).

AN OUTLINE OF PART III

The central arguments of this part of the book are that (1) the reapportionment revolution greatly affected strategic entry and exit decisions in congressional elections and that (2) strategic entry and exit decisions have always influenced the measured value of incumbency and did so even more after the reapportionment revolution. In order to elaborate this argument, we proceed in reverse order.

We first explain (in Chapter 9) how strategic entry and exit affect the measurement of the incumbency advantage. The central point is that incumbents who forecast a difficult race may choose to exit, so that the observed correlation between the incumbent party's vote share and the presence of an incumbent defending the seat may not all be due to the resources of incumbency boosting vote shares. Although previous authors (e.g., Gelman and King 1991; Levitt and Wolfram 1997) have noted this possibility, we provide systematic evidence that the problem (a form of *simultaneity bias*) is severe.

The other part of the argument, that the reapportionment revolution profoundly shaped strategic entry and exit decisions, divides into two subarguments. First, we argue (in Chapter 10) that the reapportionment decisions themselves substantially strengthened a preexisting *redistricting-induced entry cycle*. Prior to *Wesberry*, congressional candidates in many states (e.g., those expected to gain seats in the apportionment or to hold steady) might reasonably have expected that their districts would *not* be redrawn. After *Wesberry*, and especially after *Preisler*, incumbents and potential challengers both knew that virtually every district in the nation would be redrawn (at least to some extent) after every decennial census. This was a sudden change in expectations that, we argue, ought to have affected the timing of strong challenges to sitting incumbents and, relatedly, the timing of prudent departures by incumbents.

Second, we argue (in Chapter 11) that the sudden disappearance of pro-Republican bias in the nonsouthern states – a proximal effect of the reapportionment revolution documented in Part II – downshifted the Republican party's chances of securing a majority in the U.S. House of Representatives. This deepening of the party's perennial minority status, in turn, substantially affected its ability to recruit new candidates and retain incumbents. The Republicans' recruitment and retention woes, in turn, affected the measured value of incumbency to the Republicans relative to the measured value of incumbency to the Democrats.

9

Candidate Entry Decisions and the Incumbency Advantage

Previous studies of the incumbency advantage have focused on how much running an incumbent for reelection boosts the incumbent party's expected vote share. Incumbents, however, can *decide* whether to run for reelection, and their decisions are based partly on anticipation of the vote share they might win were they to run. Thus, while the presence of an incumbent may boost the incumbent party's vote share, forecasts of this vote share may determine whether there is an incumbent in the race to begin with.

All current measures of the incumbency advantage risk overestimating how much incumbency matters, by neglecting the possibility that incumbents tend to seek reelection when the prospects for their party are better, while retiring when those prospects are poorer. To the extent that incumbents are good at forecasting votes, one will find the incumbent party's vote share larger when there is an incumbent (who correctly forecast the favorable vote and hence ran for reelection) and smaller when there is no incumbent (the incumbent having retired in the face of a bad expected vote, which the nonincumbent replacing her to some extent inherits). In technical terms, the argument just given amounts to saying that there is a species of simultaneity bias afflicting current measures of the incumbency advantage.

It is not just *incumbents'* entry strategies that pose analytic challenges, however. When high-quality challengers (defined as those who have previously won elective office) enter the fray, they presumably do so partly on the basis of favorable vote forecasts. Their decisions to enter accordingly may bias estimates of how much the presence of a strong challenger boosts the challenging party's vote share.

Thus, there are two sources of potential bias: the incumbent's entry decision and the high-quality challenger's entry decision. Matters are further complicated because these two entry decisions are interdependent: the strong challenger is more likely to enter if the incumbent does not, and vice versa.

In the rest of the chapter, we proceed as follows. First, we explain the method of analysis that we shall employ to identify whether simultaneity bias is a serious problem or not. Second, we present evidence that incumbent candidates have tended to exit when faced with poor vote prospects, especially in and after the 1960s. Third, we discuss some consequences of our findings for both the positive and normative interpretations of congressional elections.

In all of our empirical analyses, we continue to focus on the non-southern portion of the United States, as in previous chapters. However, for the most part, the patterns we shall report continue to hold when the South is included in the analysis.

The main focus of this chapter is conceptual and methodological – how to think about and measure the incumbency advantage. We turn to the substantive issue of how redistricting affected the much-studied growth in the incumbency advantage in the following chapters.

MEASURING THE INCUMBENCY ADVANTAGE: METHODOLOGY

In this section, we review our previous model of the incumbency advantage (Cox and Katz 1996), and then build on it to explore the issues of entry and simultaneity bias raised in the introduction. Although it does not appear possible to estimate our amended model, at least not for all years, we show that a simpler technique exists that effectively addresses the methodological problems posed by the incumbent's entry decision.

The Cox–Katz 1996 Model

In previous work (Cox and Katz 1996), we proposed a simple path-analytic model of incumbency's effects. The presence of an incumbent candidate in the race can have two distinct effects on the incumbent party's vote share: first, a direct effect; second, an effect mediated by the quality of the challenging party's candidate. Let us consider each effect in turn.

Running an incumbent can be directly valuable because legislative resources available to incumbents (e.g., personal staff) can be used in electorally useful ways (e.g., to perform casework) or because voters view incumbency per se as an asset or as indicating competence. Running an incumbent can also be indirectly valuable. The effect here occurs in two steps.

First, the presence of an incumbent in the race tends to scare off high-quality challengers, either because these challengers know that the incumbent is an especially formidable campaigner or because they know that incumbents can derive large direct benefits from their incumbency. This scare-off effect depresses the quality of the candidate fielded by the challenging party.[1] Second, depressing the quality of the challenging party's candidate – we follow Jacobson (e.g., 1990a) in measuring quality operationally by whether the candidate has previously won elective office – boosts the incumbent party's vote to the extent that candidate quality matters in determining election outcomes. If voters always vote for their party's candidate, then the fact that incumbents scare off high-quality challengers does not matter. But the more voters vote for the person rather than the party, the more personal characteristics and campaigning ability will matter.

In our previous work, we pointed out that the incumbency advantage might have increased either through the direct or the indirect pathway. Perhaps the direct vote-boosting effects of incumbency increased – for example, because incumbents' perquisites of office increased. Alternatively, perhaps the indirect effects of incumbency increased: (1) incumbents' presence more greatly depressed challenger quality; or (2) the importance of challenger quality in determining election outcomes increased; or (3) both.

To assess both the direct and the indirect effects of incumbency, we suggested a two-equation model. The first equation predicted whether a strong challenger would enter in the *j*th district at the *t*th election, as a function of the incumbent party's vote in the previous election in that district, whether the incumbent candidate sought reelection or not, which party currently held the seat, and whether an incumbent sought reelection in the district at the previous election. The second equation predicted the incumbent party's vote in the *j*th district at the *t*th election as a function of the same variables as in the first equation, plus one more indicating whether a strong challenger had entered or not. The second equation's pedigree stretches back to early work by Erikson (1971,

---

[1] We assume that higher-quality challengers are also those with larger opportunity costs – i.e., with more to lose (their current position) by entering and failing.

1972), but it is most directly related to more recent work by Gelman and King (1990) and Cox and Katz (1996).

Adding the Incumbent's Entry Decision: a Simultaneous Equations Model

In our previous work, we did not explicitly recognize that the incumbent is also a strategic agent who must decide whether to enter the competition for another term. In this section, we take a more symmetric view of incumbents and challengers. We imagine that in each district there is an incumbent (denoted by female pronouns) and a single strong challenger (denoted by male pronouns). Just as the strong challenger in a district will be less likely to enter if he knows the incumbent will run for reelection (because then his expected vote share is lower), the incumbent will be less likely to enter when she knows the strong challenger will enter (because then her expected vote share is lower).[2] To put it another way, just as the entry of the incumbent may scare off the strong challenger, the entry of the strong challenger may scare off the incumbent. More generally, the incumbent's anticipation of a poor vote – or an insufficiently good vote – may contribute to her decision to withdraw.[3]

To incorporate the incumbent's entry decision in our econometric model, we simply add another entry equation. The full model thus has two entry equations, one for the strong challenger and one for the incumbent, plus a vote equation (that is conditional on the observed entry decisions).

If we could properly estimate the full system of three simultaneous equations, we could parse the overall correlation between the incumbent party's vote share and the incumbent candidate's entry decision into two components: (1) how much the presence of an incumbent boosts her party's vote share and (2) how much anticipation of a poor vote share drives incumbents from the field. A similar analysis of the overall

---

[2] The theoretically relevant variables are the candidates' estimates of their probabilities of victory, but we assume there is a monotonic relationship between expected vote and probability of victory.

[3] There is good evidence that candidates in general consider their chances of winning when deciding whether to enter (see Chapter 11). There is also good evidence that incumbent candidates in particular are sensitive to "bad years" for their parties (Jacobson and Kernell 1983) and to scandals (Groseclose and Krehbiel 1994; Jacobson and Dimock 1994).

correlation between the incumbent party's vote share and the strong challenger's entry decision would also be possible.

Unfortunately, we do not have the information necessary to estimate our model as a system of simultaneous equations.[4] Nor can we ignore the entry equations and estimate the incumbency advantage conditional on entry.[5] However, we can investigate whether the self-selection of incumbents into (and out of) our sample is problematic in practice by a much simpler and more tractable analysis based on identifying the reasons that seats become open.

Why Did the Incumbent Not Appear in the General Election?

In our previous discussion, we assumed that the incumbent was *deciding* whether to retire. However, incumbents do not always voluntarily forgo the chance to seek reelection. Some die. Others try but fail to secure their party's renomination. Still others are expelled from the House. In each of these cases of involuntary withdrawal, the incumbent's vote

[4] The main difficulty is finding appropriate instruments to identify each equation. Consider, for example, the strong challenger's entry equation. The standard approach to identifying this equation would entail finding variables that affect the challenger's decision to enter but do not affect either the incumbent's decision to enter or the incumbent party's vote share. One might think that the challenger's opportunity costs would be suitable instruments. However, we do not know who the potential strong challengers are in each district. Even if we did, might not the incumbent consider the challenger's opportunity costs when deciding whether to enter, if she knew them?

[5] The problem is that the errors in the entry equations are correlated with those in the vote equation. When we estimate the incumbent party's vote, given the lagged vote in the district, there will be an error. Similarly, when we estimate whether the incumbent will seek reelection, given the lagged vote in the district, there will again be an error. Suppose incumbents can forecast votes in their districts systematically better than we can, using just the incumbent party's lagged vote share. Consider the set of incumbents who expect better vote shares than a forecast based solely on lagged votes would indicate. These incumbents tend to enter more often than we expect (positive error in the entry equation) and to get higher vote shares than we expect (positive error in the vote equation). In contrast, the set of incumbents who expect worse vote shares than the lagged-vote forecast indicates tend to exit and their parties tend to do poorly (negative errors in both equations). If we estimate the incumbency advantage simply by looking at the coefficient on an incumbency dummy variable in a single vote equation, a portion of the gap we find between the incumbent party's performance with and without its incumbent candidate will be artifactual. It will be generated by the fact that all politics is local and the local politicians know it a lot better than we do, so that incumbents' entry and exit decisions reveal information about which way the electoral winds were blowing.

expectations either play no role (in the cases of death or expulsion) or should have been favorable (in the case of defeat for renomination, where she had in fact decided to seek reelection). In contrast, part of the reason for involuntary withdrawal – retirement, seeking another office, or pursuing opportunities in the private sector – may be the anticipation of doing poorly were she to seek reelection.

Thus, one expects losses in voluntarily vacated seats to exceed losses in involuntarily vacated seats – at least if the following two conditions hold. First, incumbents' anticipations of their party's vote share must play a significant role in their voluntary exit decisions. This assumption is central to the entire literature on rational entry and appears to be abundantly supported (see, e.g., Schlesinger 1966; Black 1972; Rohde 1979; Jacobson and Kernell 1983; Brace 1984; Canon 1990; Kiewiet and Zeng 1993; Hall and van Houweling 1995). Second, the incumbent party's vote share must to a significant extent be based on party, as opposed to personal, votes. That is, when the incumbent anticipates a bad vote share, it is not typically for purely idiosyncratic reasons but instead for reasons that will affect the vote of any nonincumbent who runs in her stead should she withdraw.[6]

Given these two conditions – entry is strategic, party voting in the electorate is widespread – there should be a substantial difference between the loss suffered by the incumbent party, depending on whether the incumbent withdrew voluntarily or involuntarily. Exactly how large the difference will be, however, is an empirical question.

In order to investigate whether there is in fact a significant difference in the incumbent party's vote loss, depending on the reason for the incumbent's withdrawal, we simply adapt the Cox–Katz model presented earlier. Instead of a single variable indicating the presence of an incumbent, we employ two variables, one indicating a seat that is open due to the voluntary withdrawal of the incumbent and one indicating a seat that is open due to the involuntary withdrawal of the incumbent. Thus, open seats rather than seats defended by an incumbent are the reference category. Additionally, instead of presenting a straight comparison between open and incumbent-defended seats, we contrast two categories of open seats to incumbent-defended seats and to each other. We expect the

---

[6] If the incumbent withdraws because a strong challenger enters the race or because her party is saddled with an unpopular president, the bad electoral news will be inherited by whomever replaces her. If the incumbent retires due to a personal scandal, it is debatable whether her replacement will suffer some of the blame.

average vote loss suffered by a party when it loses an incumbent due to voluntary withdrawal to exceed its average vote loss when it loses an incumbent due to involuntary withdrawal. If the difference in vote losses in the two categories of open seat is statistically discernible from zero (and substantively significant), we will conclude that self-selection is a problem.

MEASURING THE INCUMBENCY ADVANTAGE: RESULTS

The most general description of the methodological problem that one faces in estimating the incumbency advantage is simultaneity bias. However, we shall also use the term *selection bias* – more broadly than is typical in the technical literature – since a good part of the problem stems from the fact that incumbents choose whether to seek reelection or not.[7]

In the next four subsections, we argue that selection bias is indeed severe.[8] That is, incumbents are systematically more likely to exit when their party's local vote prospects are poorer. The first two subsections provide circumstantial evidence that candidate entry has been strategic, especially after the mid-1960s. The third subsection measures the size of the resulting selection bias in estimators of the incumbency advantage, finding it to be large. The fourth section speculates about selection bias in estimators of how much challenger quality matters.

Coordination of Entry

Table 9.1 cross-tabulates the frequency with which incumbents and strong challengers entered in two periods: 1946–1964 and 1966–1998. We highlight two points supported by these figures.

First, in both periods, strong challengers appear less frequently when the incumbent enters, and incumbents appear less frequently when a

---

[7] Whenever the sample that an analyst has available to analyze arises as the result of potentially strategic decisions on the part of the agents under study, the sample is said to be self-selected and the potential for selection bias in the estimation of various causal effects arises. The usual model of selection bias, however, assumes that the error terms in the entry equation(s) are not correlated with the error terms in the outcome equation – whereas we make no such assumption and, indeed, provide evidence to the contrary.

[8] Gelman and King (1990) provide an unbiased estimator of the difference in two conditional means – the incumbent party's expected vote with and without an incumbent seeking reelection. However, theirs is not an unbiased estimator of the *causal effect* of running an incumbent on the incumbent party's vote share.

Table 9.1. *Nonsouthern Incumbents' and Experienced Challengers' Entry Decisions, 1946–1964 and 1966–1998*

Does the Incumbent Seek Reelection?	Does an Experienced Challenger Enter?			
	1946–1964		1966–1998	
	No	Yes	No	Yes
No (Open Seat)	67.4%	32.6%	54.2%	45.8%
	(194)	(94)	(207)	(175)
Yes (Incumbent-Defended Seat)	72.1%	27.9%	77.4%	22.6%
	(1790)	(693)	(2596)	(757)
Likelihood-Ratio χ^2	2.77		88.16	

Note: Cell entries are the row percentage within the time period given. The numbers in parentheses are the actual number of cases in the cell.

strong challenger enters. This suggests that strong candidates are avoiding each other.

Second, there is a reduction in the frequency of "crashes" (both the incumbent and a strong challenger entering); an increase in the frequency of cases in which the incumbent enters while the strong challenger stays out; and an increase in the frequency of cases in which the strong challenger enters but the incumbent stays out. Overall, a standard measure of statistical association (the likelihood ratio χ^2) increases from 3.02 before 1966 to 89.47 after ward. This large increase suggests considerable improvement in the candidates' ability to coordinate their entries.[9] Increasingly, if one strong candidate entered, the other did not.

The Scare-Off Effect

In this subsection, we estimate the probability that a strong challenger enters as a function of two main variables: whether the seat is open and whether the seat becomes open only after the incumbent's entry, due to her subsequent death or failure to secure renomination. In all cases of voluntary withdrawal, as well as in some cases of death, the incumbent

[9] If one looks at the district level, one finds that the probability of a crash declines substantially (and statistically significantly) after 1966, controlling for the incumbent party's vote share in the previous election. It is not clear that the decline in crashes is a step-function phenomenon, as there is a downward trend over time after 1966. However, it is also clear that the process generating crashes changes in 1966, as there is no time trend at all in the period 1946–1966.

does not even enter her party's primary election contest. Thus, any strong challenger(s) in her district can know whether the incumbent is entering or not before they themselves decide to enter. In contrast, when the incumbent fails to appear in the general election because she was defeated in the primary or died after entering (and perhaps winning) the primary, strong challengers will not have known that the incumbent would not appear in the general election at the time they made their own entry decisions. Thus, to the extent that strong challengers are avoiding incumbents, we expect them to enter more frequently in *forseeably* open seats but not in *unforseeably* open seats.[10]

Our model controls for the incumbent party's lagged vote and for whether the incumbent party ran an incumbent candidate in the previous election. These two variables together help capture the normal vote that the incumbent party can expect in a given district.[11] The analysis also allows separate intercept terms for each party in each year to accommodate the fact that there are good years and bad years for each party that bring out larger than usual or smaller than usual crops of strong challengers (Jacobson and Kernell 1983).

Our results, presented in Table 9.2, show sharp differences between the pre- and post-1966 periods. In the earlier period, strong challengers were more likely to enter, both in forseeably and in unforseeably open seats, than they were in incumbent-defended seats. However, neither tendency was statistically significant at conventional levels. Moreover, there is no significant difference in the frequency of entry by strong challengers as between the two categories of open seats.

In the later period, the tendency for strong challengers to enter in forseeably open seats strengthens considerably and becomes statistically

---

[10] Operationally, we identified unforeseeable withdrawals using biographical information on each member of congress. Our sources were (1) the Inter-university Consortium for Political and Social Research and Carroll McKibbin (1997) and (2) http://bioguide.congress.gov/biosearch/biosearch.asp. Thanks also to James M. Snyder, Jr., for providing information on members for recent years.

[11] The lagged vote share obviously helps capture the normal vote. However, an incumbent party that received 60% of the vote running an incumbent in the previous election is arguably not as strong as one that received 60% contending for an open seat, which in turn is not as strong as a party that won 60% running against an incumbent of the other party. Thus, we also control for whether the incumbent party's candidate in the previous election was the incumbent (+1), contending for an open seat (0), or challenging an incumbent of the other party (−1).

Table 9.2. *Entry by Nonsouthern Challengers with Elective Experience, 1946–1964 and 1966–1998*

Independent Variables	Estimated Coefficients	
	1946–1964	1966–1998
Lagged Incumbent Vote	−0.054***	−0.037***
	(0.005)	(0.003)
Lagged Incumbency Status	−.203***	−.153***
	(.047)	(.047)
Open	0.127	0.731***
	(0.096)	(0.077)
Unforseeably Open	0.000	−0.333
	(0.229)	(0.236)
N	2658	3544
Log Likelihood	−1450.08	−1810.42

Notes: The dependent variable = 1 if a challenger who had previously won elective office enters, = 0 otherwise. Standard errors are reported in parentheses below the coefficient estimates. Three asterisks (***) indicate significance at the .001 level or better. The analysis includes separate intercepts for each party in each year (not reported). Complete estimates are available upon request.

significant. The frequency of strong challengers' entry in unforseeably open seats is intermediate between that in incumbent-defended and in forseeably open seats and is statistically distinct from neither (in two-tailed tests at the .05 level).[12]

These results suggest that, in and after 1966, strong challengers became more likely to bide their time, waiting for the incumbent to depart, before launching their own candidacies. That they *consistently* entered more frequently *only* in open seats in which the incumbent departed before the filing deadline to enter this primary contests bolsters this impression.[13]

One thing our analysis does not illuminate is how much strong challengers may be scaring off incumbents, rather than the reverse. In some cases, it may have been common knowledge that a strong

[12] When the South is included in the analysis, the distinction between forseeably and unforseeably open seats becomes statistically discernible. Strong challengers are significantly more likely to enter in forseeably open seats than in unforseeably open ones.
[13] For interview evidence showing that strong challengers are scared off by the presence of an incumbent, see Kazee (1983).

challenger had good prospects against a particular incumbent. In these cases, the challenger might have pushed the incumbent into retirement by credibly committing to enter the race. How frequently challengers scared off incumbents in this way we cannot tell from the analysis in Table 9.2. In the next subsection, we present an analysis that suggests that incumbents were more likely to withdraw voluntarily when they forecast poor vote shares (conditional on the strong challenger's entry decision).[14]

The Incumbent Party's Vote Loss Depends on Why the Incumbent Left

In this subsection, we estimate the incumbent party's vote share as a function of various control variables and two open-seat indicators: one indicating the voluntary withdrawal of an incumbent and one indicating the involuntary withdrawal of an incumbent.[15] We estimate the model separately for the pre- and post-1966 periods (see Table 9.3).[16]

In the pre-1966 period, the estimated loss to the incumbent party when the incumbent voluntarily withdraws is 2.74 percentage points (statistically discernible from zero). In contrast, the estimated loss when the incumbent involuntarily departs is 0.51 percentage points: statisti-

---

[14] The incumbent will forecast a lower expected vote when the strong challenger enters than when he does not. However, our point here is that incumbents forecast votes for both states of the world: when the strong challenger enters and when he does not. When these conditional forecasts are more favorable, they are more likely to enter. Technically, it is only when incumbents know more than analysts about their conditional-on-entry chances that selection bias due to entry decisions can arise.

[15] The basic patterns we find are apparent even when one has no controls at all and simply compares a party's average loss in its involuntarily and voluntarily open seats.

[16] Operationally, we identified involuntary withdrawals using biographical information on each member of congress (Inter-university Consortium for Political and Social Research, and Carroll McKibbin 1997). We classified as involuntary all withdrawals due to defeat in the primary election, all withdrawals due to expulsion, and all withdrawals due to death. There were two cases in the online dataset that were coded as deaths that we recoded as voluntary withdrawals, because the candidate in each case had voluntarily forgone the House race in order to contest a U.S. Senate seat in his state but died during the campaign (thus, from the perspective of the House clerk, their departure from the House was due to death, as their terms had not yet elapsed). These two cases were those of Edwin Keith Thompson and Jerry Lon Litton. All told, there were 166 involuntary withdrawals in the dataset versus 1,089 voluntary withdrawals.

Table 9.3. *Incumbent Party Vote Share,*
Nonsouthern, 1946–1998

	Estimated Coefficients	
Independent Variables	1946–1964	1966–1998
Lagged Incumbent Vote	0.739	0.717
	(0.017)	(0.014)
Lagged Incumbency Status	0.065	−2.455
	(0.198)	(0.230)
Voluntarily Open	−2.664	−7.424
	(0.413)	(0.403)
Involuntarily Open	−0.731	−2.901
	(0.739)	(1.012)
Challenger Quality	−2.195	−3.903
	(0.252)	(0.268)
N	2657	3537
R^2	0.59	0.60

Notes: The dependent variable is the incumbent party's vote share. *Challenger Quality* is coded as +1, if the challenger had held previous elective office, 0 otherwise. Standard errors are reported in parentheses below the coefficient estimates. The analysis includes separate intercepts for each party in each year (not reported). Complete estimates are available upon request.

cally indistinct from zero but distinct from 2.74 points. Thus, there is evidence of strategic entry biasing estimates of the incumbency advantage even in the early period.[17]

If the value of incumbency related simply to the perquisites of office, then the loss suffered in both kinds of open seats should be similar, as these perquisites are lost in both cases. Similarly, the use of incumbency as a cue is lost in both sorts of open seats, as the incumbent party's candidate no longer has the word *incumbent* printed next to her name on the ballot. What differs is that incumbents who withdraw voluntarily may be getting out in the face of poor vote expectations, whereas this is

[17] If one separates the involuntary withdrawals into those due to defeat in the primary and those due to death, one finds that the loss in *both* sorts of involuntarily open seat is about .51 (the pooled estimate given in Table 9.3); that the loss is statistically indiscernible from zero in both cases; and that the loss is statistically discernible from the loss in voluntarily open seats in both cases (at the .05 level for the larger category of failures to secure renomination and at the .10 level for the smaller category of deaths).

not true of incumbents who depart involuntarily (on the assumption that death, expulsion, and primary defeat are not caused by or correlated with poor general election vote expectations).

The amount of selection bias is apparently even larger in the post-1966 period. The average vote loss suffered by the incumbent party is 7.42 percentage points when the incumbent departs voluntarily but only 2.90 points when she departs involuntarily. Thus, the voluntary/involuntary gap more than doubled – from 2.23 points before 1966 to 4.52 points afterward.[18]

Different Sorts of Voluntary and Involuntary Exit

The simple contrast between seats that become open due to the voluntary as opposed to the involuntary exit of the incumbent, of course, hides the diversity within each category. Involuntary exits can be further divided into deaths and failures to win primary elections (with expulsions being in practice a negligible third category). Voluntary exits can be further divided into retirements and decisions to seek other elective office (with acceptances of federal office a small category subsumed under the retirement). What happens if we examine vote losses in open seats created by primary defeats, deaths, retirements, and progressive ambition?

Empirically, we can report that losses are largest in cases of progressive ambition, intermediate in cases of retirement, and smallest in cases of death and primary defeat. The differences here are all statistically discernible, except that between retirement losses and losses due to death (there are only 13 deaths in the dataset in this period) and that between losses following primary defeats and losses due to death.

The main new finding of this finer-grained analysis is that vote losses after the incumbent leaves to pursue other office are typically higher than losses after retirement. There are many factors within our model that might generate this difference. For example, perhaps progressive ambition is more often a push-out phenomenon than is retirement. Retire-

---

[18] If one separates the involuntary withdrawals into those due to defeat in the primary and those due to death, one finds that the loss in both sorts of involuntarily open seat is smaller than that in voluntarily open seats; that the loss in both cases is statistically discernible from the loss in voluntarily open seats (although only at the .06 significance level for the smaller category of deaths); and that the losses in the two subsets of involuntarily open seats are statistically indistinguishable from one another.

ment often occurs at the end of a long career. Perhaps the districts from which incumbents retire tend to be safer for one party, leading to relatively small vote losses pursuant to retirement. Progressive ambition, in contrast, is a midcareer phenomenon. Perhaps the districts that are launching pads for further careers in politics tend to be more competitive, leading to relatively large vote losses after a given incumbent moves on. In support of this conjecture, we can note that the probability that a strong challenger enters the race is significantly higher when the incumbent decides to seek other office than when the incumbent simply retires.[19]

Summary

The evidence presented in this section shows that parties lose more when an incumbent departs voluntarily than they do when an incumbent departs involuntarily, especially after 1966. This finding is inconsistent with the assumption, implicit in previous work, that strategic entry does not affect estimates of the value of incumbency. Thus, we can conclude that previous estimators of the incumbency advantage overstate it. In order to measure this advantage properly, a fully simultaneous estimation procedure would be necessary.

In other words, and the point is worth underlining, *conventional estimators do not provide unbiased estimates of the real value of incumbency in House elections.* A fortiori, there is no clear evidence that the real value of incumbency in House elections grew.

There are other possible estimators of the incumbency advantage besides Gelman and King's (1990) and its predecessors. For example, Ansolabehere, Snyder, and Stewart (n.d.) exploit county-level electoral data, while Levitt and Wolfram (1997) study cases in which the same pair of candidates run against each other more than once. As neither of these estimators was constructed with an eye to solving the simultaneity problem, each would have to be defended explicitly on this score before one could recommend them over the Gelman–King estimator.

Another possible estimator of the true incumbency advantage is the expected loss of open seats created by involuntary departures of the incumbents. This estimator is arguably purged of selection bias (narrowly

---

[19] This observation is based on an analysis that is identical to that in Table 9.1, except that the open seat variables are removed and replaced with indicators for progressive ambition, retirement, and involuntary departure.

construed). To see this, recall that the reference group of races consists of all those with an incumbent seeking reelection. Averaging across these cases, the vote share for the incumbent party is higher than would be expected (solely on the basis of the previous race's characteristics) because the incumbent's decision to enter is based partly on a sufficiently favorable vote forecast. Now consider the cases involving an involuntary departure of the incumbent. In almost all of these cases, the incumbent also decides to seek reelection but is either defeated in her party's primary or dies after entering. These cases are no different than the reference group of races in that the incumbent decided voluntarily to try for reelection in all of them.[20] Thus, it might seem reasonable to take the vote loss in involuntarily open seats as a selection-bias-free estimator of the incumbency advantage.

Unfortunately, one cannot defend this estimator against charges of simultaneity bias. Solving part of the statistical problem is no guarantee that the whole problem has been solved. Nonetheless, we can report that the estimated incumbency advantage by the "vote loss in involuntarily open seats" measure corresponds roughly to the figures reported in Ansolabehere, Snyder, and Stewart (n.d.). We estimate the real incumbency advantage at about .5 percentage points in the period 1946–1964, while they estimate it (or something similar) at about 2 points in the period 1932–1960. We estimate the real incumbency advantage at about 2.9 points in the period 1966–1994, while they estimate it at about 4 points in the period 1972–1988. These figures contrast with the corre-

---

[20] In a few involuntarily open races – those involving death before the filing deadline for the primary election – we do not know whether the incumbent would have decided to enter the race or not. For some fraction of these cases of early death, the incumbent would have entered had she survived; they too would thus be no different than the reference category of contests. For the rest of the cases, however, the incumbent would have decided to retire had she survived, indicating poorer than average vote forecasts. The more such cases there are, the more the comparison between involuntarily open and held seats produces an underestimate of the value of incumbency. Let's assume that the rate of voluntary departure in cases of early death would have been about what it is in cases with senior incumbents (say, at least seven terms of service) who do not die – or about 7%. Given this assumption, and the fact that there were only 16 cases of early death in the dataset, one can conclude that only about *one* of the involuntarily open races in our dataset would have had expected vote shares for the incumbent party lower than in the reference category of races (conditional on the previous race's characteristics). Thus, the incumbents' expectations are largely held constant in the comparison between the reference group of districts and the cases involving involuntary departure; however, the resources of incumbency are present in the reference group but absent in the comparison group.

sponding estimates, given in the previous chapter, of 2.40 percentage points before and 8.30 percentage points after. In each case, the estimate produced by the current state-of-the-art procedure is far more than twice our estimates (based on vote losses in involuntarily open seats).

REDISTRICTING AND THE DECISION TO SEEK REELECTION

In this section, we provide additional evidence that strategic exit by incumbents can affect the measured value of incumbency. To explain, consider the situation of incumbents whose districts have been redrawn. Some of them will have had their districts made safer; they are likely to seek reelection. Others will have had their districts, previously inefficiently safe, pushed toward a more efficient margin of safety; they too are likely to seek reelection. A third class of incumbents will have been targeted for elimination, victims of the other party's partisan gerrymander (or of bad luck in a bipartisan gerrymander); they are likely to exit. Thus, even if incumbents are no better at garnering votes than otherwise similar nonincumbents, we expect a considerably larger vote loss when incumbents voluntarily exit after their district has been redrawn than when they voluntarily exit without such redrawing.

To explain this point more fully, consider the set of incumbents with redrawn districts. Those who exit are likely to consist predominantly of those targeted for defeat, which should produce a big swing against the incumbent party. In contrast, those who stay among the set of incumbents with redrawn districts are likely to consist predominantly of those made safer or only slightly less safe, which should produce an average swing in favor of the incumbent party. All told, the incumbent party's expected vote, when one of their incumbents voluntarily departs, should be substantially less than its expected vote in districts in which the incumbent defends her seat.

Now consider incumbents with stable (not redrawn) districts. Those who exit are likely to consist predominantly of those who anticipate a high risk of defeat, which should produce a swing against the incumbent party. However, one would certainly not expect as large an average vote swing as when the incumbent's district has been redrawn to include a net addition of the other party's partisans. Those who stay (among the set of incumbents with stable districts) are likely to consist mostly of those with better electoral prospects, which should produce an average swing in favor of the incumbent party. The size of the favorable swing will, on average, fall short of that in districts made safer by redistricting but exceed that in districts pared down by redistricting; thus, whether it exceeds the overall swing in redrawn districts whose incumbents stay depends on the ratio of districts made safer to pared districts. As we have already shown that many of the 1960s redistrictings were bipartisan, the favorable swing was likely even more favorable in redrawn than in stable districts.

All told, the incumbent party's expected vote loss, when one of its incumbents voluntarily departs, should have been larger in redrawn than in stable districts. Was it?

In order to test the notion that selection bias was more severe in redrawn districts, we adapt the regression from Table 9.3, in four ways. First, we focus only on the period 1966–1970, the peak period of extraordinary redistricting action. Second, we include both redrawn and stable districts. Third, we exclude involuntarily open seats, contrasting voluntarily open to incumbent-defended seats. Fourth, we estimate the incumbency advantage separately for redrawn and stable districts.

Our results are displayed in Table 9.4. They show an average loss of open seats created by voluntary withdrawal that is about 80% larger in *redrawn* districts (11.17) than in *stable* districts (6.25).[21] This difference – statistically significant – is consistent with the notion that incumbents exit partly due to poor vote prospects. In a stable district, all kinds of short-term factors can boost or depress the incumbent's expected vote share, above and beyond the normal vote in the district. Incumbents who anticipate sufficiently good short-term shocks stay; those who anticipate sufficiently bad shocks depart. Thus, the incumbent party's vote share should decline when an incumbent voluntarily exits, even if her replacement is an equally good campaigner. The story is similar in redrawn districts except that there are two sorts of shocks: the usual short-term shocks that can affect any district, plus structural shocks due to redistricting. The structural shocks arise because the district has been redrawn to increase or decrease the incumbent party's normal vote. For present purposes, the most important point is that the variance of the shocks in

---

[21] There were no cases of *involuntarily* open seats that were also redistricted in 1966–1970, so we cannot examine the contrast between redrawn and untouched districts in this category of open seats. We do not believe there would be any difference, but it would have been worthwhile demonstrating that no systematic difference existed, had the data allowed such an analysis.

Table 9.4. *Incumbent Party Vote Losses in*
Voluntarily Open Seats, Nonsouthern, for Redrawn
and Untouched Districts, 1966–1970

Independent Variables	Estimated Coefficients
Lagged Incumbent Vote	0.727
	(.027)
Lagged Incumbency Status	−2.210
	(.379)
Voluntarily Open	−6.207
	(1.042)
Voluntarily Open ×	−5.114
Redrawn	(1.616)
Challenger Quality	−3.057
	(0.441)
N	904
R^2	0.61

Notes: The dependent variable is the incumbent party's
vote share. *Challenger Quality* is coded as +1 if the challenger
had held previous elective office, 0 otherwise. Standard
errors are reported in parentheses below the coefficient estimates. The analysis includes separate intercepts for each party
in each year (not reported). Complete estimates are available
upon request.

redrawn districts (with both short-term and structural shocks) is larger
than that in stable districts (with only short-term shocks). Thus, more
of the incumbents who exit after redistricting will have had really bad
vote forecasts (engineered most likely by their friends in the other party
who redrew their district's lines), and more of the incumbents who stay
after redistricting will have had really good vote forecasts (especially
those whose districts were chosen to be stuffed with their own party's
partisans).

Table 9.4 thus provides another sort of evidence that incumbents' exit
decisions are systematically related to their vote forecasts. Table 9.3
relied on comparing voluntarily and involuntarily open seats and
excluded redrawn districts from the analysis entirely. In Table 9.4, we
compare voluntarily open seats in districts that were and were not
redrawn and exclude involuntarily open districts. The results in both
analyses show that incumbents' exit decisions were strategic and indirectly support our claim that strategic exit can substantially inflate estimates of the incumbency advantage.

Interpreting Congressional Elections

Beginning in the 1970s, a host of scholars and other observers have noted two central changes in congressional elections. First, running an incumbent, rather than a nonincumbent, became more important in keeping the incumbent party's vote share high. Second, running a high-quality, rather than a low-quality, challenger became more important in keeping the challenging party's vote share high. These findings fit well with a larger view according to which congressional elections became more candidate-centered and less party-centered, starting in the 1960s (Wattenberg 1984).

Both of these central findings, however, are consistent with the alternative hypothesis that incumbents and strong challengers coordinated their entries more successfully. Under this hypothesis, the incumbency advantage increased because selection bias increased: incumbents got better at going when the going was good. Meanwhile, the quality effect (how much larger the challenging party's vote share is with a high- rather than a low-quality candidate) increased too, for similar reasons: challengers got better at entering when the entering was good.

Our results in this chapter support one strong and one weaker but still defensible claim. The strong claim is that strategic exit and entry, in light of vote forecasts, do seriously affect the estimation of the electoral value of incumbency. If the standard approaches (which assume that simultaneity bias is negligible) were valid, then there would be no difference in the size of the incumbent party's vote loss in open seats created by voluntary as opposed to involuntary withdrawal of the incumbent candidate. We can confidently reject the idea that simultaneity bias is negligible.

The weaker claim is that the gap in votes lost, as between involuntarily and voluntarily open seats, is a reasonable measure of how much impact strategic exit and entry have on the usual measures of the incumbency advantage.[22] This claim is weaker because simultaneity bias potentially affects the estimation of all model parameters. Nonetheless, we can and will show in the next two chapters that the size of the involuntary/voluntary gap fluctuates as we would expect, both across time

---

[22] To put it another way, the loss in involuntarily open seats is taken to indicate the true incumbency advantage reasonably accurately, while the loss in voluntarily open seats is taken to be systematically inflated by strategic entry and exit considerations.

(Chapter 10) and between the two parties (Chapter 11). Thus, although we cannot prove that this is an unbiased measure of strategic effects, we can show that it has considerable external validity.

INTERPRETING THE INCUMBENCY ADVANTAGE IN OTHER ELECTIONS

Our main argument is not confined to the U.S. House of Representatives. Consider any legislature in which (1) incumbents' entry and exit decisions are (to some extent) based on their vote forecasts; (2) those forecasts are (to some extent) relevant to any candidate the incumbent's party might run at the next election; and (3) the incumbency advantage has been estimated by one of the array of standard measures. In all such legislatures, the possibility arises that a substantial portion of whatever incumbency advantage has been found is due to selection bias.

Consider, for example, the assemblies of the U.S. states. The idea that resources underpin the incumbency advantage is plausible for these legislatures.[23] However, the state-level evidence shows that it is the larger states with more professionalized legislatures that have the larger measured incumbency advantages. This basic finding is consistent with the idea that the incumbency advantage increases with the value of the legislative seats at stake – because then incumbents are more likely to exit voluntarily only in the face of poor vote prospects.

CONCLUSION

The standard bibliography of scholarly work on Congress lists, in its two editions (Goehlert and Sayre 1982; Goehlert, Martin, and Sayre 1996), no fewer than 145 works dealing with the incumbency advantage in congressional elections.[24] Although we cannot claim to have read all these works, the many we have read all believe that incumbents increasingly

---

[23] On the incumbency advantage at the state level, see, e.g., Breaux (1990), Cox and Morgenstern (1993, 1995), Garand (1991), Holbrook and Tidmarch (1991, 1993), Jewell and Breaux (1988), King (1991a, b), Niemi, Jackman, and Winsky (1991), Weber, Tucker, and Brace (1991), and Carey, Niemi, and Powell (2000).

[24] For a sampling of work on the incumbency advantage at the federal level, see Alford and Brady (1989), Alford and Hibbing (1981), Ansolabehere, Brady, and Fiorina (1988), Born (1979), Cain, Ferejohn, and Fiorina (1987), Collie (1981), Erikson (1971, 1972), Ferejohn (1977), Fiorina (1977), Garand and Gross (1984), Gelman and King (1990), Jacobson (1987, 1990a), King and Gelman (1991), Krehbiel and Wright (1983), and Mayhew (1974).

outperformed the replacements that their parties sent forth to defend seats they vacated. When scholars observed an increasingly regular *retirement slump* – or vote loss by the incumbent party when its incumbent candidate did not reappear in the general election – they uniformly concluded that the arrow of causality ran from some aspect of incumbency to vote shares. This belief was reinforced by the regularity with which new victors won reelection by substantially increased margins when compared to their initial victory as nonincumbents (a regularity dubbed the *sophomore surge* in the literature).

Given this belief about which way the arrow of causation ran, explanations of the increased incumbency advantage have all centered on possible advantages of incumbent candidates. Perhaps incumbents leveraged the increasing size of the federal bureaucracy, and their own increasing staffs, into more casework and more grateful constituents (Fiorina 1977). Perhaps voters increasingly began to use incumbency as a voting cue (Burnham 1974; Mayhew 1974; Ferejohn 1977). Perhaps incumbents were more and more effective at scaring off high-quality challengers and/or perhaps the vote differential between high- and low-quality candidates grew as elections became more candidate-centered (Jacobson 1987, 1990a; Cox and Katz 1996).

The primary message of this chapter is that all these perspectives have seriously overestimated the electoral value of running an incumbent rather than a nonincumbent – the so-called incumbency advantage. While it is plausible and perhaps true that incumbents garner larger vote shares than nonincumbents do in similar electoral circumstances, the arrow of causality does not run in just one direction. Incumbents' anticipations of their likely vote shares have evidently always influenced their decisions on whether to seek reelection. Thus, having an incumbent in the race does boost the incumbent party's vote share, but anticipation of vote shares also affect whether there will be an incumbent in the race at all. By neglecting the impact of vote forecasts on candidates' entry decisions, scholars have overestimated the impact of the two primary race-specific variables utilized in studies of postwar congressional elections: the presence (or absence) of an incumbent and the presence (or absence) of a high-quality challenger.

In this chapter, we have shown that the extent of overestimation is large. Because we have not estimated the full system of simultaneous equations, we cannot confidently say exactly how large the real incumbency advantage is. However, we think the best estimator is the size of the vote loss in involuntarily open seats. By this estimator, the estimated value of incumbency is statistically insignificant before 1966 and less than half of conventional estimates after 1966.

One issue we have not addressed is how our findings relate to the central theme of this book – the electoral consequences of the reapportionment revolution. We take up this task in the next two chapters.

10

Redistricting and Electoral Coordination

In the previous chapter, we showed that conventional estimators over-estimate the incumbency advantage. The positive correlation between the incumbent party's vote share and the presence of an incumbent candidate seeking reelection is due not only to the strength of the campaign that the incumbent candidate can mount (using the resources of her office) but also to the fact that incumbents who forecast sufficiently poor vote shares for their party, relative to their opportunity costs, withdraw from the race. Our findings also showed that the contribution of vote forecasting to the incumbency advantage as usually measured increased in the 1960s.

In this chapter, we seek to explain why incumbents' exits might have become more reliable signals that their party would fare poorly in the ensuing open-seat election. We note that the reapportionment revolution introduced unavoidable redistricting after every decennial census that candidates could more easily anticipate. This, in turn, meant that the next redistricting increasingly provided a focal point in the entry game between strong would-be challengers and sitting incumbents.

HOW ANTICIPATIONS OF REDISTRICTING HELP COORDINATE ENTRY

The Supreme Court's decision in *Wesberry v. Sanders* should have abruptly changed politicians' expectations regarding the frequency and inevitability of redistricting. Prior to *Wesberry*, redistrictings were virtually certain only in states that lost seats in the decennial reapportionment. In the other states, those that either held even or gained in the reapportionment, district lines were often preserved. After *Wesberry*, in contrast, everyone knew that redistrictings would occur at least once every 10 years. Moreover, virtually every district would be affected because population shifts over the decade would leave almost no districts close enough to the new statewide average to satisfy the court's equal-population mandate.

At an aggregate level, the size of the change in political expectations should have been quite substantial. In 1952 and 1962, only 41% and 50% of all congressional districts were redrawn. In contrast, roughly 98% of all districts were redrawn in 1972, 1982, and 1992. Thus, the probability that a district would be redrawn after a federal census *doubled* from before the reapportionment revolution (.46) to afterward (.98).

This doubling in the scope of the typical postcensus redistricting provided a stronger focal point in the competition between incumbents and strong challengers. Consider a strong challenger and an incumbent in a district in 1970, 1980, or 1990. Both know that, two years hence, the state will likely redraw the district in which they currently sit. Will the challenger enter? Will the incumbent exit?

If the challenger enters and wins, his investment will immediately be at risk: the district might be redrawn in a way that makes it very difficult to defend. On the other hand, if the challenger waits, he can see if the redistricting brings good news and enter (or not) after the uncertainty of the redistricting has been resolved. If he does wait, get a favorable redistricting, enter, and win, his investment can be secure against redistricting shocks for up to 10 years.[1] Since it is common knowledge that the challenger's incentives to enter just before a redistricting are reduced, the incumbent is more likely to seek reelection and the strong challenger to stay out.[2]

Now consider the race just after a redistricting. The uncertainty about how the district will be redrawn has ended. Hence, the new normal vote in the district is (better, if not perfectly) known. Moreover, the time to the next redistricting shock is maximal. If the strong challenger thought that national tides would be constant across the coming decade, then he would either enter now or never. In the real world, of course, there is the possibility of waiting for a particularly large national tide or a scandal. Nonetheless, the natural investment period in a congressional

---

[1] We say "can" because states can redraw their district lines more than once in a decade if they so choose.

[2] For an explanation of this claim, see the Appendix.

district is, especially after *Wesberry*, 10 years. So, the natural or focal point of entry, ceteris paribus, is just after a redistricting.[3]

RESULTS

To test whether the anticipation of redistricting had the postulated effects, both before and after *Wesberry*, we conduct three statistical analyses that focus on strategic entry. In one analysis, the dependent variable is whether the incumbent candidate voluntarily chose not to seek reelection. In the second analysis, the dependent variable is whether the challenging party's candidate had held previous elective office. In the final analysis, the dependent variable is whether the challenging party's candidate had held previous elective office *and* the incumbent candidate voluntarily exited.

As explained in the previous chapter, the incumbent's and strong challenger's entry decisions should be highly interrelated. Thus, from an econometric standpoint, the correct procedure would be to estimate each entry equation as part of a system of simultaneous equations. Lacking the instruments that would be necessary to identify such a system, we estimate "reduced forms" of the entry equations here. We believe that plausible inferences can be made concerning how the redistricting cycle affects entry decisions on the basis of these analyses.

As in our previous analyses, we exclude the South. Southern politicians should also have been anticipating the next redistricting but, as we noted in Chapter 1, the redistricting process in the South differed significantly from that in the North. Thus, it is not surprising that our analyses reveal some substantial differences between the regions in how redistricting conditions entry and exit (noted subsequently).

---

[3] The story just sketched is complicated by the distribution of strong challengers: some districts have none, some have one, others may have more than one. Another complication concerns the distribution of opportunity costs for those strong challengers who do exist. Family considerations, the expected value of the state or local office currently held, and other factors may affect how costly it will be for a given strong challenger actually to enter the race at a given time. There is no reason to expect family-related opportunity costs to correlate with the redistricting cycle, so presumably their impact is chiefly to add white noise to the data. Similarly, opportunity costs related to local or statewide office should be unrelated to the redistricting cycle. Strong challengers whose current office is in the state legislature, however, may face their own redistricting shocks at the state level. Their opportunity costs may decline as the next congressional redistricting approaches, since the continuation value of their own seat is depressed by the looming redistricting.

The Probability of Voluntary Exit by an Incumbent

In our analysis of voluntary exit, the independent variable of primary interest is a dummy variable, equal to 1 for the first election after a state redraws its district lines, 0 otherwise. We expect this variable to have a positive coefficient: voluntary exits should be more likely just after a redistricting. (We also examine the effect of each individual district being redrawn or not.)

We control for the incumbent party's normal vote in each district (by including the incumbent party's vote share in the previous election and whether or not it ran an incumbent).[4] Additionally, we allow a separate intercept term for each party in each year. Finally, we control for the number of terms the incumbent has served and for the number of districts in the incumbent's state. The previous literature has found that incumbents are more likely to exit voluntarily as the number of terms they have served increases and as the number of districts in their state declines.

To assess the differences before and after the reapportionment revolution, we ran the analysis separately for the prerevolutionary (1948–1964) and postrevolutionary (1966–1998) periods. As can be seen in Table 10.1, before *Wesberry* voluntary exit was unaffected by whether the state redistricted. After *Wesberry*, in contrast, voluntary exit was significantly more likely in the first election after a redistricting.

Our results are similar if we include the South. They are also similar if we exclude all districts that were redrawn immediately before the election in question. Finally, if we include all districts and add a variable indicating whether the focal district was redrawn, neither the state-level redistricting nor the district-level redistricting variables are significant. This is not surprising, given that whether a particular district was redrawn and whether at least one of the districts in the state was redrawn are highly collinear. In any event, we believe that the statelevel redistricting variable is the theoretically appropriate one because our argument focuses on politicians' ability to foresee

---

[4] If a district was freshly redrawn, we identify the control variables by the following rules. First, if there is an incumbent running for reelection, we assume that the appropriate control variables come from this incumbent's previous district. Second, if there is no incumbent running for reelection, it is sometimes possible to identify the previous district on other grounds. Where this has been done in Gary Jacobson's dataset, we use that information. Otherwise, the control variables are missing and the observation is dropped from the analysis.

Table 10.1. *Voluntary Exits by Nonsouthern Incumbents, 1946–1998*

Independent Variables	Estimated Coefficients	
	1948–1964	1966–1998
Lagged Incumbent Vote	−0.022**	−0.013**
	(0.006)	(0.003)
Lagged Incumbency Status	0.123	0.167**
	(0.075)	(0.066)
Log of number of terms served by incumbent	0.140**	0.308**
	(0.053)	(0.041)
Log of number of districts in state	−0.093**	−0.176**
	(0.039)	(0.029)
State Redrawn	−0.185	0.313**
	(.131)	(.102)
N	3052	4993
Log Likelihood	−759	−1310

Notes: The method of analysis was probit. Standard errors are reported in parentheses below the estimates. Double asterisks indicate that the coefficient is statistically discernible from zero at the .05 level or better in a two-tailed test. Estimates for the year and year-party dummies have been excluded from the table. Complete estimates are available upon request.

redistricting events, and it is easier to predict whether a given state will redraw than whether that redistricting will affect a particular district in the state.

The Probability of Entry by a Strong Challenger

In our analysis of entry by strong challengers, the independent variable of primary interest is again an indicator for the first election after a redistricting. We again expect this variable to have a positive coefficient: strong challengers should be more likely to enter just after a redistricting. Our control variables are identical to those we used in the analysis of voluntary withdrawal by incumbents, except that we omit the variable tapping the number of terms served by the incumbent (which is insignificant if included and allows us to extend the analysis to 1996–1998 if excluded).

We ran the analysis separately for the prerevolutionary (1948–1964) and postrevolutionary (1966–1998) periods. Our results, displayed in

Table 10.2. *Entry by Nonsouthern Challengers Who Had Previously Won Elective Office, 1946–1998*

Independent Variables	Estimated Coefficients	
	1946–1964	1966–1998
Lagged Incumbent Vote	−0.051**	−0.036**
	(0.004)	(0.003)
Lagged Incumbency Status	−0.181**	−0.092**
	(0.043)	(0.037)
Log of number of districts in state	−0.217**	−0.231**
	(0.029)	(0.022)
State Redrawn	0.070	0.184**
	(.094)	(.074)
N	2979	4744
Log Likelihood	−1590	−2470

Notes: The method of analysis was probit. Standard errors are reported in parentheses below the estimates. Double asterisks indicate that the coefficient is statistically discernible from zero at the .05 level or better in a two-tailed test. Estimates for the year and year-party dummies have been excluded from the table. Complete estimates are available upon request.

Table 10.2, echo those presented earlier.[5] After *Wesberry* but not before, strong challengers were significantly more likely to enter in the first election after a redistricting. This finding is again robust when including the South, excluding districts that were redrawn immediately before the election in question, or adding a variable to indicate redrawn districts.

Push-Outs

Our final analysis examines what we call *push-outs* – events in which a strong challenger enters and an incumbent voluntarily exits. One way to view push-outs is that the incumbent decides, for reasons unrelated to the strong challenger's intentions, to exit, after which the strong challenger enters. Another way to view them is that the strong challenger makes clear his intention to enter, thereby lowering the incumbent's estimate of her chances of reelection and helping to "push" her out.

[5] The number of observations in the two tables differ because we have missing data on the quality of the challenging party's candidate in some cases.

The control variables in our analysis of push-outs are the same as those we used in analyzing voluntary exits. There are two points to make about our results (not reported but available on request). First, they jibe with those given earlier. Before *Wesberry*, the probability of a push-out outside the South is unrelated to redistricting. After *Wesberry*, nonsouthern push-outs are significantly more likely in the election just after a state redistricts.

Second, there are some interesting differences between the parties and the regions. In preliminary analyses, the story for the post-*Wesberry* period is as follows. The probability of a Democratic incumbent being pushed out is never significantly related to redistricting in either the southern or nonsouthern portions of the country. In contrast, the probability of a Republican incumbent being pushed out is significantly *increased* by a nonsouthern redistricting but significantly *decreased* by a southern redistricting.

The regional differences in how redistrictings affected push-outs in Republican districts presumably reflect the divergent directions of political change in the two areas. In the South, the Republicans grew from a hopeless minority in the 1960s to a new majority in the 1990s. Each redistricting brought new opportunities for them. Although they did not begin to control southern state legislatures until late in the period of study, they could hope that the constraints of dealing with Republican governors and the Voting Rights Act would force the Democrats into increasingly less profitable gerrymanders. In Alabama, for example, the redistricting plan adopted in 1992 was proposed by the Republicans and ordered into effect by a federal court. Thus, the Democrats' continuing strong majorities in both houses of the state legislature did little to help them.

We believe that redistrictings in the South were viewed by Democrats in general, and by strong Democratic challengers in particular, as no-win situations. In any event, strong Democratic challengers were *less* likely to enter right after a redistricting in the South, whereas they were *more* likely to do so outside the South. Thus, the probability of a Republican incumbent being pushed out was strongly depressed in the immediate aftermath of a southern redistricting, whereas it was increased in the aftermath of a nonsouthern redistricting.

A full exploration of this southern finding is beyond the scope of this book. We note it here for its intrinsic interest and as an illustration that our decision to exclude the South (almost) throughout the book has an empirical as well as a theoretical basis.

Related Work

The notion that candidates consider the possibility and proximity of redistricting when they decide to enter or exit congressional races is a natural one. Indeed, the idea is mentioned in standard texts on congressional elections (Herrnson 1995; Jacobson 1997). And if one simply plots the aggregate number of competitive races (as judged by the Congressional Quarterly) in each year, one finds a substantial downward trend in each reapportionment decade. There were roughly half as many competitive districts in 1990 as there had been in 1982 and, again, roughly half as many competitive districts in 2000 as there had been in 1992 (see Jacobson 2001).

So far as we know, the only other systematic statistical investigation of entry decisions at the district level is the unpublished study of Larson, Globetti, and Hetherington (2000). These authors, in an investigation of House elections from 1990 to 1998, find that there is a generally downward trend in incumbent retirements and strong challenger entries as the redistricting cycle progresses from the first election after one redistricting to the last election before the next. As their specification and control variables are considerably different from ours, yet their results are comparable, their study lends further support to the idea that the redistricting cycle has had strong effects on entry and exit after the reapportionment revolution. As their study does not include any pre-*Wesberry* elections, however, they do not provide additional evidence concerning whether the cycle's impact on entry and exit strengthened after the reapportionment decisions.[6]

CONCLUSION

Strong candidates have an incentive to avoid competing against other strong candidates. If a would-be challenger for a House seat can wait

---

[6] Other studies investigate whether the *extent* of redistricting affects retirement decisions in the first election after the redistricting. See, e.g., Alford, Teeters, Wald, and Wilson (1994) and Theriault (1998), both of which find that retirement is more likely as the extent to which the incumbent's district was revised increases. Another study that bears on our findings is that of Bauer and Hibbing (1989). They find that, after 1974, almost all incumbents who lose "do so because of adverse redistricting or a major, personal scandal" (p. 262). Thus, it is not just entry decisions – upon which we have focused – that seem to follow the redistricting cycle; actual outcomes do also.

two years and compete for an open seat against a weaker competitor, he may prefer to wait for the incumbent to withdraw. If a current incumbent believes that a strong challenger has credibly committed to entering in two years, she has another reason to pursue other options.

In Chapter 9, we noted that strong challengers and incumbents in the U.S. House became observably better at coordinating their entries after the Supreme Court's reapportionment decisions. In this chapter, we have sought to explain why they became better. Our explanation has two steps: first, redistricting provides a focal point for the congressional entry game; second, the Supreme Court's decisions made the redistricting focal point easier to anticipate and rely on, hence improving strong candidates' ability to avoid competing against each other.

Before *Wesberry*, redistricting was not a certainty. A randomly chosen district had about a 50–50 chance of being redrawn in 1952, for example. After *Wesberry*, politicians knew that virtually all districts would be redrawn at least every 10 years. Our empirical results show that, since *Wesberry*, incumbents have been more likely to exit and strong challengers have been more likely to enter just after a redistricting (controlling for the normal vote in each district, the number of terms served by the incumbent, the number of districts in the state, and year effects).

The increased utility of redistricting as a focal point in congressional entry led not just to the entry/exit pattern just noted but also, we believe, to a subtler effect in the years surrounding redistricting. In particular, if one finds a push-out – with the incumbent voluntarily exiting and a strong challenger entering – in the years before or after a redistricting, the expectation is that this event was motivated by an even stronger signal about these two candidates' chances than would be needed in a redistricting year. Push-outs in nonredistricting years should, ceteris paribus, have been even worse news for the incumbent party (than they had been before the introduction of more regular redistricting). Thus, the correlation between voluntary exits by incumbents and vote losses by the incumbent party – that is to say, the incumbency advantage as usually measured – should have increased.

We are not arguing that the redistricting focal point provides the only route by which the reapportionment revolution affected electoral coordination (see Chapter 12). However, we are arguing that it provides one such route and that it had a substantial effect. Thus, the incumbency advantage (as traditionally measured) increased partly as a distal consequence of the Supreme Court's landmark decisions in *Baker v. Carr* and *Wesberry v. Sanders*.

Appendix: Some Thoughts on Entry in
Congressional Elections

In this appendix, we briefly elaborate on the claim made in the text that a decline in the expected value of winning a seat would lower the frequency of exit by incumbents and entry by strong challengers. We assume that the incumbent usually moves first, deciding to seek reelection or not, with the strong challenger reacting to that decision. If the strong challenger enters (and the incumbent has already), then the incumbent's probability of victory is p_{lo} and the cost is c_{hi} (for both candidates). The strong challenger enters (after the incumbent has) only if $(1 - p_{lo})V + p_{lo}b - c_{hi} > b$, where V is the expected value of the seat and b is the *reservation wage* (see Chapter 11 for a fuller exposition of this condition – derived from a standard decision-theoretic entry model). In the last election before a redistricting, V is lower for both the incumbent and the strong challenger (because the redistricting may make the seat untenable for whoever wins the election). Indeed, we assume that V is often low enough so that neither the incumbent nor the strong challenger would wish to enter if they knew the other was going to do so. If the players moved simultaneously, the result would be a game of Chicken. As the incumbent can typically move first, she enters knowing the strong challenger will then stay out.

This analysis generates the result stated in the text: voluntary exits and strong challenges are less likely just before a redistricting. However, the key to the result is our assumption that the incumbent moves first. Were the sequence of moves reversed (challenger first, then incumbent), a lowering of V would increase, not decrease, voluntary exits and strong challenges.

It is beyond the scope of our current project to explore fully how incumbents (or strong challengers) can credibly commit to enter the next race. However, we can state that we believe this is a key consideration and note that it casts a new light on many topics. For example, once the Federal Election Commission began requiring candidates to file reports on their contributions and expenditures, a commitment mechanism was created. Incumbents could credibly signal their intent by never closing their accounts, building large war chests, and the like. Once the law changed and incumbents could no longer cash out their campaign funds, the credibility of war chests should only have been enhanced.

I I

Redistricting, the Probability of Securing a Majority, and Entry

I'm [not running for reelection]. It reflects a lack of confidence on my part that we'll be a majority party in the House any time soon.

Rod Chandler (R-Washington) (quoted in Ansolabehere and Gerber 1997)

In Chapter 8, we showed that the incumbency advantage (as measured by the standard methodology) tended to be larger for Republicans than for Democrats after the mid-1960s. In this chapter, we seek to explain this and other party differences.

In outline, our argument is as follows. First, the abrupt disappearance of pro-Republican bias in the translation of congressional votes into congressional seats (outside the South) led to an abrupt structural decline in the short- and medium-term probability that the Republicans would be able to secure a majority in the U.S. House of Representatives. This decline in the Republicans' chances of securing a majority raised the expected value of a House seat for Democrats but depressed it for Republicans, leading to a syndrome of entry and selection effects that, among other things, explain the party differences uncovered in Chapter 8.

The rest of the chapter proceeds as follows. The first section outlines a simple model of a candidate's decision to enter a House race. We then use that model to explain why candidates of the two parties should have had different valuations of a House seat and how the *valuation gap* evolved over the post-World War II era. The key variable in this discussion is the probability that each party would secure a majority in the House. The third section explains the consequences that should have followed as the valuation gap rose and fell. We then test these predictions, discuss our findings, and conclude.

THE DECISION TO ENTER

Consider a candidate deciding whether to enter a race for a House seat. To model this decision, we follow the standard approach in the literature on political ambition and rational entry (e.g., Schlesinger 1966; Black 1972; Rohde 1979). Although ultimately it would be useful to construct a full game-theoretic model of entry in congressional elections, here we confine ourselves to the decision-theoretic building blocks that a game model might employ.

At the time of the decision, the potential candidate knows p, the probability of winning should she enter; V, the value of winning a House seat; and c, the cost that will have to be paid during the election in order to obtain the probability p.[1] The potential candidate also knows the value of her best opportunity, other than entering the House race, which we denote by b. This best alternative opportunity could be running for another office (also characterized by a probability, a value, and a cost), taking employment in the private sector, or even retiring. We assume that, if the candidate seeks election to the House but fails, then she either retires or takes a job in the private sector. We denote the value of this fallback option by r. Note that $b \geq r$, with equality in case the fallback is also the best outside option.

The candidate enters if the expected value of doing so exceeds the value of the best alternative opportunity, that is, if $pV + (1 - p)r - c > b$. Three theoretical conclusions about how entry responds to changes in the value of a House seat (V) follow straightforwardly from this inequality if one holds all else constant. First, a potential candidate is more likely to enter in pursuit of a more highly valued seat (entry is more likely as V increases). Second, a candidate will accept tougher odds in pursuit of a more valued seat (the larger is V, the smaller is the minimum probability that can induce the candidate to enter).[2] Third, a potential

---

[1] It is of course quite unlikely that a politician deciding to enter in the real world will have a point estimate of her election costs and the resultant probability this will buy her. But more realism is purchased only at the cost of more complex notation and does not yield any new insight, at least for present purposes.

[2] To clarify the second claim, let $p^* = (b - r + c)/(V - b)$ and note that the candidate will enter if $p > p^*$, stay out if $p < p^*$, and be indifferent between the two courses of action if $p = p^*$. The value p^* is the minimum probability that can induce entry. (The formulation "minimum probability that *can* induce entry" is shorthand for "minimum probability of victory that induces a positive probability of entry." We assume that, when $p = p^*$, the candidate has some chance of entering. Alternatively, p^* is the infimum of the set of probabilities that induce entry with certainty.) As V increases, the value p^* declines – all else constant.

candidate will forgo more attractive outside options in pursuit of a more valued seat (the larger is V, the larger is the maximum opportunity cost that the candidate will bear and still enter).[3,4]

THE EXPECTED VALUE OF A HOUSE SEAT

A key parameter in the decision to enter is V, the value of a House seat. It is important to note that this value, judged at the time politicians decide to enter or not, depends on the probability that the potential candidate's party will secure a majority of seats in the House. If one accepts the argument made by Cox and McCubbins (1993, in press), the majority party's members have always enjoyed better procedural powers than the minority party's members, making majority seats distinctly more valuable than minority seats. The *expected value* of a House seat to a candidate thus depends on the probability that the candidate's party will secure a majority.[5]

To clarify this last point, we can introduce some simple formulas. Let M be the value of a House seat if the member's party holds a majority, m be the value of a House seat if the member's party is in the minority,

---

[3] To clarify the third claim, let $b^* = p(V - r) + r - c$ and note that the candidate will enter if $b < b^*$, stay out if $b > b^*$, and be indifferent between the two courses of action if $b = b^*$. Thus, b^* is the largest opportunity cost that the candidate will bear and still enter (with positive probability). As V increases, the value b^* increases – all else constant.

[4] It is important to note the theoretical limitations of these conclusions. One might plausibly take the values V, b, and r as exogenous to the entry decisions made in a particular year. However, the other factors in the entry decisions – the cost c and the probability p – are endogenous. Thus, when V increases, we cannot imagine that all of the response to this change occurs in just one of the variables.

[5] Another study that emphasizes the importance of the probability of majority status is Ansolabehere and Gerber (1997). Although our argument shares many steps with theirs, key steps are different and our substantive conclusion is in some respects opposite to theirs. They assume that the increased incumbency advantage, as measured by standard methods, reflected a real resource advantage of some sort and take this as the premise on which the rest of their argument is based. They further assume that the advantage was uniform across the parties. We, in contrast, view the incumbency advantage, as previously measured, as mostly a product of strategic entry and consequent selection bias. Moreover, we find that the incumbency advantage varied substantially between the parties. Thus, while Ansolabehere and Gerber conclude that "a higher incumbency advantage led to a lower retirement rate [especially for the majority]" (p. 171), we essentially reverse the causal direction: differential retirement rates (and incentives) between the parties, produced by their differing chances of majority status, generated entry and selection phenomena that produced a higher apparent incumbency advantage.

and P be the probability that the Democrats will secure a majority. In this notation, the expected value of a House seat to a Democrat is $V_{dem} = PM + (1 - P)m$, while the expected value of a seat to a Republican is $V_{rep} = (1 - P)M + Pm$. Thus, the gap between the parties – how much more valuable a seat is to a typical Democrat than to a typical Republican – is $V_{dem} - V_{rep} = (2P - 1)(M - m)$. The partisan gap increases as (1) the probability that the Democrats will win a majority, P, increases (assuming $P > .5$) and (2) the difference in the value between holding a majority seat and a minority seat, $M - m$, increases (assuming $M > m$).

The Reapportionment Revolution and the Probability of a Democratic Majority

In this subsection, we consider how the reapportionment revolution affected the valuation gap. There is no reason to expect that it would have affected how much more valuable a majority seat was than a minority seat $(M - m)$. But there is reason to expect that 1960s redistrictings affected the probability of a Democratic majority (P). The abrupt redistricting-induced eradication of pro-Republican bias outside the South meant that the Republicans' expected number of seats, for any given vote, dropped by about 20. By a crude calculation, this reduction in expected seats would have reduced the Republicans' chances of attaining a majority by 11 percentage points.[6] Moreover, the effects were long-lasting, given that redistricting after the 1970 and 1980 censuses ended in a partisan draw. Thus, we expect that the reapportionment revolution widened the valuation gap more or less permanently (at least until the 1992 redistrictings).

We are not arguing that the reapportionment revolution was the only factor affecting Democratic fortunes. But we do view it as the most important change in their fortunes with a clearly structural underpinning. To make the distinction between long-term or structural changes and short-term nonstructural changes, consider some of the elections

---

[6] Over the period 1946–1964, the Republicans averaged 189 seats, with a standard deviation of 32. Assuming that their seat share was normally distributed, the probability of winning a majority was .17, which implies 1.7 wins over the 10 elections in 1946–1964 (as compared with their actual record of 2 wins). A permanent decrease in the mean number of seats they win, from 189 to 169, combined with a continuation of the same standard deviation, would reduce their probability of winning a majority to .06.

traditionally viewed as causing particularly large changes in party fortune: those of 1958, 1974, 1980, and 1994.

From 1946 to 1956, the Republicans averaged 207 seats in the House, attaining a majority in two out of six elections. Plausibly, the average chance of a Republican majority in this period was relatively high: one-third on a simple frequency count.

In 1958, the Republicans suffered an enormous midterm setback, falling to 153 seats. The conventional wisdom regarding their loss is simply that there was a very severe recession in 1958 and the Republicans, as the party of the president (Eisenhower), suffered the consequences, losing votes and seats. Looking simply at a graph of the Republicans' seats over time, one might be tempted to think that 1958 represents a structural break of some sort, as the next three elections give them only 174, 176, and 140 seats, well below their 1946–1956 average of 207.

However, none of these elections are outliers in the standard predictive models of congressional votes and seats. Moreover, the usual story that goes along with them has to do with presidential politics and the economy.

Here's the story. The Republicans gain back 21 seats in 1960, leaving them at the low end of their previous distribution. They do not gain more because the Democrats take the presidency, with John F. Kennedy defeating Richard M. Nixon. The Republicans gain back a further two seats in 1962, an anemic showing explained by the Democrats' good fortune to preside over one of the most robust midterm economies of the postwar era. Finally, the Republicans lose 36 seats in 1964, suffering the consequences of LBJ's crushing victory over Barry Goldwater. Thus, there does not appear to be a structural break in 1958, although certainly party fortunes shifted greatly.

Another disastrous but temporary setback for the Republicans occurred in the Watergate election of 1974. While this electoral drubbing certainly created a hole for the Republicans to climb out of, as had the midterm election of 1958, there is again no evidence of a structural break. That is, there was no reason to suspect that their seat share would be permanently lower.

An election that seems clearly to have raised Republicans' hopes of taking the House (and marking some sort of structural shift to the right in public opinion) was Reagan's victory in 1980. They won 192 seats. To find a higher total, one has to go back to 1956. Also, notions of a Reagan revolution fueled thoughts that the American public had permanently shifted in a conservative direction. The recession of 1982, however, produced a strong Democratic resurgence, and Republicans' hopes of a majority quickly faded.

It is not until 1994 that the Republicans finally did secure control of the House again. This election clearly produced a shift in prevailing estimates of the Republicans' chances of taking the House again (in 1996 and 1998). Indeed, during this period the Republicans, not the Democrats, had the better odds. Moreover, the shift in the Republicans' fortunes was arguably structural, a product of the 1992 redistricting and of a sort of balloon payment on the emergence of the Republican party in the South (Jacobson 1996).

All in all, we perceive only two elections that produce what could be called structural breaks in the probability of a Democratic majority in the House: 1966 and 1994. The other elections – those of 1958, 1974, and 1980 – all produced sizable but temporary vote and seat swings.

OPERATIONALIZING THE VALUATION GAP: THE DEMOCRATIC MARGIN OF CONTROL

The gap between the parties in the expected value of a House seat, given by the product $(2P - 1)(M - m)$, is our main independent variable in this chapter. In this section, we consider how to measure it.

Our approach is to focus on P, the probability of a Democratic majority in the House, and proxy this by the Democratic margin of control in the previous Congress. Although we believe it may be theoretically important to distinguish between short-term fluctuations in P and longer-term structural shifts, per the previous discussion, we cannot in practice quantify both separately. Thus we focus on a proxy for the probability of a Democratic majority resulting from the current election.

To explain our proxy measure, suppose that the Democrats control 60% of the House seats in a particular Congress. We say that their margin of control is 60% – 50% = 10%. More generally, the Democrats' margin of control is their percentage of seats less 50%. Thus, negative margins of control arise when the Republicans have a majority of seats, positive values arise when the Democrats have a majority, and a value of zero indicates a hypothetical result in which each party has exactly half the seats.

The larger the Democratic margin of control, the more likely it is that the Democrats will secure a majority at the next election. The Democratic margin of control thus provides a suitable proxy for the

Democrats' probability of securing a majority (P). However, the valuation gap is a function not just of P but also of the difference in values between a majority and a minority seat $(M - m)$. Unfortunately, we cannot measure $M - m$ on a year-by-year basis. We can, however, divide the postwar years into periods, with the boundaries defined by shifts in the majority's procedural advantage. Following this approach, we shall postulate a "low" value of $M - m$ in the period 1948–1964 (whose end corresponds roughly to the famous packing of the Rules Committee) and a "high" value thereafter (1966–1998).[7] Given that the valuation gap is the product of $2P - 1$ and $M - m$, *we expect that variations in the Democratic margin of control* (our proxy for P) *will have a more substantial impact in the later than in the earlier period.*

CONSEQUENCES OF THE VALUATION GAP BETWEEN THE PARTIES

In this section, we explain how variations in the valuation gap should have affected entry decisions, campaign expenditures, and votes. As explained earlier, our primary measure of the valuation gap is the probability that the Democrats will secure a majority, proxied by the Democratic margin of control.

The Minority Investment Disadvantage

Imagine a hypothetical increase in the probability of a Democratic majority (P) and consider what happens in Republican open seats as a consequence. The Republicans should have a harder time recruiting candidates with high opportunity costs (hence high campaigning ability) to defend their open seats, because potential defenders know that their chances of being in the majority are poorer. Relatedly, whoever does defend the seat should have a harder time raising money, because potential contributors know that his or her chances of being in the majority are poorer. These factors should combine to produce larger vote losses.

We shall label this syndrome of predicted difficulties – over recruitment, money, and votes – the *minority investment disadvantage*.[8] *Our*

---

[7] Our results are quite similar if the last year in the first period is 1962 rather than 1964. On the packing of the Rules Committee, see Cummings and Peabody (1969).

[8] Note that the minority investment disadvantage becomes acute in cases of one-party regimes, such as that in the American South described by Key (1949).

main hypothesis is that the minority's investment disadvantage worsens as its chance of securing a majority worsens.

As for the majority – the Democrats for most of the time – one expects the opposite pattern. As their probability of securing a majority improves, they should have an easier time finding well-qualified (high-opportunity-cost) candidates to defend their open seats, and these candidates should find it easier to raise money and win votes.

The Majority Retirement Slump

Increases in the probability of a Democratic majority affect not just recruitment, money-raising, and votes in open seats, per the minority investment disadvantage hypothesis, but also the meaning of incumbents' exit decisions. To see this, consider the signal about future vote prospects that is sent when an incumbent voluntarily exits. From the formula presented earlier, we know that an incumbent will exit voluntarily if and only if $p < p^* = (b - r + c)/(V - r)$. In other words, an incumbent will exit if and only if her probability of victory is too low. Thus, an incumbent's decision to exit suggests that her party's expected vote share at the next election, $E(v)$, must be bounded above: $E(v) < v^*$, say.

Suppose, however, that $p^* > 1$. In this case, an incumbent's exit says *nothing* about her probability of winning the next election. Exit implies $p < p^*$ but, since $p^* > 1$, $p < p^*$ is equivalent to $p \leq 1$, which merely says that the incumbent's probability of victory is bounded above by 100%. We already knew that. The incumbent's exit has revealed no new information. Evidently, her alternative opportunities are of such high value that she will exit even if guaranteed victory in the House race.

Extreme cases in which $p^* > 1$ may not be likely, but they illustrate an important general point. The higher is p^*, the less we can infer about the incumbent's vote forecast for her party from her decision to exit. The lower is p^*, in contrast, the more we can infer from exit – in particular, that the incumbent's vote forecast indicates a poor showing for her party. Put in terms of the retirement slump – that is, the expected vote loss a party suffers when one of its incumbents voluntarily exits – the point is that the retirement slump should increase the lower is p^*.

Which party has the higher cutoff probability, $p^* = (b - r + c)/(V - r)$? Assuming that $b - r + c$ will not differ systematically between the parties, the party with the higher cutoff probability is the one with the smaller value of $V - r$. In other words, the party whose members tend to value House seats less highly relative to their outside opportunities will have the higher cutoff probability.

From the literature on professionalization (e.g., Fiorina 1994, 1997) and recruitment (e.g., Ehrenhalt 1991), it appears that Republicans (especially nonincumbents) generally have not had lower opportunity costs (r). Due to their near-constant minority status, they also have had lower valuations (V) of House seats for most of the postwar era. Putting these observations together, we conclude that the Republicans should have had generally higher cutoff probabilities.

Now we can state the punch line: at least before 1994, *Republican incumbents' decisions to exit voluntarily should convey less information about the expected vote at the next election than do Democratic incumbents' decisions.* Because House seats are less valuable relative to their outside opportunities, Republican incumbents may exit even if they have a *good* chance of reelection. In contrast, if a Democratic incumbent voluntarily exits, it is more likely that a bad vote forecast prompted the decision.

In terms of the previous chapter's discussion, the parties' different seat valuations generate the following prediction: selection bias will be more severe in estimating the Democrats' incumbency advantage than in estimating the Republicans'. The Democrats' expected vote loss when one of their incumbents *voluntarily* exits will be substantially larger than their expected loss when an incumbent *involuntarily* exits. The analogous difference will be smaller for the Republicans.[9]

More generally, we expect the amount of selection bias in a party – measured by the difference between its expected vote losses in involun-

---

[9] Another hypothesis is that selection bias arising from strong challengers' decisions to enter works differently from that arising from incumbents' decisions to exit. If a strong Democratic candidate decides to enter, we know that $p > p_{dem}*$. This may not say much, however, if $p_{dem}*$ is quite low, as it is more likely to be for Democrats. In contrast, a strong Republican candidate's decision to enter is more informative, since $p_{rep}* > p_{dem}*$. Such a candidate's entry is a better signal that he had favorable vote forecasts. We thus expect the entry of a strong Republican to have a bigger selection bias component than the entry of a strong Democrat. This does not necessarily mean that the observed vote loss to the incumbent party will be larger, however, because Democratic candidates are likely to be of higher quality. Since V is higher for Democrats, the highest opportunity cost that a candidate will bear and still enter is higher for the Democrats. Assuming that quality and opportunity cost are highly correlated, a strong Democrat's entry signals less but produces more of a real impact. Meanwhile, a strong Republican's entry signals more but produces less impact. We cannot test the selection bias hypothesis because, unlike for incumbents, we cannot contrast voluntary and involuntary entries.

tarily and voluntarily open seats – to increase as the party's prospects of securing a majority improve. Better prospects of a majority raise the expected value of a seat, hence depressing p^*. When an incumbent does exit voluntarily, therefore, it is more likely to have been due to poor vote prospects.

We should note that our expectations for the period 1994–1998 are ambiguous. If the Republicans' outside opportunities in this period continued to exceed the Democrats' in value, then it is not clear which party's $V - b$ values were lower. Hence, it is not clear which party should have the greater amount of selection bias. What is clear, however, is that the Republicans' selection bias in 1994–1998 should be greater than it was before, while the Democrats' should be less.

Summary

We have stated four predictions regarding how the Democrats' probability of securing a majority of House seats, P, should affect entry, expenditures, votes, and selection bias. In a nutshell, for the years in which the Democrats held a majority, we predict that higher values of P should worsen the minority (i.e., Republican) investment disadvantage: it should be harder for the minority party to recruit well-qualified candidates to defend its open seats, those candidates should have a harder time raising money for their campaigns, and – as a result of the first two factors – the minority should suffer greater vote losses in its open seats. Moreover, higher values of P should also lessen the difference between the minority's expected vote loss in involuntarily and voluntarily open seats. The majority party, meanwhile, should react to increases in P in exactly the opposite fashion on all four scores.

In the next four sections, we survey evidence bearing on each of these four predictions. Throughout our discussion, we shall focus on the period during which the Democrats were the majority party. For the period 1994–1998, our discussion needs to be modified to account for the Republicans' takeover of the House.

EVIDENCE: DO VARIATIONS IN P AFFECT ENTRY DECISIONS?

Several studies in the literature provide evidence that politicians' estimates of their chances of being in the majority do affect their career decisions. Gilmour and Rothstein (1993) and Ansolabehere and Gerber

(1997) both assume that majority seats, are more valuable than minority seats, and both argue that this disparity in value, along with the Republicans' generally poor prospects of securing a majority, explain why Republicans were more likely to exit the House voluntarily from the mid-1950s to the early 1990s. In a study of voluntary retirement from 1938 to 1998, Snyder and Ting (2000) find that minority party members were more likely to retire, holding constant age, seniority, ideological position, and previous vote share. Schansberg (1994) shows that increases in the Democratic margin of control lead to statistically significant increases in the rate at which Republicans exit the House to seek higher office.

Finally, Hall and Van Houweling (1995) provide somewhat more nuanced evidence based on comparisons of retirement rates *within* the two parties. Within the majority party, they find that voluntary exit is less likely for leaders, committee chairs, and those likely to become chairs. Within the minority party, the analogous relationships do not hold: neither leaders nor ranking members nor those likely to become ranking members are any less likely to retire. These patterns make sense if being the ranking minority member of a committee does not confer much power but being the chair does. Hall and Van Houweling's work thus supports the notion that procedural power is monopolized by the majority party but also suggests that it is not at all evenly divided within the party.[10]

This brief survey suffices to show that there is general evidence that variations in P affect entry decisions for the reason suggested earlier: higher values of P mean that the Democrats' expected value of a seat is higher and the Republicans' lower, because the procedural advantage of the majority party is substantial. We cannot add to this general evidence much specific evidence that *minority entry in open seats* is affected. We have found that the probability of the Republicans' fielding an experienced defender (one who has previously won an election at some level) is depressed by increases in the Democratic margin of control – but the effect is not statistically significant. These results presumably reflect the small pool of minority open seats available for analysis but, in any event, they do not lend independent support to this part of the minority investment disadvantage hypothesis.

---

[10] They do not specifically consider whether the retirement-depressing effect of holding a chair or being in the majority leadership fluctuates with the Democrats' probability of retaining their majority.

EVIDENCE: DO VARIATIONS IN *P* AFFECT CAMPAIGN EXPENDITURES?

There is clear evidence that members of the majority party have an advantage in attracting contributions from access-oriented political action committees (PACs). When the Republicans gained a majority in the House in 1994, for example, their estimated gain in PAC contributions per member was $36,000 (Cox and Magar 1999). Another bit of evidence is the way that PACs respond to changes in a candidate's incumbency status (over the period 1978–1996). A candidate who runs as a nonincumbent, wins, and then runs again as an incumbent increases his or her campaign war chest by about $191,000 on average. However, "legislators who enter the majority party see their campaign funds grow by $133,000 more than legislators who enter the minority party" (Ansolabehere and Snyder 2000, p. 83).

No one has previously investigated whether variations in the probability of a Democratic majority have affected the *size* of the Democrats' fund-raising advantage. However, there is anecdotal evidence. For example, there was a reduction in PAC giving to Democrats in the aftermath of Reagan's victory in 1980, followed by a resurgence of such giving after the 1982 midterm elections reinstated a substantially larger Democratic majority (Jackson 1988).

To provide more systematic evidence, we considered how total expenditures (in constant dollars) respond to two different sorts of closeness (local and global) over the period during which standardized reports of campaign expenditures in House races are available (1974–1998).[11] The measure of local closeness, or how close the race in a particular district might be, is simply the incumbent party's vote percentage in the previous election. The measure of global closeness, or how close the contest for majority control of the House might be, is the absolute value of the Democratic margin of control. To control for the different levels of expenditure that might be expected in New York City as opposed to rural Louisiana, we include the lagged total expenditure in each district as a regressor. To control for the upward trend in campaign expenditures over time (even in constant dollars), we include a time trend variable.

It is well known that total expenditures vary with local closeness. Thus, it is not surprising to find that total expenditures decline by about

---

[11] Only races held in nonsouthern districts that were not redistricted are included in the analysis.

$16,500 for each additional percentage point increase in the incumbent party's previous vote percentage.

What has not been shown previously is that total expenditures also consistently decline as the fight for majority control in the House becomes less close. This suggests that the parties believe majority status is worth fighting for. To indicate the size of the effect, consider two districts, A and B, matched in terms of previous vote share and expenditures. In district A, the election is held in the context of a global dead heat (a 218–217 split in the previous Congress), while in district B the election is held in the context of a previous margin of control in Congress of 10% (or a 261–174 split). Our estimates indicate that expenditures in district A would be on average $58,000 greater than those in district B (a statistically significant boost).

In sum, it is clear that members of the majority party are better able to raise money, and it also appears that closer fights for majority status in the House boost total expenditures. At a general level, money and majority status are closely linked. We do not, however, have clear evidence that the minority party in the House has had special difficulties with money in its open seats. Given the paucity of open seats and the notorious difficulties in measuring the impact of expenditures on House election outcomes (cf. Jacobson 1980, 1990b; Krasno and Green 1988), this is not surprising.

EVIDENCE: DO VARIATIONS IN P AFFECT HOW MUCH THE INCUMBENT PARTY LOSES IN ITS OPEN SEATS?

In this section, we examine how open seat losses for the two parties vary as a function of the Democratic margin of control in the previous Congress. A higher margin of control should increase the Democrats' probability of securing a majority. This, in turn, should raise the typical Republican's value of p^* – the minimum probability of victory sufficient to induce entry – but lower the typical Democrat's.

An increase in the cutoff probability p^* for Republicans means two things. First, the Republicans should have a tougher time finding qualified defenders of the districts their incumbents have vacated (voluntarily or involuntarily). Only candidates with relatively small opportunity costs will choose to enter. To the extent that opportunity costs and quality are correlated, the expected vote loss in both sorts of open seat should increase. Second, voluntary exits by Republican incumbents signal less in the way of poor vote forecasts, so that the gap in vote losses between the Republicans' voluntarily and involuntarily open seats should shrink.

A decrease in the cutoff probability for Democrats should produce opposite patterns. First, the Democrats should have an easier time finding qualified defenders of the districts their incumbents have vacated (voluntarily or involuntarily). Even candidates with relatively high opportunity costs will choose to enter. To the extent that opportunity costs and quality are correlated, the expected vote loss in both sorts of open seat should decrease. Second, voluntary exits by Democratic incumbents signal more in the way of poor vote forecasts, so that the gap in vote losses between the Democrats' voluntarily and involuntarily open seats should grow.

How Open-Seat Losses Vary with the Democratic Margin of Control

We have stated clearly different expectations regarding how the two parties' electoral fates should vary with the Democratic margin of control. In order to test the first of these expectations – that Republican open seat losses worsen as the Democratic margin of control increases, while Democratic open seat losses improve – we modify one of our previous analyses. The dependent variable is the incumbent party's vote share in a particular district. The control variables include the lagged vote share of the incumbent party in that district, whether there was an incumbent running in the previous election (and of which party), whether an experienced challenger contests the seat, and the nationwide swing to the incumbent party (i.e., the party that holds that particular seat, not the party that holds the presidency). The variables of primary interest are *DMC* (the Democratic margin of control in the previous Congress), *Open* (a dummy variable indicating open seats), and *DMC*Open*. If our hypothesis is correct, then the interaction term will have a negative coefficient for the Republicans (indicating that their open seat losses worsen as the Democratic margin of control in Congress increases) but a positive coefficient for the Democrats (indicating that their open seat losses decrease as their margin of control increases). The effect should be especially pronounced after 1965.

We run separate regressions for each party in each of the two time periods (before and after 1965). For the Republicans, we find that they lose more in their open seats, as the Democratic margin of control increases, in both periods (see Table 11.1). The effect is smaller and

Table 11.1. *Republican Vote Losses in Their Open Seats, as a Function of the Democratic Margin of Control in Congress, 1946–1998*

Independent Variables	Estimated Coefficients	
	1946–1964	1966–1998
Lagged Incumbent Vote	0.644**	0.550**
	(0.023)	(0.021)
Lagged Incumbency Status	−0.026	−1.219**
	(0.223)	(0.286)
Swing to Incumbent Party	0.911**	1.054**
	(0.047)	(0.055)
Challenger Quality	−2.098**	−3.909**
	(0.277)	(0.337)
Open	−2.292**	−4.279**
	(0.560)	(0.871)
Democratic Margin of Control	0.001	0.007
	(0.028)	(0.033)
Open × Democratic Margin of Control	−0.093	−0.465**
	(0.064)	(0.082)
N	1458	1911
R^2	0.54	0.51

Notes: Standard errors are reported in parenthesis below the estimate. Double asterisks indicate that the coefficient is statistically discernible from zero at the .05 level or better. Year effects were included but are not reported here. Complete estimates are available upon request.

statistically insignificant before 1965, larger and statistically significant afterward. The substantive impact of variations in the Democratic margin of control is large after 1965. The Republicans' expected open-seat loss was a mere 1.26% at the minimum margin of control (−6.5%) and statistically indistinguishable from zero. In contrast, their expected loss was 12.55% at the maximum margin of control (+17.8%).

The results for the Democrats (Table 11.2) are similar to those for the Republicans. Before *Wesberry*, the Democrats' open-seat losses (unexpectedly) worsen as their margin of control increases (the effect being significant at the .10 level). After *Wesberry*, their losses – in line with our expectations – decline as their margin of control increases (the effect being significant at the .05 level). The substantive impact of variations in the Democratic margin of control is, again, large. The Democrats' expected open-seat loss was 9.87% at their minimum margin

Table 11.2. *Democratic Vote Losses in Their Open Seats, as a Function of the Democratic Margin of Control in Congress, 1946–1998*

Independent Variables	Estimated Coefficients	
	1946–1964	1966–1998
Lagged Incumbent Vote	0.800**	0.739**
	(0.020)	(0.016)
Lagged Incumbency Status	0.299	−2.830**
	(0.278)	(0.297)
Swing to Incumbent Party	1.055**	0.946**
	(0.064)	(0.057)
Challenger Quality	−1.141**	−4.282**
	(0.436)	(0.371)
Open	−2.391**	−8.452**
	(0.858)	(0.955)
Democratic Margin of Control	−0.001	−0.065*
	(0.038)	(0.035)
Open × Democratic Margin of Control	−0.156*	0.217**
	(0.094)	(0.082)
N	1092	2333
R^2	0.70	0.59

Notes: Standard errors are reported in parentheses below the estimates. Double asterisks indicate that the coefficient is statistically discernible from zero at the .05 level or better in a two-tailed test. A single asterisk indicates significance at the .10 level. Year effects were included but are not reported here. Complete estimates are available upon request.

of control (−6.5%) but only 4.58% at their maximum margin of control (+17.8%).

How the Signal Sent by Voluntary Exit Varies with the Democratic Margin of Control

In this subsection, we investigate the second hypothesis given earlier, that the majority party should have a larger gap between its losses in voluntarily and involuntarily open seats – and that this gap should grow with the margin of control. The analysis is similar to that in the previous section, except that, instead of a single indicator for open seats (*Open*), we now include separate indicators for involuntarily open (*OpenI*) and voluntarily open (*OpenV*) seats. We also include two new interaction terms: *DMC*OpenV* and *DMC*OpenI*. In the case of the Republicans, we expect that $DMC*OpenV$ and $DMC*OpenI$ should both have negative coefficients (the Republicans should suffer greater losses in their open seats as DMC increases, because they have a tougher time recruiting good candidates to defend their seats). More to the point, we expect that the coefficient on $DMC*OpenI$ should be a larger negative than the coefficient on $DMC*OpenV$ (the gap between the Republicans' expected loss in the two categories of open seats should diminish as DMC increases, because Republican incumbents' decisions to exit are less and less informative signals as DMC increases). As for the Democrats, our expectations are the opposite of those stated for the Republicans.

Our expectations hold for both the early period (1948–1964) and the later period (1966–1998) but are stronger for the latter because the advantage of holding a majority rather than a minority seat $(M - m)$ should be greater then. We can report that the gap between a party's losses, in voluntarily and involuntarily open seats, is not statistically related to the Democratic margin of control prior to 1965. In what follows we present results only for the post-1965 period.

Our results are given in Table 11.3. The Republican results provide slight support for our predictions. As expected, the coefficients on the two interactive variables, $DMC*OpenV$ and $DMC*OpenI$, are both negative and significant: Republicans suffered larger losses in both kinds of open seat as the Democratic margin of control increased. More to the current point, the coefficient on $DMC*OpenI$ is a larger negative (−.50) than is that on $DMC*OpenV$ (−.46). Although this difference is not statistically significant, it does imply a reduction of the gap in expected losses between the two categories of open seat. At the high-water mark of Democratic dominance (a margin of control of 17.8), the Republicans could expect to lose only about 1.8 percentage points more in their voluntarily open than in their involuntarily open seats. In contrast, at the high-water mark of Republican power (a Democratic margin of control of −6.5), the Republicans could expect to lose 2.7 percentage points more in voluntarily open as opposed to involuntarily open seats. As the expected value of the seat increased, Republican incumbents' exit decisions became more informative about their party's likely performance at the next election.

The results for the Democrats provide stronger support for our expectations. The coefficients on $DMC*OpenV$ and $DMC*OpenI$ are both positive – Democrats suffered smaller and smaller losses in both kinds of open seat as their margin of control increased. Moreover, the coeffi-

Table 11.3. *Party Vote Losses in Their Open Seats, as a Function of the Democratic Margin of Control in Congress, 1966–1998*

Independent Variables	Estimated Coefficients	
	Republicans	Democrats
Lagged Incumbent Vote	0.549**	0.737**
	(0.021)	(0.016)
Lagged Incumbency Status	−1.198**	−2.774**
	(0.286)	(0.296)
Swing to Incumbent Party	1.054**	0.945**
	(0.055)	(0.056)
Challenger Quality	−3.900**	−4.192**
	(0.337)	(0.369)
Voluntarily Open	−4.555**	−8.627**
	(0.917)	(0.989)
Involuntarily Open	−2.089	−8.693**
	(2.537)	(3.112)
Democratic Margin of Control	0.007	−0.065*
	(0.033)	(0.035)
Voluntarily Open × Democratic Margin of Control	−0.458**	0.144*
	(0.085)	(0.085)
Involuntarily Open × Democratic Margin of Control	−0.496**	0.714**
	(0.248)	(0.261)
N	1911	2333
R^2	0.51	0.60

Notes: Standard errors are reported in parentheses below the estimates. Double asterisks indicate that the coefficient is statistically discernible from zero at the .05 level or better in a two-tailed test. Year effects were included but are not reported here. Complete estimates are available upon request.

cient on *DMC*OpenI* is a larger positive (.71) than is that on *DMC*OpenV* (.14). This difference is statistically significant at the .05 level. Moreover, it produces a fairly substantial predicted increase of the gap in expected losses between the two categories of open seat. At the high-water mark of Democratic dominance (a margin of control of 17.8), they could expect to lose about 10.1 percentage points more in their voluntarily open than in their involuntarily open seats (a statistically significant difference). In contrast, at the high-water mark of Republican power (a Democratic margin of control of −6.5), the Democrats could expect to lose 3.8 percentage points *less* in voluntarily as opposed to involuntarily open seats (a statistically insignificant difference). As the expected value of the seat increased, Democratic incumbents' exit decisions became more informative about their party's likely performance at the next election.

Discussion

Two additional features of our results are worth stressing. First, selection bias is more severe for the Democrats than for the Republicans. That is, Democrats tend to lose more in their voluntarily open seats than in their involuntarily open seats. This is especially evident after 1966 in years with large Democratic margins of control.

Second, the estimated incumbency advantage for the Democrats – measured by their expected vote loss in involuntarily open seats – is statistically insignificant in both periods (albeit substantively large in the second). In contrast, the Republicans' incumbency advantage is both substantively large and statistically significant in the second period. For Democratic margins of control of 0%, 3%, 6%, 9%, 12%, and 15%, the estimated Republican incumbency advantages (and associated t-tests) are 2.1 (0.8), 3.6 (1.8), 5.1 (3.3), 6.6 (4.7), 8.0 (4.9), and 9.5 (4.5). For all margins of control greater than about 3.3% (i.e., when the Democrats have more than 224 seats), the Republican incumbency advantage is statistically discernible from zero and substantively large.

It is worth stressing what we have just found. *The Democrats never have a statistically significant incumbency advantage by our measure, while the Republican incumbency advantage grows the fewer seats they have in the House.* These patterns are inconsistent with the notion that growing office resources or increasing use of incumbency as a voting cue can explain the increasing incumbency advantage.

THE INCUMBENCY ADVANTAGE IN OTHER LEGISLATURES

Might the emphasis placed here on the value of majority status be relevant in other legislatures? Consider the United Kingdom. Katz and King (1999) find that the largest incumbency advantage belongs to the party with the poorest chance of getting into government: the Liberals. It is hard to believe that Liberal members of the House of Commons get more resources than do Labour or Conservative members. More plausible is the notion that the Liberals suffer a substantial drop in the quality and perceived viability of their candidate when one of their incumbents withdraws.

CONCLUSION

In this chapter, we have explored how the reapportionment revolution produced a syndrome of differences between the two parties. The starting point of the argument is the observation that the eradication of pro-Republican bias (documented in Chapter 4) reduced the short- and medium-term probability that the Republicans would secure a majority in the House of Representatives. Two main conclusions follow from this premise. First, the Republicans' lowered chance of controlling the House made it harder to recruit good candidates to defend their open seats, harder to raise money in defending these seats, and thus harder to prevent substantial vote losses when incumbents departed the scene. Simply put, the minority faced an investment disadvantage because the expected value of the seat was lower to its members. Second, the Republicans' lowered chance of controlling the House also meant that Republican incumbents' decisions to exit voluntarily were less likely to reflect poor vote forecasts, while Democratic incumbents' exit decisions were more likely to reflect such forecasts.

Our argument is not that the reapportionment revolution's lessening of pro-Republican bias was the only event affecting the probability of a Democratic majority. Certainly there were many others. We merely assert that this was one of the key structural changes affecting congressional elections, one that should have affected forecasts of House control for the next generation.

The evidence for our main claims is not confined to contrasting the two parties before and after the reapportionment revolution. Our argument asserts that variations in the Democrats' probability of securing a majority should have affected a range of variables, with the parties responding in opposite fashions. Thus, our analytic strategy has been to measure variations in the probability – via the Democratic margin of control in the House – on an election-by-election basis, looking for the predicted patterns.

The Minority Investment Disadvantage

Our results provide strong support for the notion of a minority investment disadvantage, at least after 1966. The Republicans' open seat losses *increased* and the Democrats' open seat losses *decreased* as the Democratic margin of control increased. The most plausible explanation of this pattern is that the Republicans found it harder and harder to find good candidates and raise money as their prospects for a majority waned.

Selection Bias

We also find considerable support for the notion that selection bias is a direct function of each party's probability of securing a majority in the House. We stress four points in particular.

First, the amount by which a party's expected loss in voluntarily open seats exceeds its expected loss in involuntarily open seats – its *open seat gap* – increases as its chances of securing a majority improve. It appears that as the expected value of a seat increases (with improving chances of securing a majority), incumbents' exits are more and more likely to be prompted by poor vote forecasts.

Second, the Democrats – the party with the better chance of securing a majority for most of the postwar era – exhibit more selection bias than the Republicans. Thus, selection bias varies not only across time within each party as the chances of securing a majority fluctuate, but also across parties at any given time – again in accord with which party has the better chance of attaining a majority.

Third, in the only extended period in which the Republicans clearly have better or roughly equal chances of securing a majority, 1994–1998, they show a statistically significant selection bias for the only time in the entire postwar era. They lose on average 7.5 percentage points when one of their incumbents withdraws voluntarily versus only 2.7 percentage points following involuntary withdrawals. A difference of this size would arise by chance alone less than 6 times out of 100.[12]

Fourth, the probability that a strong Republican challenger will contest a Democratic open seat increases significantly if the seat was vacated voluntarily by the previous incumbent. This is consistent with the notion that the Democratic incumbent, with her high valuation of a House seat, was departing in part due to a poor vote forecast. The same forecast then helps bring the strong Republican challenger into the race. In contrast, the probability that a strong Democratic challenger will

[12] The Democrats remain competitive during the 1994–1998 period and continue to show a substantial gap in how much they lose in their voluntarily and involuntarily open seats. One would not necessarily expect the Republicans to show *more* selection bias than the Democrats, since the Republicans typically have higher opportunity costs – or so one might infer from the literature on professionalization.

contest a Republican open seat does not increase significantly if the seat was vacated voluntarily. This is consistent with the notion that the Republican incumbent, with a lower valuation of a House seat, was departing to pursue other opportunities rather than being scared off by a poor vote forecast. Accordingly, there is nothing to distinguish the voluntarily from the involuntarily open seats as far as attractiveness to strong Democratic challengers is concerned.

The Incumbency Advantage

If one measures the incumbency advantage by the expected loss suffered by a party when one of its incumbents involuntarily departs, *the Democrats never show a statistically significant incumbency advantage.* In contrast, the Republican incumbency advantage is significant after the reapportionment revolution. These findings are hard to reconcile with standard accounts of the incumbency advantage, which view the advantage as sourced either in the resources of office or the value of incumbency as a cue.

Even harder to reconcile with such accounts is our finding that a party's incumbency advantage, measured by the standard Gelman–King estimator, *decreases* as its probability of winning a House majority increases. For example, the Republican incumbency advantage is largest when the party is deepest in the hole in terms of winning a majority in the House and smallest when the party controls the House. Why should a party's incumbency advantage decline with the probability that it will control Congress if this advantage stems from the resources of office or the value of incumbency as a cue?

Both of these contrary findings can be explained naturally from our approach, as shown earlier. Thus, we believe that most of the phenomena that the previous literature has understood as an incumbency advantage strongly reflect strategic entry decisions, with perhaps little in the way of real advantage.

12

Reassessing the Incumbency Advantage

In this chapter, we review the line of argument we have pursued in this part of the book. First, we contrast our view of the increasing incumbency advantage and the vanishing marginals with previously dominant notions. Second, we argue that the question to ask is at least as much about improved electoral coordination as it is about any increase in the "real" incumbency advantage. Third, we review our explanation of why electoral coordination improved and briefly consider some possible alternatives. Fourth, we review our explanation of why the two parties' patterns of vote loss in open seats were so different, both across time and cross-sectionally. Fifth, we reconsider the normative stakes involved in the increasing incumbency advantage.

THE INCUMBENCY ADVANTAGE, THE VANISHING MARGINALS, AND DEMOCRATIC DOMINANCE OF THE HOUSE

The 1960s brought a remarkable complex of changes to House elections: a sudden increase in the incumbency advantage, a sudden decrease in the number of marginal districts, and a sudden eradication of pro-Republican bias outside the South. The dominant way of viewing these changes is still probably that suggested in the work of Erikson (1972) and Mayhew (1974). In (one reconstruction of) their view, the causal sequence was as follows. (1) The incumbency advantage in House elections – a vote premium that accrued to incumbents per se – increased.[1]

---

[1] We note that the incumbency advantage in Senate elections, estimated by a version of the standard Gelman–King estimator, does not show a sharp increase in or near the mid-1960s. Instead, the estimated advantage drifts upward at a shallow rate

(2) The incumbency advantage increased because one or more of the following events took place: (a) voters sharply dealigned from the parties during the turbulent 1960s, increasing the value of incumbency as a cue (Burnham 1974; Ferejohn 1977); (b) the staff and other resources of House members increased just as the expansion of the federal bureaucracy generated more opportunities to provide ombudsman services to constituents (Fiorina 1989); (c) the importance of money in congressional elections and incumbents' advantages in raising money increased sharply in the 1960s (an extension of the view offered by Ansolabehere and Snyder 2000). (3) The increased incumbency advantage led to a decrease in the proportion of marginal districts, and hence to a decrease in the swing ratio, or what we call *responsiveness*. (4) The permanently more sluggish response of congressional seat shares to congressional vote shares allowed the Democrats to retain their gains from the 1960s indefinitely. (5) The Democrats' good fortune to possess a majority of seats just when the incumbency advantage increased explains why pro-Republican bias disappeared.

Our work directly challenges points (1), (2), and (5) and bears on point (4) as well. Regarding point (1), by our estimates the real incumbency advantage has never been statistically discernible from zero for the Democrats. Hence, we deny the initial premise: there was no increase in the real incumbency advantage to lock in the Democrats' gains.[2]

Regarding point (2), our results are inconsistent with any theory that sees the incumbency advantage growing larger primarily because the resources of office grew. One resource of office is the proportion of the electorate prepared to use incumbency as a voting cue. Other resources include staff and opportunities to provided casework. Still another resource is the ability to perform services for PACs in exchange for campaign contributions.

The first of these resource-based explanations suffers a unique difficulty, indicated in the following question. If the dealignment of the electorate in the 1960s produced more voters willing to use such a cue, why has the realignment of the electorate since the 1970s (cf. Bartels 2000)

---

throughout the early postwar era until the late 1960s and then declines thereafter. (This characterization is based on unpublished figures and analyses performed by Gary King.)

[2] Another way to put this is that, given the simultaneity bias problem that we show to exist, there is no unbiased estimator of the real incumbency advantage that shows it to be statistically different from zero.

not produced fewer voters willing to use such a cue – and hence a decline in the incumbency advantage?

All three resource-based explanations share the following problems. First, there should be no difference in a party's losses in its voluntarily and involuntarily open seats, because the resources (whether the incumbency cue, the staff and casework opportunities, or the fund-raising advantages) are lost in either case. Yet we know there is such a difference (Chapter 9). Second, the majority party should not have a smaller incumbency advantage than the minority party, because majority-party members either have the same resource advantage (in the case of the incumbency cue or personal staff allocations) or a demonstrably larger resource advantage (in the case of committee staff allocations or the ability to raise PAC money). Yet we know that the minority party tends to have the larger measured incumbency advantage after the mid-1960s (Chapter 8). Third, the incumbency advantage should not vary with the size of the Democratic contingent in the House. Yet we know that it does (Chapter 11).

We have also addressed point (5) – the claim that the increasing incumbency advantage explains the disappearance of pro-Republican bias – in Chapter 4. Essentially, we argued that the argument fails on purely logical grounds.

Finally, consider the often-made claim that the increased incumbency advantage helped entrench the Democrats in power – a cousin of claim (4). In Chapter 8, we showed that standard estimators give the Republicans a larger incumbency advantage than the Democrats. In Chapter 9, we noted that our own estimator suggests that the Democrats have never had a statistically discernible incumbency advantage, whereas the Republicans have. But if the Republicans have the larger advantage, then how could the incumbency advantage entrench the Democrats in power?

In our view, the causal sequence was much different than that articulated earlier. We see two main causal pathways. First, the Supreme Court's reapportionment decisions led immediately to a wave of court-supervised redistricting actions in the 1960s. These actions tended to undo preexisting Republican gerrymanders and also, in states under divided control, to be more favorable to incumbents – by padding their districts with their own partisans. Thus, redistricting led both to the eradication of pro-Republican bias outside the South and to a reduction in responsiveness.

Second, the Court's decisions also strengthened the redistricting-induced entry cycle, so that strong challengers and incumbents became better at avoiding one another's company. A side effect of this strategic avoidance was that the presence of an incumbent became a better indicator of a high vote share for the incumbent party, while the presence of a strong challenger became a better indicator of a high vote share for the challenging party.

ASK NOT JUST WHY THE INCUMBENCY ADVANTAGE INCREASED; ASK ALSO WHY ELECTORAL COORDINATION IMPROVED

The question that has dominated studies of congressional elections for the past 30 years is why the incumbency advantage increased. Previous scholars have taken it as established that most of the increase was real. Accordingly, their theories have concerned real resources that incumbents possess and that may plausibly have become more plentiful or valuable over time – primarily the incumbency cue (Mayew 1974), personal staff able to do casework favors for constituents (Fiorina 1989), and personal and committee staff able to do legislative favors for PACs (Ansolabehere and Snyder 2000). Our emphasis, in contrast, has been on the reverse direction of causality. In explaining the correlation between the presence of an incumbent candidate and the incumbent party's vote share, we stress strategic exit – that is, the tendency for incumbents to retire in the face of poor vote prospects (which are then inherited by their replacements).

We believe that we have clearly established (in Chapter 9) that a substantial portion of the incumbency advantage as conventionally measured is due to strategic exit. Thus, we feel justified in saying that the striking changes in strategic exit and entry that emerged in the 1960s are at least as much a puzzle worthy of explanation as is the increase in the real incumbency advantage. Put another way, an important puzzle to explain is the relatively sudden improvement in electoral coordination between incumbents and strong challengers.

WHY DID ELECTORAL COORDINATION IMPROVE?

Our Explanation

Much of the third part of the book has explored the improvement in electoral coordination just noted. In this section, we first review our ideas and the evidence for them, and then consider (more speculatively) some possible alternatives.

Our primary explanation of the improvement in electoral coordination – that is, strong challengers and incumbents getting better at avoiding one another – is that the reapportionment decisions increased the frequency and predictability of redistricting, thus strengthening the redistricting-induced cycle of entry/exit. The evidence in favor of this view starts with the sheer size of the macro change: the frequency of postcensus redistricting roughly doubled. After the reapportionment decisions, all candidates could count on virtually every district being redrawn after every census. That candidates did respond to this change in their environment is indicated in our analyses of voluntary exits by incumbents and entries by strong challengers: both were significantly influenced by the redistricting cycle – after but not before the reapportionment revolution.

Another sort of evidence that the redistricting cycle has been important in recent congressional elections concerns money. Contributions by PACs to challengers are relatively dispersed in the immediate aftermath of a redistricting (years ending in "2"), but they become steadily more concentrated as the redistricting cycle progresses toward its end (see Jacobson 2001). This pattern in contributions is visible only for the last three decades, as systematic data on campaign contributions have been collected only since 1972. Thus, we cannot say that money in congressional elections became *more* redistricting-related after the reapportionment revolution. However, we can say that the pattern of increasingly concentrated giving to challengers fits with the coordination theme that we have repeatedly sounded in this part of the book.

Alternative Explanations

The literature affords no explicit alternative explanations of why electoral coordination increased abruptly in the 1960s for the simple reason that no one else has previously argued that the increasing incumbency advantage stemmed from (increasingly) strategic entry and exit. Nonetheless, several alternatives – variously related to the reapportionment revolution – seem plausible.

The first alternative hypothesis begins by noting that the wave of 1960s redistricting broke some very long-standing traditions in American politics. Although redistricters were in principle free to draw congressional districts that cut across county lines, incorporating parts of many and wholes of none, there were two ironclad regularities in practice. First, outside the large cities, congressional districts were typically composed of whole counties. Second, even in the large cities, congressional districts were typically proper subsets of counties. The observance of these constraints by parties enjoying unified control of state government entailed real costs in terms of forgone gerrymandering opportunities. It is only logical to assume that there were countervailing forces that prevented the seizure of these opportunities. We believe that the countervailing force in question was the power of county-level party organizations. When *Wesberry* brought with it the increasingly widespread violation of these norms of redistricting, it also disrupted partisan recruitment mechanisms and career paths.

In particular, one might conjecture that the wave of 1960s redistricting actions led to *more isolated decisions on entry*. What we mean by this is that the local parties could less often entice a reasonably good candidate to run against long odds, with the promise of payment elsewhere (e.g., a local position of some sort), or perhaps they less often had the incentive to do so. In an increasingly candidate-centered world, more entry decisions were made strictly on the merits of the opportunity at hand and the opportunity costs it would entail for the individual candidate. Thus, the odds of winning the congressional race played a larger role – and voluntary exits by incumbents were more often bad tidings for their party.

The second alternative hypothesis begins by noting that it was not just congressional districts but all state legislative districts as well that were affected by the reapportionment revolution. Indeed, the changes in the state legislative districts were often substantially larger than those at the congressional level because the preexisting malapportionment was even greater. Conceivably, state-level redistricting opened up some career paths for would-be professional politicians that had not previously existed, increasing the pool of serious potential challengers. This may also have contributed to the professionalization of state legislatures, which in turn affected the opportunity costs of potential congressional entrants.

In favor of this sort of idea, we note two bits of evidence. First, the proportion of members of the U.S. House who had previously been state legislators increased substantially, from 28% after the election of 1946 to near 50% in the 1990s. Moreover, the single largest election-to-election increase in this proportion occurred between 1964 (32%) and 1966 (38%). Second, recent studies have shown that state legislators are more strategic (i.e., more sensitive to the odds of winning) in their entry decisions, especially if they are from more professionalized states

(Berkman and Eisenstein 1999; Maestas, Maisel, and Stone 2000). Thus, perhaps the reapportionment revolution at the state level – in combination with other factors – shook up state politics in such a way as to produce more careerist politicians in the state legislatures, who made up an increasingly large share of the pool of *serious* candidates for House seats. These state-level career politicians were more strategic in their entry decisions, with the net effect of improving electoral coordination between strong challengers and incumbents.

The final alternative hypothesis centers on television and money. If the rapid spread of television viewing raised the fixed cost of entry into a congressional race (to run a serious campaign, one needed increasingly expensive television ads), then candidates and their supporters would have had to think harder about entering a given race. This presumably would have led to an increasing concentration of political money on competitive races, with increased national coordination of funds.[3]

We cannot conclusively reject these alternatives at this point. We do wish to note three points, however. First, regardless of the explanation, the improvement in electoral coordination just reviewed is an important and understudied feature of postwar congressional elections. Second, the first two alternative explanations presented also hinge on the reapportionment revolution. Thus, were either of these alternatives to pan out, this would be consistent with the broad thrust of our argument. Third, each of these alternative explanations can be further probed by seeing how well they explain interparty differences, something we pursue in the next section.

WHY DID THE PARTIES DIFFER?

Our Explanation

In this section, we review several differences between the parties, along with our explanations for them. There are four key differences to explain. First, the Democrats fared significantly worse in their voluntarily than in their involuntarily open seats, especially after 1966; in contrast, the Republicans fared about the same in both sorts of open seat. Second, after *Wesberry* the Republicans' open-seat losses were larger when the Democrats' margin of control in Congress was larger, while the Democrats' open-seat losses were smaller. Third, the Republicans'

---

[3] For an alternative view on the importance of television, see Pryor (2000).

vote loss in their involuntarily open seats increased significantly from before to after *Wesberry*, whereas the analogous figures for the Democrats did not increase significantly. Fourth, the Democrats' vote loss in involuntarily open seats is never statistically discernible from zero, whereas the analogous figure for the Republicans is (after *Wesberry*). Fifth, after *Wesberry* the Republicans suffered from a minority investment disadvantage, which made it systematically more difficult to (1) recruit candidates, (2) raise money, and hence (3) win.

To explain this quintet of party differences, we note that the reapportionment decisions led to the eradication of pro-Republican bias outside the South, which downshifted the Republicans' chances of securing a majority in the House. Because the value of a House seat was typically higher for the majority party, the *voluntary* retirement of a Democrat usually came about only in the face of particularly poor vote prospects. Thus, the Democrats tended to lose substantially more votes in seats that became open due to the voluntary as opposed to the involuntary withdrawal of the incumbent. In contrast, the value of a House seat was substantially lower for Republicans, and thus they more often abandoned such seats, even when they had good vote prospects. Thus, the Republicans tended *not* to lose much more in voluntarily as opposed to involuntarily open seats (until 1996–1998, when, for the first time, they do).

A related argument explains why the two parties' open-seat losses responded in opposite fashion to a strengthening of the Democratic margin of control in Congress. When the Democratic margin increased, the expected value of a House seat for Republicans declined even further, making it even harder for them to recruit good candidates and defend their seats but easier for the Democrats. Thus, the Republicans suffered larger and larger open-seat losses as the Democrats' control of Congress strengthened, while the Democrats' losses became smaller and smaller.

Why did the Republicans' vote loss in involuntarily open seats increase substantially after *Wesberry*? Our explanation is that the party had increasing difficulties in recruiting high-quality candidates to defend those seats, because the expected value of a House seat was lower (due to the diminished probability of a Republican majority following the eradication of pro-Republican bias outside the South). In contrast, the Democrats had excellent prospects of retaining their majority and thus had little difficulty in recruiting strong candidates to defend their involuntarily open seats.

The same argument explains why the Democrats' vote loss in involuntarily open seats never differed statistically from their vote loss in seats defended by an incumbent Democrat. The high expected value of a House seat was sufficient to pull in a talented politician to defend the seat.

Finally, a few comments on the minority investment disadvantage. The syndrome of ailments afflicting the Republicans after *Wesberry* was typical of oppositions in dominant-party systems, though not as severe. In U.S. terms, the minority investment disadvantage extrapolates to southern politics à la V. O. Key (1949). In the old days of the Solid South, the Republicans could not recruit any good candidates, as all serious would-be politicians entered the Democratic party. Presumably, they could also not raise any money from would-be favor-seekers. Finally, they won seats only in a relatively few areas the Democrats were content to abandon.

The predicament of Republicans in the House of Representatives was never so dire as it had been for the Republican party of Alabama or Georgia. However, they did have well-known recruitment difficulties; they did have well-known frustrations with corporate PACs' tendency to give to the Democrats; and they did have trouble winning the open seats they needed to take or keep the House (cf. Jacobson 1990a). Their problems might, in a more unitary system, have become self-reinforcing – leading to a one-party regime at the national level. In part due to our separated-powers system, the Republicans at the national level continued to compete, and all their problems decreased substantially after their stunning victory in the midterm elections of 1994 put paid to their status as the perennial minority.

Alternative Explanations

In this subsection, we consider the alternative explanations of electoral coordination offered previously to see if they also might explain party differences in entry and exit. Two of the alternative theories do *not* seem to provide natural explanations of the party differences. If, per the first alternative, redistricting's disruption of local party ties is the key, then interparty differences would presumably stem from substantial differences between the two parties in the extent of such disruption. However, there is no evidence that this was the case. If, per the third alternative, television is the key, then interparty differences would stem from sustained differences between the parties in their ability to adapt to the new electoral world. Again, there is no evidence to this effect.

This leaves the second alternative explanation, which focuses on how state redistricting and professionalization affected career paths. We already know (cf. Fiorina 1994, 1997) that the professionalization of state legislatures seems mostly to have benefited Democrats. This at least provides a starting point for theorizing, though we are not sure how this initial party difference would ramify into the pattern of open-seat differences that is to be explained.

NORMATIVE CONSEQUENCES OF THE INCREASE IN THE INCUMBENCY ADVANTAGE

As noted in the previous section, the dominant explanations of why there is an incumbency advantage attribute it to resources intrinsic to incumbency. By one line of argument, the resources of office can be electorally beneficial – for example, staff can be located in the member's district and act as a perpetual campaign organization. By another line of argument, the relevant resource might simply be the right to have the word *incumbent* printed next to one's name on the ballot.

By either of these accounts, the incumbency advantage is potentially dangerous to democratic governance, because incumbents can win reelection for reasons other than the assiduity with which they serve the nation's or their constituents' interests. Prominent analysts have repeatedly viewed the increasing incumbency advantage as evidence of *dysfunction* in our body politic.

One argument sees incumbents as insulated from popular wrath and increasingly in bed with special interests. This belief has probably always existed. But it has certainly been a mainstay of op-ed essays on what ails the country over the last generation or so. Moreover, in the 1990s this belief, partly sustained by incumbents' fat margins of victory since the 1960s, was an important impetus behind the term limits movement in America. The logic seemed to be: if incumbents have an unfair advantage because they can use the (bloated) resources of their office as election subsidies, and if this unfair advantage frees them to ignore their constituents and serve special interests, then put a stop to it all by limiting the number of terms they can serve.

A second argument sees the increasing incumbency advantage primarily as evidence that members have succeeded in carving out a larger and larger "personal vote." Incumbents turn congressional resources, by dint of hard work, into a successful but very personal relationship with their constituents (Fenno 1978). They may be in bed with the special interests, but the real problem is that they have become ever more narrowly focused on their constituents' concerns to the detriment of national concerns. In a nutshell, the incumbency advantage allows members to ignore their parties in pursuit of the parochial interests of their constituents. As the parties are the primary agencies, along with the presidency, through which broad national goals are addressed, the result is a failure of collective responsibility in American politics (Fiorina 1980).

A third argument sees the incumbency advantage as the reason that the Democrats succeeded in maintaining majorities in the House of Representatives throughout most of the postwar era, despite many Republican victories at the presidential level. Here, Democratic incumbents are able to support their party's benighted programs without paying the just price at the polls, because they have an unfair electoral bonus just for being in office (for a review of this argument, see Jacobson 1990a, pp. 1–2).

Each of these arguments assumes that the increasing incumbency advantage was real. Incumbents were granted an increasingly valuable set of resources just for being incumbents, and this allowed them to pay less heed to some political actors (the good guys) in order to pay more heed to other political actors (the bad guys). What changes in the stories is the identity of the good guys and the bad guys. In story 1, incumbents ignore the virtuous citizenry in their districts in order to pay more attention to evil but wealthy special interests. In story 2, incumbents ignore the virtuous parties in Congress in order to pay more attention to the greedy and shortsighted citizenry in their districts. In story 3, incumbents ignore the enlightened citizenry voting for Republican presidential candidates in order to pay more attention to the evil congressional empire, formerly known as the Democratic party.

The light touch with which we have exposed these arguments notwithstanding, they are all important. Indeed, the question of whom representatives of the people heed is central to democratic theory and practice. When incumbents adjust their role, paying less heed to X in order to pay more heed to Y, the consequences are potentially important, even if the adjustments are marginal. Moreover, exactly how much attention incumbents pay to party, constituents, and interest groups is constantly in flux, constantly contested by these groups and their champions. Thus, the logic of the stories previously told – that incumbents given a cushion of safety may redress the balance of forces on them in ways unhealthy for democratic governance – is perennial.

But what if the premise is false? What if incumbents did not acquire a cushion setting them free from electoral pressures? What if they only have the appearance of a cushion and not the reality?

If the cushion is more apparent than real, then the arguments just reviewed cannot get off the ground, logically speaking. Their conclusions may still be true. Maybe incumbents have paid relatively more attention to special interests and relatively less to their constituents. Maybe they have paid more attention to local yokels and less to parties. Maybe they have paid more attention to their parties and less to their constituents. Whatever the empirical merit of these competing conclusions, one cannot explain them by referring to an increasing incumbency advantage if there was no such increase.

We are not the first to suggest that incumbents' electoral safety did not increase. Jacobson (1987) has noted that, at the same time that incumbents' margins of victory increased on average, the size of their vote swings from election to election also increased on average, leading to almost no improvement in their probability of victory (until the late 1980s). But it is safety in the sense of a high probability of victory, not safety in the sense of winning big when you do win, that matters in all of the normative arguments given previously. Hence, Jacobson's work directly undermines the key premise of these arguments.

Note that Jacobson (1987) also conflicts with the conventional notion that incumbency confers a premium of so-and-so many percentage points. Logically, such a vote premium would also entail a premium in the probability of victory. If the vote premium grew, as conventionally asserted, then so should the probability-of-victory premium have grown. However, how could incumbents' probabilities of victory increasingly have outdistanced their nonincumbent replacements' chances, while at the same time incumbents have not become any more likely to win reelection when they seek it? One cannot both believe Jacobson (1987) and also believe the conventional wisdom on the vote-denominated incumbency advantage.

Our work provides further support for the Jacobsonian view and resolves the apparent conflict just noted. We deny that incumbency even confers a substantial vote premium (or, more modestly, assert that the evidence that it does is not compelling). There is thus no inconsistency between our view of the vote-denominated incumbency advantage (it increased little, if at all) and Jacobson's view of incumbents' probabilities of victory (they also increased little, if at all, until the late 1980s).

PART IV

Conclusion

13

Final Thoughts

Jurisprudentially, the Supreme Court's reapportionment decisions have long been recognized as revolutionary. Administratively, they led to a wave of extraordinary court-supervised redistricting actions in the mid-1960s whose ostensible purpose was to eradicate then-massive levels of malapportionment. Politically, however, they seem not to have sparked much change.

Some claimed that court-mandated redistricting in the 1960s favored the Democrats, others that it favored the Republicans, but the near-consensus of the literature has been that redistricting did not produce substantial net gains for either party. Some suspected that redistricting in the 1960s sparked the storied growth of the incumbency advantage, but the consensus of the literature is that it did not. Almost everyone expected a substantial change in policy, from a pro-rural to more pro-urban stance, but the near-consensus of the literature is that no such change was forthcoming (for a dissenting view, see McCubbins and Schwartz 1988).

This book has reexamined the electoral consequences of the reapportionment revolution. In this chapter, we first review three major proximal effects: the wave of redistricting in the 1960s, the change in the frequency and regularity of redistricting, and the change in the reversionary outcome of the redistricting process. We then tie these proximal changes to fundamental changes in the nature of electoral competition, both between Democrats and Republicans and between incumbents and challengers.

Conclusion

PROXIMAL EFFECTS

Redistricting in the 1960s

The first proximal effect of the Court's decisions was that most of the nation's congressional (and state legislative) districts were redrawn in a series of extraordinary redistricting actions. These actions were extraordinary not just in the sense of not being triggered by a reapportionment but also in the sense of being the first in the nation's history to be conducted under court supervision. Because virtually all of the nation's congressional districts were to some extent malapportioned, the Court's "one person, one vote" principle required that virtually all be redrawn, resulting in the most comprehensive remaking of the electoral map that the nation had ever seen.

The Regularity of Redistricting

The second proximal effect of the Supreme Court's reapportionment decisions was that the frequency and regularity of redistricting increased. Before *Wesberry*, redistricting was a relatively rare event, especially in states that did not lose seats in the reapportionment. After *Wesberry*, the "one person, one vote" principle required congressional districts of equal population. Because equality of districts would almost never be preserved from one reapportionment to the next in a nation with the dynamic population growth typical of the United States, redistricting became unavoidable – a congressperson's equivalent of death and taxes – and regular – occurring every 10 years after the decennial census.

Reversions to Redistricting

The third proximal effect of the Court's decisions was to alter what happened at law should a state government fail to enact a new districting statute after a decennial reapportionment. The previous literature has largely failed even to mention this change in the reversionary outcome of the redistricting process, much less stressed its fundamental importance.

Endowing the lower courts with the power to set the reversion meant that the courts became players in all subsequent redistricting actions. The possibility always existed that a state's plan would be litigated. Thus, those devising new redistricting plans had to consider which court would hear the case and its likely view of matters. Whereas failure to produce a plan acceptable to both legislature and governor had previously often left the old plan in force, the new reversionary outcome of the redistricting process in the 1960s was whatever the supervising court said it was (subject to the constraint that districts be of equal population). This ability of the supervising court to set the reversion systematically affected the nature of redistricting plans produced in the 1960s (and, plausibly, beyond).[1]

DEMOCRATS VERSUS REPUBLICANS

Consider now how the first and third proximal effects discussed earlier – the wave of redistricting in the 1960s and the redefinition of the reversion to the redistricting process – contributed to redressing the balance of congressional power between Democrats and Republicans. It is clear that the balance *was* redressed. Prior to the 1960s, the Republicans enjoyed about a 6% bias: for 50% of the nonsouthern vote they could expect about 56% of the seats. After the mid-1960s, the pro-Republican bias was gone. The eradication of this bias was worth about 20 seats per election. The previous literature has recognized that pro-Republican bias did abruptly disappear in the 1960s, but it has not viewed redistricting as the causal force pushing the change.

Redistricting is thought unlikely to produce net partisan gains nationwide because – as Butler and Cain (1992, pp. 8–9) put it – (1) partisan gerrymanders occur only when one party enjoys unified control, making them relatively rare given the frequency of divided government in the states; (2) partisan gerrymanders sometimes fail; and (3) Republican gerrymanders in some states balance Democratic gerrymanders in other states. We agree that the conditions that must be met before a substantial national partisan gain via redistricting becomes likely are hard to meet. However, we would state the key conditions differently, especially for the post-*Wesberry* period. First, there must be a substantial *shift* in the distribution of partisan control at the state level relative to the distribution of control reflected in the current districting plans. Second, there must be a substantial and correlated dominance of the federal judiciary.

---

[1] Although we here emphasize the ability of the courts to set the reversion, the broader point is that the court could influence the redistricting process – through the setting of deadlines, the decision whether to accept a plan in principle or in practice, the setting of reversions, and possibly in other ways as well.

Both of these conditions were met in the 1960s. First, most of the *old* plans (those being replaced) were products of past episodes of unified Republican government (sometimes updated under bargaining conditions that, due to the conservative reversions that obtained prior to *Baker*, favored the Republicans). Thus, most nonsouthern states renegotiated their districting plans under structural bargaining conditions that were more favorable to the Democrats. The result was a substantial opportunity for net partisan gain. Second, the same party that benefited from the shift in partisan control at the state level also dominated the supervising courts.

The conditions that arose in the 1960s – old plans favoring the Republicans; a strong shift in partisan control of state government away from unified Republican control (relative to the distribution of partisan control implicit in the plans in force); and Democratic dominance of the federal judiciary – will probably not be repeated soon. However, they obtained in the 1960s and combined to produce a substantial and sudden net partisan gain – not merely in the form of seats gained at a particular election but also in the form of permanently reequilibrating the distribution of districting plans outside the South, hence permanently recalibrating the translation of congressional votes into seats.[2]

Corroborating evidence of how large a partisan effect redistricting in the 1960s had can be garnered by looking at district-by-district data. Most changes in districting plans in the 1960s were from more to less favorable for the Republicans. That is, most Republican incumbents found their districts packed with surplus Republican identifiers, while a few saw their districts cracked (entailing a large reduction in the share of Republican identifiers). Meanwhile, most Democratic incumbents found their districts pared of excess Democratic identifiers. In terms of vote shares, this pattern of district-level changes meant the following. First, redrawn districts tended to show a decline in the expected Demo-

---

[2] The main qualification we need to make of the discussion just given is to note that the disappearance of pro-Republican bias started in 1962, before the reapportionment decisions. This is consistent with the preceding discussion, in that the 1958 election was a Democratic landslide, one that pushed the distribution of control in the states in their favor just before the 1962 redistricting. Thus, the first condition – the existence of a large shift in partisan fortunes – obtained. Since redistricting actions in 1962 predated the reapportionment revolution, the partisan complexion of the courts at this time is irrelevant. However, the conservative nature of the reversionary outcome helps explain why only the states that were newly under unified Democratic control adopted plans that were markedly different in partisan bias from those that had previously obtained.

cratic vote share relative to otherwise comparable but untouched districts. This reflects the fact that most districts were either pared of excess Democrats or packed with excess Republicans (with only a few substantial reductions in the share of Republican voters in the cracked districts). Second, redrawn Republican-held districts tended to show a larger variance in vote share relative to otherwise comparable but untouched districts. This reflects the stark difference between packed and cracked Republican districts.

INCUMBENTS VERSUS CHALLENGERS

In this section, we consider how the proximal effects of the reapportionment revolution affected competition between incumbents and challengers. A preliminary but fundamental point concerns how to conceptualize the incumbency advantage – and we take that up next.

How to Conceptualize the Incumbency Advantage

It is well known that the incumbent party's vote share in a congressional district is usually larger when the incumbent candidate seeks reelection than when she does not. The conventional explanations of this correlation between who enters the race and the incumbent party's vote share all posit that the incumbent candidate benefits from one or more resources of office: perhaps incumbency per se is a positive cue for voters; perhaps personal staff and institutional positions allow members to cater to constituents' casework needs or to PACs' legislative needs. Thus, the incumbency advantage is based on a real resource advantage of one sort or another.

Our view is that the loss suffered by parties in their open seats, relative to their incumbent-defended seats, largely reflects strategic exit by incumbents. It is widely accepted that (serious) candidates in general are strategic. That is, they decide whether to enter a race on the basis of their chances of winning, the value of the office at stake, and their opportunity costs. We merely insist that the same logic be applied to incumbent candidates in particular. In this we follow the spirit of Jacobson and Kernell's (1983) analysis of the important systemic consequences of strategic entry (their focus being more on strong challengers).

There is good evidence that incumbents' exit decisions *are* strategic – that is, that they depend inter alia on their perceived chances of victory. For example, incumbents whose districts were redrawn unfavorably in the 1960s prudently exited, and their parties suffered substantially larger losses than would have been expected solely on the basis of past vote shares and the fact of being redistricted. Also, losses in seats that become open due to the voluntary departure of the incumbent – where poor vote forecasts can play a role in the exit decision – are systematically larger than those in seats that become open involuntarily – where poor vote forecasts play no role.

Because forecast vote shares affect who enters, and because who enters affects realized vote shares, there is a problem of simultaneity bias in estimating the incumbency advantage. Indeed, currently there is no unbiased estimator that shows that the real incumbency advantage is statistically discernible from zero. Thus, substantively, our conclusion is that there may not be much growth in the real incumbency advantage (i.e., the impact of entry on vote share) to explain, only growth in the impact of anticipated vote shares on entry and exit. Methodologically, our conclusion is that the literature on the incumbency advantage cannot avoid going the route taken by the literature on campaign expenditures: a fully simultaneous equation approach, keeping track of both the incumbent's and any strong challenger's entry decisions, along with the subsequent votes received, will be necessary.[3]

Redistricting, Majority Status, and the Incumbency Advantage

Now consider how the first two proximal effects – the wave of extraordinary redistricting in the 1960s and the increased regularity of postcensus redistricting – indirectly affected measurements of the incumbency advantage. We have already discussed how the changed reversion to the redistricting process, Democratic dominance of the federal judiciary, and the erosion of Republican strength in nonsouthern state governments combined to eradicate pro-Republican bias. The disappearance of this bias raised the short- and medium-term probability that the Democrats would secure a majority of the House, emphatically confirming the Republicans' status as the perennial minority and driving a wedge between the parties' valuations of House seats. This, in turn, led to (1) a larger minority investment disadvantage and (2) a larger majority

---

[3] This comment pertains to all methods that use district-level electoral data as the basis for estimation. Methods that use subdistrict data, such as that of Ansolabehere, Snyder, and Stewart (2000), may be able to deal with issues of endogeneity better.

retirement slump (i.e., vote losses pursuant to the voluntary exit of an incumbent).

The minority investment disadvantage arose because individual Republican politicians placed a lower expected value on winning a House seat than did individual Democratic politicians: the Republicans were likely to languish in the minority and knew it, while the Democrats could hope for long careers culminating in committee chairs or leadership positions. The minority disadvantage consisted in the following: the Republicans found it relatively harder to recruit qualified candidates (why abandon a successful state or local career for a minority seat in the House?); to raise money (why invest in someone almost sure to be in the minority?); and hence to win votes (because of the first two problems).[4]

The majority's retirement slump (in the case of voluntary exits) arises as the flip side of the minority investment disadvantage. The likely majority party's incumbents attach a high expected value to the seat and will therefore rarely give it up voluntarily except in the face of particularly poor vote prospects. The likely minority party's incumbents attach a lower expected value to the seat and will more often not seek reelection, even when they have relatively good prospects of winning. Thus, the majority party's losses in its voluntarily open seats should substantially exceed its losses in its involuntarily open seats, whereas the difference should be milder for the minority. We find that this pattern does hold in U.S. House elections after 1966 and, moreover, that the interparty difference increases as the Republicans' minority status intensifies. The more hopeless the Republicans, the larger the vote loss differential between voluntarily and involuntarily open seats for the Democrats, and the smaller the differential for the Republicans.

Redistricting-Influenced Entry

Scholars have learned much about congressional career decisions from simple rational entry models of the sort first studied by Schlesinger (1966) and Black (1972). Taking the same basic approach, we have

---

[4] The investment problem faced by the Republicans, and exacerbated by the eradication of bias in the 1960s, is only a special and relatively mild form of a more general problem faced by minority parties. Truly hopeless minorities, such as the Republicans were for so long in the South, suffer much larger investment problems. Such parties see ambitious and talented politicians who might otherwise join their ranks seek instead to compete within the majority party (Epstein 1986; Cox 1997).

stressed that the Supreme Court's reapportionment decisions rather abruptly changed politicians' expectations about the frequency of congressional redistricting, and hence about the expected value of winning House seats. Once efforts to reverse the Court's decisions had failed (by late 1965), politicians should have realized that district lines in force at any given time were unlikely to survive past the next decennial reapportionment. The near-certainty that every district would be redrawn after every reapportionment, however, should have affected the expected value of winning a House seat at different points in the redistricting cycle. We show that it apparently did – or at least that there is a regular entry and exit rhythm associated with the redistricting cycle, one that strengthened after *Wesberry*. Moreover, we argue that the increased regularity of redistricting improved electoral coordination in the sense that incumbents and strong challengers became better at avoiding each other. This increased coordination was one significant factor increasing the correlation between the incumbent candidate's exit/entry decision and the incumbent party's vote share.

THE 1960S AND U.S. POLITICAL HISTORY

The *methodological* points we have made in this book, concerning how to model the redistricting process and how to measure the incumbency advantage, are not confined to the 1960s and in some ways not even to the United States. The main *substantive* argument of this book, however, is specific to U.S. political history.

We hope to have convinced the reader that the Supreme Court's reapportionment decisions powerfully shaped congressional elections in America for the succeeding generation. The only other contemporary event with a comparably far-reaching (but quite different) electoral effect was the passage of the Voting Rights Act in 1965.

The Court's decisions mandated the single most important set of procedural changes in the long history of redistricting in the United States. They led directly to that rara avis, a large net partisan gain nationwide produced by redistricting. They indirectly – but profoundly – changed the calculus of strategic entry (and exit) in such a way as to widen gaps both between Democrats and Republicans and between incumbents and challengers.

It has long been puzzling to survey the vast literature on the incumbency advantage, all of which agrees that this advantage increased abruptly in the mid-1960s, and discover that redistricting has been dismissed as playing any important role. It has long been puzzling to survey the literature on bias in congressional elections, all of which agrees that this bias changed abruptly in the mid-1960s, and again discover that redistricting has been dismissed as the explanation. The fish was plainly in the milk. In this book, we have identified the cat.

References

Abramowitz, Alan I. 1983. "Partisan Redistricting and the 1982 Congressional Elections." *Journal of Politics* 45:776–770.

Alford, John R., and David W. Brady. 1989. "Personal and Partisan Advantage in U.S. Congressional Elections." In Lawrence C. Dodd and Bruce I. Oppenheimer, eds., *Congress Reconsidered*, 4th ed. Washington, D.C.: Congressional Quarterly.

Alford, John R., and John R. Hibbing. 1981. "Increased Incumbency Advantage in the House." *Journal of Politics* 43:1042–1061.

Alford, John, Holly Teeters, Daniel S. Ward, and Rick K. Wilson. 1994. "Overdraft: The Political Cost of Congressional Malfeasance." *Journal of Politics* 56:788–801.

Ansolabehere, Steve, David W. Brady, and Morris P. Fiorina. 1988. "The Vanishing Marginals and Electoral Responsiveness." *British Journal of Political Science* 22:21–38.

Ansolabehere, Stephen, and Alan Gerber. 1997. "Incumbency Advantage and the Persistence of Legislative Majorities." *Legislative Studies Quarterly* 22:161–178.

Ansolabehere, Stephen, and James M. Snyder, Jr. 2000. "Money and Office: The Sources of the Incumbency Advantage in Congressional Campaign Finance." In *Continuity and Change in House Elections*. Palo Alto: Stanford University Press.

Ansolabehere, Stephen, James M. Snyder, Jr., and Charles Stewart III. 2000. "Old Voters, New Voters, and the Personal Vote: Using Redistricting to Measure the Incumbency Advantage." *American Journal of Political Science* 44(1):17–34.

Apportionment Act. 1941. *Statutes At Large*. Vol. 55, sec. 1, p. 762.

Apportionment Act. 1982. *U.S. Code*. Vol. 4, sec. 2a, p. 64.

Aronow, Geoffrey F. 1980. "The Special Master in School Desegregation Cases: The Evolution of Roles in the Reformation of Public Institutions through Litigation." *Hastings Constitutional Law Quarterly* 7:739.

Badham v. March Fong Eu, 568 F. Supp. 156 (1983).

Baker, Gordon E. 1966. *The Reapportionment Revolution: Representation, Political Power, and the Supreme Court*. New York: Random House.

References

Baker v. Carr, 369 U.S. 186 (1962).

Barone, Michael, and Grant Ujifusa. 1991. *The Almanac of American Politics 1992*. Washington, D.C.: National Journal.

Bartels, Larry M. 2000. "Partisanship and Voting Behavior, 1952–1996." *American Journal of Political Science* 44(1):35–50.

Bauer, Monica, and John R. Hibbing. 1989. "Which Incumbents Lose in House Elections: A Response to Jacobson's 'The Marginals Never Vanished'." *American Journal of Political Science* 33:262–271.

Berkman, M., and J. Eisenstein. 1999. "State Legislators as Congressional Candidates: The Effects of Prior Experience on Legislative Recruitment and Fundraising." *Political Research Quarterly* 52:481–498.

Bicentennial Committee of the Judicial Conference of the United States. 1983. *Judges of the United States*. Washington, D.C.: Superintendent of Documents, U.S. Government Printing Office.

Beiser, Edward. 1968. "A Comparative Analysis of State and Federal Judicial Behavior: The Reapportionment Cases." *American Political Science Review* 62:788–804.

Black, Gordon. 1972. "A Theory of Political Ambition: Career Choices and the Role of Structural Incentives." *American Political Science Review* 66:144–159.

Born, Richard. 1979. "Generational Replacement and the Growth of Incumbent Reelection Margins in the U.S. House." *American Political Science Review* 73:811–817.

——— 1985. "Partisan Intentions and Election Day Realities in the Congressional Redistricting Process." *American Political Science Review* 79:305–319.

Brace, Paul. 1984. "Progressive Ambition in the House: A Probabilistic Approach." *Journal of Politics* 46:556–569.

Brady, David W., and Bernard Grofman. 1991. "Sectional Differences in Partisan Bias and Electoral Responsiveness in U.S. House Elections, 1850–1980." *British Journal of Political Science* 21:247–256.

Breaux, David. 1990. "Specifying the Impact of Incumbency on State Legislative Elections." *American Politics Quarterly* 18:270–286.

Bullock, Charles S., III. 1975. "Redistricting and Congressional Stability." *Journal of Politics* 37:569–575.

Burnham, Walter D. 1974. "Communication." *American Political Science Review* 68:207–213.

Butler, David, and Bruce E. Cain. 1992. *Congressional Redistricting: Comparative and Theoretical Perspectives*. New York: Macmillan.

Cain, Bruce E. 1985. "Assessing the Partisan Effects of Redistricting." *American Political Science Review* 79:320–333.

Cain, Bruce E., John A. Ferejohn, and Morris Fiorina. 1987. *The Personal Vote*. Cambridge: Harvard University Press.

Campagna, Janet, and Bernard Grofman. 1990. "Party Control and Partisan Bias in 1980s Congressional Redistricting." *Journal of Politics* 52:1242–1257.

Campbell, James E. 1996. *Cheap Seats: The Democratic Party's Advantage in U.S. House Elections*. Columbus: Ohio State University Press.

References

Canon, David T. 1990. *Actors, Athletes, and Astronauts: Political Amateurs in the United States.* Chicago: University of Chicago Press.

1999. *Race, Redistricting, and Representation: The Unintended Consequences of Black-Majority Districts.* Chicago: University of Chicago Press.

Carey, John, Richard G. Niemi, and Lynda Powell. 2000. "Incumbency and the Probability of Reelection in State Legislative Elections." *Journal of Politics* 62:671–700.

Chase, Harold, Samuel Krislov, Keith O. Boyum, and Jerry N. Clark. 1976. *Biographical Dictionary of the Federal Judiciary.* Detroit: Gale Research.

Colegrove v. Green, 328 U.S. 529 (1946).

Collie, Melissa P. 1981. "Incumbency, Electoral Safety, and Turnover in the House of Representatives, 1952–76. " *American Political Science Review* 75:119–131.

Congressional Quarterly. 1962. *Weekly Report.* Washington, D.C.: Congressional Quarterly.

1966. *Weekly Report.* Washington, D.C.: Congressional Quarterly.

1968. *Weekly Report.* Washington, D.C.: Congressional Quarterly.

1969. *Weekly Report.* Washington, D.C.: Congressional Quarterly.

Cover, Albert D. 1977. "One Good Term Deserves Another: The Advantage of Incumbency in Congressional Elections." *American Journal of Political Science* 21:523–541.

Cox, David. 1970. *Analysis of Binary Data.* London: Methuen.

Cox, Gary W. 1997. *Making Votes Count: Strategic Coordination in the World's Electoral Systems.* Cambridge: Cambridge University Press.

Cox, Gary W., and Jonathan N. Katz. 1996. "Why Did the Incumbency Advantage in U.S. House Elections Grow?" *American Journal of Political Science* 40:478–497.

1999. "The Reapportionment Revolution and Bias in U.S. Congressional Elections." *American Journal of Political Science* 43:812–841.

2001. "Strategies for Modeling the Politics of Redistricting." Unpublished typescript. University of California, San Diego.

Cox, Gary W., and Eric Magar. 1999. "How Much Is Majority in the U.S. Congress Worth?" *American Political Science Review* 93:299–309.

Cox, Gary W., and Mathew D. McCubbins. 1993. *Legislative Leviathan: Party Government in the House.* Berkeley: University of California Press.

In press. "Agenda Power in the U.S. House of Representatives." In David Brady and Mathew D. McCubbins, eds., *Theoretical Explorations on the History of Congress.* Palo Alto: Stanford University Press.

Cox, Gary W., and Scott Morgenstern. 1993. "The Increasing Advantage of Incumbency in the U.S. States." *Legislative Studies Quarterly* 18:495–514.

1995. "The Incumbency Advantage in Multimember Districts: Evidence from the U.S. States." *Legislative Studies Quarterly* 30:329–349.

Cummings, Milton C., and Robert Peabody. 1969. "The Decision to Enlarge the Committee on Rules: An Analysis of the 1961 Vote." In Nelson W. Polsby and Robert Peabody, eds., *New Perspectives on the House of Representatives.* Chicago: Rand McNally.

Davis v. Bandemer, 478 U.S. 109 (1986).

References

Dixon, Robert G., Jr. 1968. *Democratic Representation: Reapportionment in Law and Politics.* New York: Oxford University Press.

Ehrenhalt, Alan. 1991. *The United States of Ambition: Politicians, Power, and the Pursuit of Office.* New York: Times Books.

Elliott, Ward. 1970. "Prometheus, Proteus, Pandora, and Procrustes Unbound: The Political Consequences of Reapportionment." *University of Chicago Law Review* 37:474–492.

Engstrom, Erik. 2001. "Redistricting and American Electoral Development, 1840–1940." Unpublished Ph.D. dissertation, University of California, San Diego.

Epstein, Leon. 1986. *Political Parties in the American Mold.* Madison: University of Wisconsin Press.

Erikson, Robert S. 1971. "The Advantage of Incumbency in Congressional Elections." *Polity* 3:395–405.

———. 1972. "Malapportionment, Gerrymandering, and Party Fortunes in Congressional Elections." *American Political Science Review* 66:1234–1245.

Fenno, Richard F., Jr. 1978. *Home Style: House Members in Their Districts.* Boston: Little, Brown.

Ferejohn, John A. 1977. "On the Decline of Competition in Congressional Elections." *American Political Science Review* 71:166–176.

Fiorina, Morris P. 1977. "The Case of the Vanishing Marginals: The Bureaucracy Did It." *American Political Science Review* 7:177–181.

———. 1980. "The Decline of Collective Responsibility in American Politics." *Daedalus* Summer, 25–45.

———. 1989. *Congress, Keystone of the Washington Establishment,* 2nd ed. New Haven: Yale University Press.

———. 1994. "Divided Government in the American States: A Byproduct of Legislative Professionalism?" *American Political Science Review* 88:304–316.

———. 1997. "Professionalism, Realignment, and Representation." *American Political Science Review* 91:156–162.

———. 1999. "Further Evidence of the Partisan Consequences of Legislative Professionalism." *American Journal of Political Science* 43:974–977.

Fisher, Jeffrey. 1997. "The Unwelcome Judicial Obligation to Respect Politics in Racial Gerrymandering Remedies." *Michigan Law Review* 95:1404–1442.

Friedman, Milton. 1953. *Essays in Positive Economics.* Chicago: University of Chicago Press.

Garand, James C. 1991. "Electoral Marginality in State Legislative Elections, 1968–86." *Legislative Politics Quarterly* 16:7–28.

Garand, James C., and Donald A. Gross. 1984. "Changes in the Vote Margins for Congressional Candidates: A Specification of Historical Trends." *American Political Science Review* 78:17–30.

Gelman, Andrew and Gary King. 1990. "Estimating Incumbency Advantage without Bias." *American Journal of Political Science* 34:1142–1164.

———. 1991. "Systemic Consequences of Incumbency Advantage in United States House Elections." *American Journal of Political Science* 35:110–138.

References

Gilmour, John, and Paul Rothstein. 1993. "Early Republican Retirement: A Cause of Democratic Dominance in the House of Representatives." *Legislative Studies Quarterly* 18:345–365.

Glazer, Amihai, Bernard Grofman, and Marc Robbins. 1987. "Partisan and Incumbency Effects of 1970s Congressional Redistricting." *American Journal of Political Science* 31:680–707.

Goehlert, Robert U., Fenton S. Martin, and John R. Sayre. 1996. *Members of Congress: A Bibliography.* Washington, D.C.: Congressional Quarterly.

Goehlert, Robert U., and John R. Sayre. 1982. *The United States Congress: A Bibliography.* New York: Free Press.

Gray v. Sanders, 372 U.S. 368 (1963).

Greene, William H. 1993. *Econometric Analysis,* 3rd ed. Upper Saddle River, N.J.: Prentice Hall.

Grofman, Bernard. 1993. "Would Vince Lombardi Have Been Right If He Had Said: 'When It Comes to Redistricting, Race Isn't Everything, It's the Only Thing'?" *Cardozo Law Review*: 14:1237.

Groseclose, Timothy, and Keith Krehbiel. 1994. "Golden Parachutes, Rubber Checks, and Strategic Retirements from the 102nd House." *American Journal of Political Science* 38(1):75–99.

Gourieroux, C., A. Monfort, and A. Trongon. 1984. "Pseudo Maximum Likelihood Methods: Applications to Poisson Models." *Econometrica* 52:701–720.

Hacker, Andrew. 1963. *Congressional Districting: The Issue of Equal Representation.* Washington, D.C.: Brookings Institution.

———. 1964. *Congressional Districting: The Issue of Equal Representation,* rev. ed. Washington, D.C.: Brookings Institution.

Hall, Richard L., and Robert P. van Houweling. 1995. "Avarice and Ambition in Congress: Representatives' Decisions to Run or Retire from the U.S. House." *American Political Science Review* 89:121–136.

Herrnson, Paul S. 1995. *Congressional Elections: Campaigning at Home and in Washington.* Washington, D.C.: Congressional Quarterly.

Holbrook, Thomas M., and Charles M. Tidmarch. 1991. "Sophomore Surge in State Legislative Elections, 1968–1986." *Legislative Politics Quarterly* 16:49–63.

———. 1993. "The Effects of Leadership Positions on Votes for Incumbents in State Legislative Elections." *Political Research Quarterly* 46:897–909.

Inter-university Consortium for Political and Social Research and Carroll McKibbin. 1997. *Roster of United States Congressional Officeholders and Biographical Characteristics of Members of the United States Congress, 1789–1996: Merged Data* [Computer file]. 10th ICPSR ed. Ann Arbor, MI: Inter-university Consortium for Political and Social Research [producer and distributor].

Jackman, Simon. 2000. "Estimation and Inference via Bayesian Simulation: An Introduction to Markov Chain Monte Carlo." *American Journal of Political Science* 44:375–404.

Jackson, Brooks. 1988. *Honest Graft: Big Money and the American Political Process.* New York: Knopf.

Jacobson, Gary C. 1980. *Money in Congressional Elections*. Boston: Little, Brown.

———. 1987. "The Marginals Never Vanished: Incumbency and Competition in Elections to the U.S. House of Representatives, 1952–1982." *American Journal of Political Science* 31:126–141.

———. 1990a. *The Electoral Origins of Divided Government: Competition in U.S. House Elections, 1946–1988*. Boulder: Westview Press.

———. 1990b. "The Effects of Campaign Spending in House Elections: New Evidence for Old Arguments." *American Journal of Political Science* 34: 334–362.

———. 1996. "The 1994 House Elections in Perspective." *Political Science Quarterly* 111:203–223.

———. 1997. *The Politics of Congressional Elections*, 4th ed. New York: Longman.

———. 2001. "Congress: Elections and Stalemate." In Michael Nelson, ed., *The Elections of 2000*. Washington, D.C.: Congressional Quarterly.

Jacobson, Gary C., and Michael Dimock. 1994. "Checking Out: The Effects of Bank Overdrafts on the 1992 House Elections." *American Journal of Political Science* 38(3):601–624.

Jacobson, Gary C., and Samuel Kernell. 1983. *Strategy and Choice in Congressional Elections*, 2nd ed. New Haven: Yale University Press.

Jewell, Malcolm E., and David Breaux. 1988. "The Effect of Incumbency on State Legislative Elections." *Legislative Studies Quarterly* 13:495–514.

Karcher v. Daggett, 462 U.S. 725 (1983).

Karlan, Pamela. 1993. "The Rights to Vote: Some Pessimism about Formalism." *Texas Law Review* 71:1705–1740.

Katz, Jonathan N., and Gary King. 1999. "A Statistical Model for Multiparty Electoral Data." *American Political Science Review* 93:15–32.

Kazee, Thomas A. 1983. "The Deterrent Effect of Incumbency on Recruiting Challengers in U.S. House Elections." *Legislative Studies Quarterly* 8:469–480.

Key, V. O., Jr. 1949. *Southern Politics in State and Nation*. New York: Alfred A. Knopf.

Kiewiet, Roderick, and Langche Zeng. 1993. "An Analysis of Congressional Career Decisions, 1947–1986." *American Political Science Review* 87:928–941.

King, Gary. 1989. *Unifying Political Methodology: The Likelihood Theory of Statistical Inference*. New York: Cambridge University Press.

———. 1990. "Electoral Responsiveness and Partisan Bias in Multiparty Democracies." *Legislative Studies Quarterly* 15:159–181.

———. 1991a. "Constituency Service and Incumbency Advantage." *British Journal of Political Science*. 21:119–128.

———. 1991b. "Political Gerrymandering and Pairing Incumbents: A Proposed Threshold for Legal Action." Unpublished typescript. Harvard University.

King, Gary, and Robert X. Browning. 1987. "Democratic Representation and Partisan Bias in Congressional Elections." *American Political Science Review* 81:1251–1273.

References

King, Gary, and Andrew Gelman. 1991. "Systematic Consequences of Incumbency Advantage in U.S. House Elections." *American Journal of Political Science* 35:110–138.

King, Gary, Robert O. Keohane, and Sidney Verba. 1994. *Designing Social Inquiry: Scientific Inference in Qualitative Research.* Princeton: Princeton University Press.

Kirkpatrick v. Preisler, 394 U.S. 526 (1969).

Krasno, Jonathan S., and Donald P. Green. 1988. "Preempting Quality Challengers in House Elections." *Journal of Politics* 50:920–936.

Krehbiel, Keith, and John R. Wright. 1983. "The Incumbency Effect in Congressional Elections: A Test of Two Explanations." *American Journal of Political Science* 27:140–157.

Larson, Bruce, Suzanne Globetti, and Marc J. Hetherington. 2000. "The Redistricting Cycle and Strategic Candidate Decisions in U.S. House Races." Paper presented at the American Political Science Association Meetings, Washington, D.C., August 31–September 4.

Levitt, S. D., and C. D. Wolfram. 1997. "Decomposing the Sources of Incumbency Advantage in the U.S. House." *Legislative Studies Quarterly* 22:45–60.

Lloyd, Randall. 1995. "Separating Partisanship from Party in Judicial Research: Reapportionment in the U.S. District Courts." *American Political Science Review* 89(2):413–420.

Lockerbie, Brad. 1999. "The Partisan Components to the Incumbency Advantage." *Political Research Quarterly* 52:631–646.

Maddala, G. S. 1983. *Limited-Dependent and Qualitative Variables in Econometrics.* Cambridge and New York: Cambridge University Press.

Maestas, Cherie, L. Sandy Maisel, and Walter J. Stone. 2000. "When to Risk It? State Legislators and the Decision to Run for the U.S. House." Paper presented at the American Political Science Association Meetings, Washington, D.C., August 31–September 4.

Mann, Thomas E. 1977. *Unsafe at Any Margin: Interpreting Congressional Elections.* Washington, D.C.: American Enterprise Institute.

Marbury v. Madison, 5 U.S. 137 (1803).

Martis, Kenneth C. 1982. *The Historical Atlas of United States Congressional Districts, 1789–1983.* New York: Free Press.

Mayhew, David. 1974. "Congressional Elections: The Case of the Vanishing Marginals." *Polity* 6:295–317.

McCubbins, Mathew M., Roger G. Noll, and Barry R. Weingast. 1995. "Politics and the Courts: A Positive Theory of Judicial Doctrine and the Rule of Law." *Southern California Law Review* 68:1631–1683.

McCubbins, Mathew D., and Thomas Schwartz. 1988. "Congress, the Courts, and Public Policy: Consequences of the One Man, One Vote Rule." *American Journal of Political Science* 32:388–415.

McDonald, Michael P. 1999. "Redistricting, Dealignment, and the Political Homogenization of Congressional Districts." Ph.D. dissertation, University of California, San Diego.

Meeks v. Anderson, 229 F. Supp. 271 (1964).

References

Murphy, Walter F. 1964. *The Elements of Judicial Strategy*. Chicago: University of Chicago Press.

Niemi, Richard G., Simon Jackman, and L. R. Winsky. 1991. "Candidacies and Competitiveness in Multimember Districts." *Legislative Politics Quarterly* 16:91–109.

Niemi, Richard G., and Laura Winsky. 1987. "Membership Turnover in U.S. State Legislatures: Trends and Effects of Districting." *Legislative Studies Quarterly* 12:115–123.

Noragon, Jack L. 1973. "Redistricting, Political Outcomes, and Gerrymandering in the 1960s." *Annals of the New York Academy of Sciences* 219:314–24.

O'Brien, David M. 1984. *Storm Center: The Supreme Court in American Politics*. New York: W. W. Norton.

Owen, Guillermo, and Bernard Grofman. 1988. "Optimal Partisan Gerrymandering." *Political Geography Quarterly* 7:5–22.

Prendergast, William B. 1965. "Memorandum on Congressional Districting." In Glendon Shubert, ed., *Reapportionment*. New York: Charles Scribner's Sons.

Prior, Markus. 2000. "The Incumbent in the Living Room: The Rise of Television and the Incumbency Advantage in U.S. House Elections." Unpublished typescript. Department of Communication, Stanford University.

Rae, Douglas W. 1971. *The Political Consequences of Electoral Laws*, rev. ed. New Haven: Yale University Press.

Ranney, Austin. 1971. "Parties in State Politics." In Herbert Jacob and Kenneth N. Vines, eds., *Politics in the American States*, 2d ed. Boston: Little, Brown.

Reynolds v. Sims, 377 U.S. 533 (1964).

Roberts v. Babcock, 246 F. Supp. 396 (1965).

Rohde, David. 1979. "Risk-Bearing and Progressive Ambition: The Case of Members of the United States House of Representatives." *American Journal of Political Science* 23:1–26.

Rosenberg, Gerald N. 1991. *The Hollow Hope: Can Courts Bring About Social Change?* Chicago: University of Chicago Press.

Schansberg, Eric D. 1994. "Moving Out of the House: An Analysis of Congressional Quits." *Economic Inquiry* 32:445–456.

Schlesinger, Joseph. 1966. *Ambition and Politics: Political Careers in the United States*. Chicago: Rand McNally.

Short, Lloyd M. 1931. "Congressional Redistricting in Missouri." *American Political Science Review* 25:634–649.

Silver v. Reagan, 63 Cal 2d 270 (1965).

Snyder, James M., Jr., and Michael M. Ting. 2000. "An Informational Rationale for Political Parties." Paper Presented at the 2000 Annual Meeting of the American Political Science Association, Washington, D.C., August 31–September 3.

Solimine, Michael E. 2001. "Federal Court Involvement in Redistricting Litigation." *Harvard Law Review* 114:878–901.

Theriault, Sean M. 1998. "Moving Up or Moving Out: Career Ceilings and Congressional Retirement." *Legislative Studies Quarterly* 23:419–433.

References

Tufte, Edward R. 1973. "The Relationship Between Seats and Votes in Two-Party Systems." *American Political Science Review* 67:540–554.

Wattenberg, Martin P. 1984. *The Decline of American Parties, 1952–1984*. Cambridge: Harvard University Press.

Weber, Ronald E. 1995. "Redistricting and the Courts: Judicial Activism in the 1990s." *American Politics Quarterly* 23:204–228.

Weber, Ronald E., Harvey J. Tucker, and Paul Brace. 1991. "Vanishing Marginals in State Legislative Elections." *Legislative Politics Quarterly* 16:29–47.

Wesberry v. Sanders, 376 U.S. 1 (1964).

Author Index

Subject Index